STARTING UP

DAVID HASLEY

STARTING UP

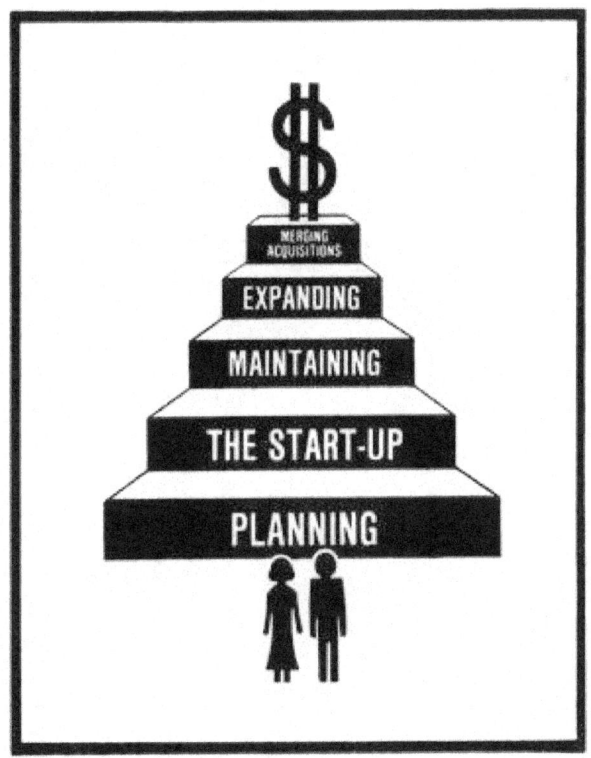

The Complete Guide to Starting
and Maintaining Your Own Business

ISBN-13: 9780692853511
ISBN-10: 0692853510
Library of Congress Control Number: 2017903145
David D. Hasley, Pittsburgh, PA

I would like to dedicate this text to my son, Darren, who has recently completed his education as a mechanical engineer, and who is beginning his career path in parallel with the republication of this book. Good luck and God bless you and your generation.

Introduction

The Industrial Age brought with it new standards that have now become second nature to most of us. During industry's rise to prominence, society's rank and file were enticed to leave their farms and crafts for the promise of a better life. Subsequently, we evolved from a decentralized to a centralized society. What followed was not necessarily a major step forward, but more a parallel to the feudal system popularized during the advent of the Agricultural Age. Wealthy land barons gave rise to wealthy industrialists, and serfs to industrial laborers who, rather than sell the fruits of their labor, simply began to sell their labor.

Undoubtedly, many of the harder tasks of the industrial era's earlier stages have long since been eliminated, and we have further evolved into a corporate society of skilled laborers and middle managers. Survival in this society has not necessarily become any easier. The inflationary characteristics proceeding the past three recessions have forced women into the workplace as yet another afflicted minority. Lifestyles that could once be supported by one salary now are difficult to maintain with two, and our stress levels continue to escalate during this process. As an outgrowth we have experienced the breakup of the family unit, and a general decline in religious beliefs and moral standards. Couple this with the fear of nuclear or terroristic holocaust and the deterioration in our cities, and it's easy to understand why today's generations are searching for a new direction.

The last few years have seen a mass exodus from within the corporate ranks because of downsizing and automation, and with it the resurrection of the entrepreneurial spirit. This phenomenon transcends social and economic class, race, and gender. It also closely parallels the end of the Industrial Age, despite business and political leaders' attempts to prolong it in an attempt to maintain their basis for power and control. Today's leaders refuse to recognize that their era is ending. It is giving way to a generation of embryonic entrepreneurs who are charting a new course.

We are witnessing the reemergence of a decentralized society on a national scale. This new generation of entrepreneurs is retaking control of their lives and destinies, taking a more active part in their children's development and rejuvenating the family unit. In short, they are pioneering a giant evolutionary step forward that two decades ago was dubbed the Informational Age.

Unfortunately, and in many cases intentionally, political and business leaders continue to suppress this transition. They see their traditional power bases slipping away, and grope blindly for a means to hold on. Present day political leaders prey on another afflicted group, the displaced worker who has lost his or her job to automation or industrial closures. While these leaders profess a return to the good life of the 1950s, they are in reality furthering a facade to maintain a continuation of their political and economic dominance.

Today's leaders blame current industrial woes on foreign competition. They fail to disclose the blame rests squarely with them and their short-sighted, short-term management philosophies, which has all but eliminated the middle class and turned America into a two-class society—the haves and the have-nots. In reality, our political business leaders have no plans for the displaced workers other than to suppress and control them through fear and misinformation.

If we are to survive, both individually and as a nation, it behooves us to expose this trend. We must act as the conscience for those leaders who have a moral obligation to retrain and reintroduce into this new society those who have been, and are being displaced. Yesterday's Industrial Age is for the most part already behind us. We must let its remnants go, and act as the catalyst to fuel the final transition into the Informational Age. Individuals and small businesses have fueled this transition to date and, in all likelihood, will continue to lead this movement in the future.

What follows is not a new manifesto, but merely a self-help guide for those pioneers who are forging this new path. A forty-year career in commercial banking, investment management, and private enterprise has afforded me the opportunity to be involved with hundreds of businesses in every size, shape, and form imaginable. I have studied the operations of all of these businesses and have served as an advisor to many. These include retail and restaurant operators ranging in size from one location to national concerns, independent gas stations to full-scale distributors and refiners, individual doctors and dentists to hospitals, and real-estate investors from one property to international holdings.

All of these concerns, large and small, share parallels in operating trends, both good and bad, which will be discussed during the course of this text. These trends can be studied by the budding entrepreneur to improve his or her management skills, and to avoid common operating pitfalls. Whether you are currently in the planning, start-up, or operating phase, this guide will help you to employ the most advanced management technologies available today. In short, it will greatly improve your chances for success. Consider this my gift to you, at a slight tax-deductible price, as you head start into the future.

Contents

PART I
THE PERSONAL PLANNING STAGE

CHAPTER 1
So You Want to Go into Business?

A t one time or another we have all dreamed of starting our own business. After all, what better way to break up the doldrums of a nine-to-five workday than to picture ourselves as successful entrepreneurs? No more stifling our imaginations to conform to corporate policies, or concerning ourselves with corporate politics. No more training recent MBAs only to have them reappear as pushy subordinates or, worse yet, as superiors. Conversely, no more taking orders from a boss whose only true asset is the ability to kiss one. No more salary or promotional gripes. Best of all, no more hour-long commutes at the beginning and end of each work day.

The daydreams can linger for minutes, hours, months, or even years. They can affect blue-collar workers, management trainees, middle managers, and vice presidents alike. Daydreams can prove therapeutic by helping to relieve much of the accompanying stress, but for most of us presently conjuring up images of self-employment, the dreams are no longer enough. For us, it's time to turn the dreams into reality.

Before jumping onto your desk to declare your independence, however, consider the consequences carefully. Although self-employment can ultimately prove more rewarding, initially it can be more of a burden than ever imagined. Some of us may even be better suited to remain as employees. Before we answer the question, "Who is right for the job?" and discuss what starting and maintaining an independent business entails, let's first define a small business.

Defining a Small Business
In designing eligibility requirements for Small Business Administration (SBA) assistance, the SBA defines a small business as an independent business having fewer than five hundred employees. By the federal government's own estimation, 99.7% of all businesses in the United States, roughly 27,900,000, fall into this category.

The small-business segment employs nearly one half of the country's workforce, and it accounts for nearly one half of its annual business revenues. Additionally, small business accounts for 64% of net new jobs annually. So realize that starting a small business does not by any stretch of the imagination mandate remaining small. The contributions made by this business segment to the overall well-being of this country as well as to the entrepreneur are considerable.

Annual Business Starts

Today there are roughly 543,000 new businesses starting each month with the vast majority being formed in the Sunbelt region. The primary emphasis is in Texas, Florida, and California. New York and New Jersey lead the charge of new business starts in the Rustbelt region with university-based states like Massachusetts, Maryland, and North Carolina growing in popularity.

The service industry leads all other industries in the number of annual business starts accounting for approximately 47% of the total. Retailers account for 19%; financial, insurance, and real estate account for 9%; construction 8%; wholesaling 6%; manufacturing 5%, and agriculture 2%. The remaining 4% fall into mining and transportation. Home-based businesses account for 52% of all new businesses started, and 73% are sole proprietorships.

Annual Business Starts by Industry

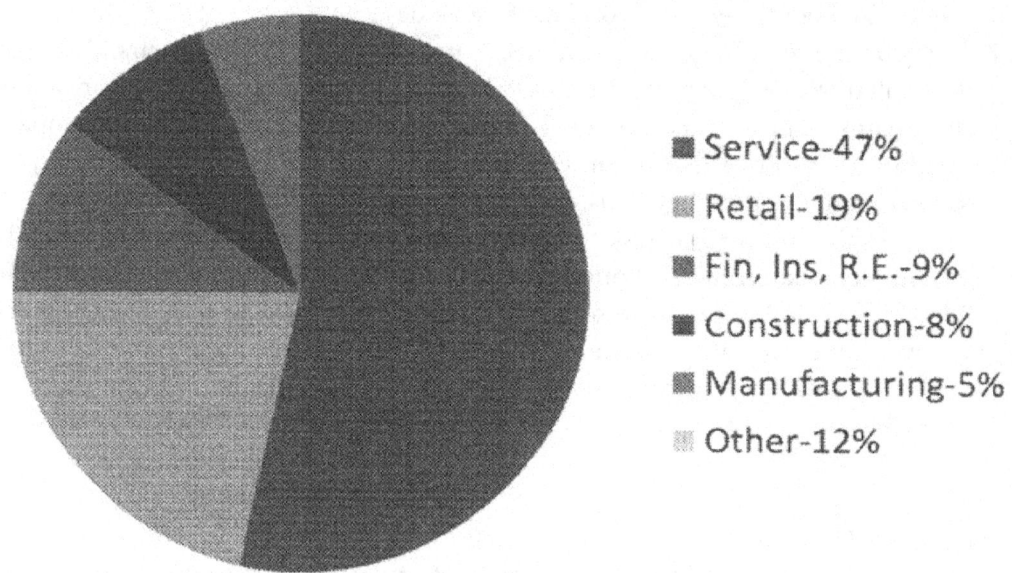

- Service-47%
- Retail-19%
- Fin, Ins, R.E.-9%
- Construction-8%
- Manufacturing-5%
- Other-12%

Business Dissolutions

Competition is admittedly fierce among new business ventures, but the landscape has improved dramatically over the past twenty-five years. When the first edition of this book was published in 1984, the SBA had estimated that 50% of all business start-ups would fail within the first year, and that 80% would fail within the first three years. By 2016 SBA estimated that only 20% of new start-ups fail in the first year, 50% survive at least five years, and 33% survive at least ten years.

The road to success will not be easy. Those who do survive will have to overcome personal frustration, the increased demands of undercapitalization, extended working hours, the trials and tribulations of an ongoing learning phase, and quite possibly decreased financial rewards, at least initially. There will be periods of self-denial and the constant fear of failure, but for the survivors there will be victory and tremendous rewards of accomplishment. Welcome to the world of self-employment.

While the odds against long-term success are considerable, the reasons for failure are in most cases avoidable. This, of course, is the major thrust of this book. By the time you finish it, you'll know all of the pitfalls associated with starting or purchasing a business. More importantly, you'll be aware of the steps necessary to avoid them.

A. Am I the Right Person for the Job?

Taking into consideration the high degree of business failures and the hardships that might be encountered along the way, you may by now be asking yourself, "Is it worth it?" For most of you, the answer will be a resounding yes! The positive aspects of self-employment far outweigh the negative. The reasons for this answer will tie into our earlier question, "Am I the right person for the job?"

We have all heard the Horatio Alger rag-to-riches stories. Interestingly enough, in talking with both clients and business associates, riches were never mentioned as the primary motivation for going into business. What was, more than any other motive, can be summarized into one word, independence.

Entrepreneurial Qualities

There were other rationales too. Most entrepreneurs are nonconformists. They don't like to follow orders, and don't lend well to regimentation. Most picture themselves as individualists and free thinkers who abhor team play unless, of course, they get to be coach and quarterback. All entrepreneurs classify themselves as hard workers who couldn't imagine expending their energies for someone else's gain. All share a sense of pride knowing, even if they fail, they have at least attempted to fulfill their dreams. All expect to be successful though, and while not expressing riches as a primary motive, all expect that one of the rewards of success will be financial freedom.

The Decision for Self-Employment

"Sounds like me," you say. "But what about the high degree of business failures?" Well, if your primary motivation is security, then you best remain an employee. I've always been a sucker for lists, and for those of you still undecided, I can think of a simple and possibly obvious solution.

Take a blank sheet of paper and title it, "The Decision for Self-Employment." Now divide the page into two columns. Title the first, "Why I Want to Go into Business," and the second, "Why I Should Work for Someone Else." Now list the advantages to each alternative. Once your list is complete, simply weigh the advantages associated with each choice. Therein lies your answer.

A Personal Evaluation

For those who made it past the first list, I propose one further and possibly more difficult form of self-analysis, "A Personal Evaluation." The first column of this insert contains personal attributes other entrepreneurs consider valuable to their success. The second column will contain your own evaluation as to whether you feel the attribute is a personal strength or weakness.

A PERSONAL EVALUATION

ENTREPRENEURIAL ATTRIBUTES	PERSONAL STRENGTHS OR WEAKNESSES
1. Self-confidence	1. ☐ Strength ☐ Norm ☐ Weakness
2. Determination	2. ☐ Strength ☐ Norm ☐ Weakness
3. Initiative	3. ☐ Strength ☐ Norm ☐ Weakness
4. Perseverance	4. ☐ Strength ☐ Norm ☐ Weakness
5. Problem solving	5. ☐ Strength ☐ Norm ☐ Weakness
6. Common sense	6. ☐ Strength ☐ Norm ☐ Weakness
7. Flexibility	7. ☐ Strength ☐ Norm ☐ Weakness
8. The ability to delegate	8. ☐ Strength ☐ Norm ☐ Weakness
9. The ability to learn	9. ☐ Strength ☐ Norm ☐ Weakness
10. Experience	10. ☐ Strength ☐ Norm ☐ Weakness

The first attribute is self-confidence. If you don't believe in yourself, no one else will either, and you'll find running a business will prove next to impossible. The second attribute is determination, which is necessary to transfer your belief in your business and yourself to others. The third, initiative, is an important quality since you will be the primary motivator for yourself and your employees. Certainly there will be periods of self-doubt, which is where the next attribute, perseverance will come into play.

The ability to solve problems is another important attribute because as Murphy's Law states that what can go wrong usually will. The ability to foresee and solve problems takes a certain amount of common sense and flexibility, two more important attributes. Remember that corporate rigidity you were always putting down? Don't give your own employees the opportunity to accuse you of the same practices.

Even for those who begin as a one-person show, eventually you will need employees if you wish for your business to grow. Once those employees have gained your trust, you will need to be able to delegate effectively for your business to continue to grow. This will require the ability to listen, and to distribute authority effectively. You'll find listening skills are invaluable in all areas of your business, including dealings with customers, suppliers, and business associates. Every business is a people business, and your ability to listen to others will prove vital to your success.

You must always be willing to learn, even if it means making a few mistakes along the way. Everyone makes mistakes; accept them and learn from them. When you learn not to repeat your mistakes, you will gain that final entrepreneurial attribute and experience.

A Form of Constructive Criticism

Don't be overly concerned with shortcomings pointed out by the personal evaluation, unless of course it brought about a realization that you really don't have what it takes to be a successful entrepreneur. It's better to realize it at this stage than beyond the point of no return. For the rest of you, use the evaluation for what it is, a form of constructive criticism or self-help tool. Learn to capitalize on those attributes you've identified as strengths, and set out to improve upon and minimize the attributes identified as weaknesses.

Minority Misconceptions

For the member of a minority, entrepreneurial independence can carry a special significance. While the business world has made great strides in becoming an equal opportunity employer, it's no secret that senior management positions are elusive if you're female or a member of a minority. Those who are lucky enough to make it to the senior management positions are still often faced with wage discrimination. In 2015, it was estimated that for every dollar a male employee earned, a female in a similar position earned just $0.78. For every dollar a white employee made, a black employee in a similar position made just $0.71. Pay inequities are just as great for members of other minorities and for seniors.

A Rapid Rise in Minority-Owned Businesses

For many self-employment may offer the best alternative to these discriminating practices. The US Department of Commerce reported that minority-owned businesses, excluding women-owned firms, grew by 37.8%—from 5.8 million in 2007 to 8 million in 2012. Hispanic-owned firms increased by 46.3%—from 2.4 to 3.3 million. Black or African American–owned firms rose from 1.9 to 2.6 million, and the number of Asian-owned firms climbed from 1.5 to 1.9 million. From 2007 to 2012, the percentage of minority-owned firms increased from 22% to 29% of the total number of US firms.

Firms owned by women increased by 26.8% from 7.8 to 9.9 million during this period, and they produced $1.4 trillion in revenues in 2012.

The Credit Climate

Today's credit climate is the best in years for starting or purchasing a business. For those who haven't heard or may not yet believe it: credit standards must, and are, being applied equally to whites, blacks, Native Americans, those of Asian descent, and homosexuals, whether they are male or female. In fact, being a member of a minority can present opportunities not readily available to the average Anglo. Many federal agencies maintain special lending programs geared to assist minority-owned businesses. Many local, city, and state governments also maintain assistance programs, as do many banks and large corporations, either on a direct basis or through support of nonprofit foundations.

While the remainder of this text will highlight special considerations that could affect women and members of minorities, the book itself was written for anyone and everyone wanting to go into business. After all, self-employment could very well offer the best alternative to discriminating corporate practices, whether you are a woman, a member of a minority, or an oppressed member of the majority.

B. The High Degree of Business Failures and Why

While the high degree of new-business failures as touched upon earlier may prove surprising, the underlying causes will prove even more startling.

The vast majority of new-business failures are caused by self-inflicted wounds. Most are readily avoidable with proper planning and operating controls. The remainder of this text is designed to ensure that those of you who have made the commitment to self-employment do not become one of those casualties.

Since most new-business failures occur within the first three years, for most of you, the keys to success will be to make it past this first stage of development. The best means to assure this success will be through a form of preventative maintenance. By examining the most common causes of business failure, we can plan management controls to avoid these common pitfalls.

While the percentages vary slightly, depending upon the study, every survey on business failures concurs that the primary reasons for failure are as follows:

1. Disaster—1.0%
2. Fraud—1.3%
3. Neglect—1.6%
4. Management Error—93.1%
5. Unknown—3.0%

Disaster: Though not the most likely cause, a disaster could result in your business failure. Fire accidents account for nearly 85% of all businesses lost through disaster. The remaining 15% is distributed evenly between floods and burglaries. While many disasters are unavoidable, an owner's investment can be protected by maintaining proper insurance coverage. Additionally, business interruption insurance can help cover operating expenses during the recovery process.

Fraud: Like disaster, a business closure due to fraud is highly unlikely, but it can happen. The most common causes of fraud are the irregular disposal of assets, and falsified accounting documents. Either could result from dishonest employees or partners who might misreport revenues, pilfer inventory, or falsify receivable records. The chances of fraud occurring can be greatly reduced by performing adequate background checks on applicants for employment, and by installing proper operating monitors and controls.

Neglect: The primary cause of neglect is poor health. This discussion should not dissuade those of you with disabilities or with health-related issues; however, I have been involved with several successful businesses that were started and managed by those classified as disabled. The demands of self-employment are taxing to say the least, especially in the start-up phase; but anyone with enough initiative can persevere.

Failure through neglect usually occurs at a stage beyond start-up. It can be triggered by health-related disorders like heart conditions and mental disorders, or through causes such as alcohol or drug abuse. Though not always avoidable, proper planning can help to prevent neglect-related failures from occurring.

Written ownership agreements, formal employee training, ownership succession plan, projection forecasting models, operating trends analyses, and adequate insurance coverage can help to minimize the burdens placed upon family members and employees when such disorders do arise. Additionally, these planning procedures can often eliminate the underlying causes for such disorders, and even help to prevent them from occurring.

The next most common cause for neglect is marital strife. The financial burdens and time restraints associated with building a successful business are both common causes of marital difficulties. While these strains may not be entirely avoidable, acknowledging them from the outset can help to lessen their impact. Starting a business should be a family decision from the outset. Quite possibly your families' involvement, both financially and as administrative and operational support, will be critical for your business to succeed.

Management Error: This is by far the major cause of business failure, yet as a business analyst, one I find inexcusable. Business management is, after all, a learned science, and those who make the commitment to go into business, should be ready and willing to learn. It's true that theory isn't always as easily applicable in the real world, but having the theoretical knowledge will usually enable the identification and correction of most operational problems before they can seriously impact your business.

Management error encompasses a multitude of sins, the most common of which is inadequate sales or revenue generation. Some may contend that sales have little to do with management abilities, yet your chances for success could very well hinge upon your ability to project and obtain adequate sales levels. Realistic sales projections will enable effective safeguards to help lessen the operating burdens that often arise prior to attaining a profitable sale level. Likewise calculating the effects of various sales levels can help predetermine the operational changes, which might be necessitated if actual sales lag or grow at a faster pace than anticipated. Later, we will devote an entire chapter to forecasting and projection models.

Competitive weakness is the next most common cause of management error. Unfortunately, when this cause occurs, it may already be too late to take corrective action. This error is usually the result of choosing a highly competitive field or choosing a poor location. This error may also occur because of ineffective marketing techniques, or overestimating the market for your product or service. This emphasizes the need for effective research, a subject that will be discussed in great detail during our next chapter.

In order of their appearance, the next most common causes of failure due to management error are uncontrolled operating expenses, receivables or inventory difficulties, and excessive fixed-asset expenditures.

Each of these areas will also be an important component in our projection modeling. Additionally, methods for determining and maintaining optimal operating levels for each of these categories will be discussed during the course of this text.

C. The Patterns of Success

Just as studying the causes of failure can serve as a form of preventative maintenance, studying the patterns of success can serve as a role model to help pattern your own successful operation. Dun & Bradstreet compiles an annual listing of the patterns of success of successful businesses. Each of these areas will prove a key element in ensuring your business's success. The patterns are as follows:

Gain Knowledge: This of course will be a continuing process beginning with the business conception and continuing throughout the business lifecycle.

Adequate Capitalization: This pattern will be discussed at length in two upcoming chapters. The importance of sufficient capitalization cannot be overemphasized. Undercapitalization can result in having to play catch-up, which often necessitates taking operational shortcuts that can prove detrimental to a business's success.

The Proper Location: A handy reminder is any money saved by choosing an inexpensive and out-of-the-way location will usually be more than offset by increases in marketing and advertising expenses to inform the public of your existence. This is especially true for retailers. The experienced business owner doesn't look for the cheapest location, but rather for the best location.

Learn Proper Buying: All aspects of inventory control are essential to success. Knowing what to buy is only the beginning. Maintaining optimal inventory levels and ensuring rapid inventory turnover are both essential components of precise cash-flow management.

Control Working Capital: This is another area that is essential to your business's success. It is also one of the most misunderstood aspects of managing a successful business. Fear not, by the time you have completed reading this text, your understanding of working capital will surpass many of the top executives at major corporations.

Sound Credit Management: Like sound buying practices, proper credit management is optimizing accounts receivable levels and turnover. This is another area that is essential to precise cash-flow management.

Plan for Expansion: One of the most common business fallacies is that an increase in sales will provide an equivalent increase in pretax profit. There are, of course, costs involved with sales generation, which must be factored into the calculations for how an increase in sales impacts the bottom line. We will cover this area in depth during our projection modeling, as well as discuss the impact of inadequate sales and the dangers of uncontrolled growth.

Keep Adequate Records: Keeping and understanding accurate accounting records may be the most important aspect to building a successful business. Don't rely on your bookkeeper or accountant to keep the engine fine-tuned. Understand the information these allies provide, and be proactive in the record keeping function.

Learn to Take Advice: There is a world of information at your disposal, adaptable through books, magazines, seminars, government agencies, and business associates, which is easily accessible through Google. While the amount of information available is nearly inexhaustible, remember to analyze it thoroughly and implement only what you believe to be accurate and relevant.

Recognize Limitations: This can be just as true for your business as it can be for yourself. As you proceed, you may uncover limitations in capital or products, or even operational procedures. As with personal limitation, these can be minimized, improved upon, and even turned into strengths.

D. Chapter Summary

The remainder of this text will be dedicated to the techniques involved in managing a small business, and to improving and reinforcing your management skills. Keep in mind, it's not always the smartest person who becomes the most successful. Oftentimes it's the person who's willing to take a chance and has the perseverance to succeed. If you've decided to take the plunge, then this is the right decision for you. Rather than dwelling on the possible implications, feel good about your decision. After all, you've already taken the first step to ensure your success. Look now to the future with excitement.

CHAPTER 2
At the Beginning

L et's now start up the stairway to building a successful business. Since most of you will have to borrow to start or purchase that business, our first step will be to complete a personal financial statement. Like buying a car, before you can choose the right business, you must first determine what you can best afford. Your personal net worth will serve as a barometer to gauge or estimate your borrowing capacity. In this instance we preface borrowing capacity with the word "estimate" because, for those of you who purchase an existing business, that business will serve as a means of increasing your borrowing capacity.

A. Preparing a Personal Financial Statement

I don't know anyone who enjoys preparing a personal financial statement, including those who have them finalized by an outside accountant. Nevertheless, every potential lender will require one, and anyone who has lent you, will expect it updated on an annual basis. For those of you who are unfamiliar with the personal financial statement format, it consists of a simplified balance sheet and income statement. Most creditors will also want you to supplement your valuations with listings of deposit accounts, securities, real estate, insurance coverage, personal property, and outstanding debt including leases.

Calculating Your Personal Net Worth

A sample personal financial statement has been provided for your convenience. Sample forms can be obtained from most lending institutions as well as through online sources. To complete your own personal balance sheet, list what you own under the appropriate category under the asset section, and what you owe in the appropriate category under the liability section. Next, total each section. Then, subtract your total liabilities from your total assets. The remainder will be your personal net worth. To test your result, add your total liabilities to your net worth. That total should equal your total assets.

HARRY P. SAMPLE
PERSONAL FINANCIAL STATEMENT
JULY 31, 20XX

ASSETS

Cash-Checking Account	$10,500
Cash-Money Market Account	$25,000
Accounts Receivable	$1,500
Listed Securities	$50,000
Real Estate-Residence	$375,000
Cash Surrender Value-Life Insurance	$5,000
Automobile:	
2017 BMW M 2	$46,500
Other Personal Property	$50,000
TOTAL ASSETS	$467,500

LIABILITIES

Notes Payable	0
Sales Contracts	0
Charge Accounts	$2,500
Installment Account (Auto)	$35,000
Installment Account (Others)	0
Real Estate Loans-Residence	$295,000
Loans on Life Insurance	$2,500
Unpaid Taxes	0
Other Liabilities	0
TOTAL LIABILITIES	$335,000
PERSONAL NET WORTH	$132,500
TOTAL LIABILITIES AND NET WORTH	$467,500

MONTHLY INCOME

Salary & Commissions	$5,500
Dividends & Interest	$250
Rental Income	0
Spouse's Salary	$3,500
TOTAL MONTHLY INCOME	$9,250

MONTHLY EXPENDITURES

Real Estate Payments	$1,225
Rent	0
Federal and State Income Taxes	$725
Property Taxes	$545
Insurance Premiums	$425
Installment Payment (Auto)	$675
Charge Accounts	$50
TOTAL MONTHLY EXPENDITURES	$3,645

The next portion of the personal financial statement is the income and expense section. To complete this section, simply calculate your ongoing monthly income and expenses. In all likelihood your expenses will exceed your income during the first few months of operation. Still, you will have to determine how best to pay these expenses until the business is able to support itself and you. The most logical ways will be as follows:

1. Personal savings
2. Increased borrowing
3. Alternative income sources such as continued employment, or spousal support
4. The sale of personal assets
5. Purchasing an existing business with proven profitability

Additional Assistance

For those of you who may need additional assistance completing the personal financial statement, there may be no better time to establish relationships with your personal banker. A bank can be much more than a deposit or lending institution. It can be a ready source of professional advice and assistance, as well as a strong business ally. Also, sharing your intentions at this stage will afford time to establish a working relationship prior to the actual need to borrow. This can help improve your chances for loan approval as well as provide a knowledgeable resource for shaping your initial business proposal.

B. Evaluating the Personal Financial Statement

Let us now dissect the personal financial statement, the way a lender does, to give you an understanding of how they will determine your borrowing capacity. After reviewing the totals, the first area that will attract a lender's attention will be the liquid asset section. These are assets that are readily convertible to cash, including cash accounts, stocks and bonds, marketable securities, and negotiable instruments.

B.1 Liquid Asset Financing

Lenders take great assurance in readily marketable assets, and most lenders will be anxious to discuss a loan collateralized by a deposit account such as a CD, or a stock portfolio. The key component here of course is collateral, which is any asset pledged as security for a loan. Like the personal financial statement itself, the term collateral will become second nature. In most cases you will be unable to obtain a loan without some form of collateral. The exception will be those of you with a personal net worth large enough to infer collateralization by itself.

As a general rule, you will be able to borrow up to 90% of the value of any readily marketable security. This percentage will decrease for less marketable securities, and could drop to as low as 60% for over-the-counter stocks. Why the ratios, you ask? To ensure that, in the event of default, there will be enough monies available from the liquidation of the collateral to pay off both the principal balance and any unpaid interest that has accrued.

When borrowing against readily marketable deposit accounts, expect the interest rate to be between 1% and 3% above the rate of interest being paid on the deposit account. If the collateral is stocks or bonds, expect the interest rate to be between 15% and 3% over prime. Because most liquid assets are so easily disposable, repayment terms will be much more lucrative than with other types of borrowing. Usually, payment can be arranged on an interest-only basis, if so desired, to keep your monthly outlay at a minimum.

B.2 Notes Receivable Financing

The next line item of the personal financial statement to attract the lender's attention will be any notes receivable. A lender's willingness to lend against such notes will depend upon several factors: Is the note seasoned, is it secured, when it will mature, and what is the payee's capacity to continue to make payments? By seasoned, we allude to the length of time the note has been in existence, and the payee's payment history to date.

Lenders prefer a note to be seasoned for at least one year. They also prefer a note to be collateralized, preferably with real estate. This isn't to say a lender won't lend against a note secured by another form of collateral, only that they may reduce the maximum amount they are willing to lend against the note.

You will be able to borrow between 70% to 80% of the equity value of a note secured by real estate, at an interest rate between 2% and 3% over prime. For a note secured by readily marketable equipment, the maximum loanable amount will approximate 70% of the liquidation value. If the equipment is less marketable, like restaurant equipment, the maximum loan amount will not exceed 50% of the liquidation value, and the interest rate will increase to 4% or 5% over prime. The lender will also want to structure the maturity of a loan secured by a note to coincide with the maturity of the note, and will frown upon lending against a note with a large balloon payment at the end.

B.3 Borrowing against Real Estate

Do not despair if you are devoid of a large-stock portfolio or notes receivable. I've seen many fortunes amassed without the aid of a huge pool of liquid assets. Real property holding will be the next line item a lender looks to when reviewing your personal financial statement. This is an area that many potential entrepreneurs overlook, but don't underestimate its potential. The unrealized appreciation of any real-estate holding, including your home, could be the ticket for financing your own business.

Typically you can borrow up to 80% of the equity value of improved property, and 50% of the equity value of unimproved property. Your ability to service the debt will also be weighed heavily in determining the maximum loanable amount, especially if the collateral is your home. Interest rates will be lowest if you take out a home equity loan or line of credit, and 2% to 3% above home loan rates if you structure a business loan secured by real estate. A major advantage of this type of financing is that repayment terms can be structured for as long as fifteen years, affording the borrower a lower monthly payment than in most other types of loans.

Cash Value of Life Insurance

The next area of evaluation for your personal financial statement will be the cash value of any whole life-insurance policies. This is a great way to borrow because the interest rate charged by the insurance company will usually be much lower than on most other type of loan. Why, because the insurance company will lend to you at about 4% to 5% over the interest rate being paid to you on the policy itself. That rate is probably as low as 1% or 2%. Most bankers and financial planners will recommend borrowing as much a possible against the cash value of any whole life policies.

B.4 Personal Property Financing

The final area of the personal financial statement that could serve as collateral is the personal property section. This should be a last resort, however, and will necessitate your owning items of value like an exotic car, a stamp or coin collection, or expensive jewelry. The maximum loan amount against an auto would be 70% of the wholesale value at the prevailing used car rate and terms. As for other items, estimate 50% of the liquidation value as the maximum loan amount with a rate of around 5% over prime.

For those who have to borrow against their personal net worth, remember you will be incurring a new monthly obligation, so budget accordingly. Though eventually you will expect your business to make the payment during the start-up stage, this isn't always possible. As an additional safety factor, I would recommend not incurring a monthly payment any larger than what you can afford to pay on your present salary: in the unlikely you may have to return to it someday.

B.5 Those with a Nominal Net Worth

For those of you with a nominal personal net worth, borrowing won't be impossible, but it will prove more difficult. Those in this category should pare your expectations to the bare minimum. You can also greatly improve your chances to borrow by purchasing an existing business. Lending institutions will give much more credence to a loan request to purchase an existing business, because the business's net worth will serve as a form of collateral and its past performance as a source of repayment. You may even find a seller who is willing to carry all or a portion of the financing personally, both as an incentive to buy and to differ the tax obligation from the sale.

There are additional avenues available as well. There are federal programs available that give special consideration to applicants who display the necessary management skills, but lack the sufficient capital base to borrow. Investment firms and individual investors represent two other alternative loan sources. We will discuss all of these avenues and more later in this text. The point is, don't get discouraged, even if you have little or no personal net worth. The most important asset of all is the will to succeed. Opportunity will follow.

The Part Time Commitment

There is one other alternative that bears mentioning at this time, because it may influence the business choice for some of you. Some businesses are well suited for an initial part-time commitment, particularly for a husband and wife team. A retail store is a perfect example. The team can share the business responsibilities, and one or both can remain at their present employment temporarily, until the business can provide full support. Despite what many bestselling authors are professing, there aren't any get-rich-quick schemes that work. For many of you, financial rewards will have to wait, so get ready for some initial belt tightening.

C. Evaluating Business Opportunities

Assessing Capital Limitations

Choosing the most compatible industry will be the second step to building a successful business. Now that you have estimated your personal financial capabilities, you are in a much better position to more realistically evaluate business opportunities. Again, capital limitations will play a heavy role in this determination. Undercapitalization is one of the major contributors to business failure. Don't get caught short from the outset, particularly those of you with visions of grandeur. You may not be able to begin your journey with the business of your dreams, but you can quickly grow into it and gain invaluable experience along the way. Just as home equity grows, so too can business equity, allowing for expansion and further opportunity.

Relying on Past Experience

There is another important and often deadly pitfall to avoid when choosing a business. We all have hobbies we dream of turning into careers, but when evaluating business opportunities, you must determine if you are truly knowledgeable enough in that particular field to turn it into a successful business. We can all cite exceptions such as Mrs. Field's Cookies or even KFC, but the success of these businesses was more an outgrowth of the advice and capital injections of professional investment bankers than one man or woman's favorite pastime. Your best chance for success will come from incorporating your past experience with your choice for a business endeavor.

D. Researching Business Markets

There are, of course, more variables involved in choosing the right business venture than just personal experience and personal preferences. An equally important consideration will be whether or not a market exists for that product or service, which, in turn, raises the geographic and distribution considerations. To determine if a market exists, or how best to create, one will require extensive market research. There are firms that specialize in this type of service but, for those of you who can't afford a private research firm, there is more than enough information available to undertake an in-depth analysis on your own. In fact, you could easily bury yourself in research materials if you aren't careful.

The trick to effective market research is to find the right research aids, and then extract from them the best possible conclusions. I will try to direct you to those few organizations and publications that can serve all of your needs in a minimal amount of time. We will engage in a two-pronged marketing approach, utilizing both financial and market statistical data. I caution you to take this research phase seriously. Identifying the strongest available market will greatly ease and enhance your initial success.

D.1 Sources of General Topic Information

There are two sources of general topic information that will be of benefit to many of you. The first will be your local library. Many libraries will offer a handy list of books and publications for the aspiring entrepreneur. Even if a list is unavailable, most libraries usually have a section reserved for business-oriented books.

Most libraries also carry a host of business-related publications that can prove of benefit in evaluating business trends. Most of these appear both in print and online editions. A few of my personal favorites are: *The Harvard Business Review, Business Week, U.S. News and World Report, Fortune, Forbes, and Entrepreneur.* These are more general-topic publications, so once you've narrowed your choice to a particular industry, you may also wish to peruse its trade journals. This will help to further your understanding of the industry and its trends. This can also serve as a starting point for locating suppliers, who themselves can serve as a valuable research source.

The second source of general information is the United States Small Business Administration (SBA). You can find direct assistance at a local SBA office or a local bank that provides SBA loan programs. You can also find a wealth of information online at SBA.gov. The headings at the SBA's home page include the following: Starting and Managing a Business, Loans and Grants, Contracting, Learning Center, and Local Assistance. Each heading has a drop-down menu with more specific information. The SBA is a gold mine of statistical research for all budding entrepreneurs.

D.2 Sources of Financial Statistics

I would highly recommend *Robert Morris Associates (RMA) Annual Statement Studies* for financial statistical information, which heads the list of publications. As the name implies, the publication is updated annually to provide current and accurate financial information segregated by the industry. This publication contains data on nearly one thousand industries formatted by business size into a handy common-sized financial statement analysis including balance sheet, income statement, and key financial ratios. It also includes industry information for the preceding five years that can prove extremely beneficial in trend analysis and guarding against entering an industry that may be on the decline.

Your local library and your bank will most likely have copies, which can enable you to photocopy the appropriate pages. You may also purchase a copy online at **www.rmahq. org/annual-statement-studies/**.

Another publication that can prove extremely beneficial is *Dun & Bradstreet's Key Business Ratio Guide.* This book is similar in both content and format to the RMA guide, although of the two, I find RMA easier to interpret. Dun & Bradstreet does have one advantage, however. It includes a category for businesses with a smaller asset range than does RMA, which might prove more accurate for smaller businesses. Your library and local bank should have a copy. Information is available online at **www.mergent.com/ solutions/research/key-business-ratios-(kbr)**

Another series of publications worth noting is the *Small Business Reporter* published by Bank of America. Bank of America also publishes pamphlets on *How to Buy and Sell a Business, Establishing a Professional Practice, Financing a Small Business*, and *Applying for Minority Business Loans.* Like the SBA's *Starting and Managing* series, these pamphlets are segregated by industry and include all phases of the business cycle from start-up to maintaining. Of the two, you will find Bank of America's series much more informative and timely than the SBA's. Information can be obtained online at **http://newsroom. bankofamerica.com/press-kit/bank-america-small-business-owner-report**.

A simple Google search will, of course, provide additional sources for statistical data as will asking for assistance from your local librarian, banker, and accounting friends.

Utilizing Your Financial Research

Studying the balance sheet for the industry or industries you are considering will help to determine the size of the capital investment required, the average percentage of borrowing to capital, and the percentage of capital to borrowing invested into given asset groups.

The income statement information will help to determine the average annual operating expense levels, profit margins, and owner salary levels. The key financial ratios (see the Ratio Analysis Work Sheet—chapter 6) will also be of assistance, and can help to determine the average return on investment, working capital requirements, and average receivables and inventory levels.

Reviewing the Statement Studies in conjunction with the general industries pamphlets obtained from Bank of America or the SBA will provide valuable insight in helping to narrow your choice of industries. Before making a final industry determination though, it will be necessary to study available marketing data as well.

D.3 Sources of Marketing Statistics

The most diverse source of marketing statistics is the US Census Bureau, which publishes information on a national, state, county, and city basis. Information is available detailing consumer buying habits and purchasing power. Data is also available on social and economic characteristics, including failure rates and national trends. Although census figures are only updated on an average of every five years, most applicable publications have been updated in the last two years. Online resources are available at **https://www. census.gov/library/publications.All.html**.

Marketing statistics are also prepared by the Department of Commerce, which can be accessed online at **www.commerce.gov/topics**. The next source of market research is the *Survey of Buying Power* published by Sales and Marketing Management. This guide is indexed by state, locale, and metropolitan areas, and contains information on consumer buying habits and purchasing power. Your local library may stock this publication. It's also available online at **https://salesandmarketing.com/**.

There is also an abundance of information available at the state and local level. Most states have their own Commerce Departments that compile statistics on a state and local basis. Your local Chamber of Commerce and local government can also prove to be valuable resources for marketing data, and they can be useful later when determining locations. Local trade association such as the Lions Club or Rotary may also prove beneficial. A quick Google search can put you in touch with any of these sources' online resources.

One final research suggestion is to visit or contact competing businesses located out of the area. Most business owners enjoy talking about their business and personal success, and most will be willing to help in a reasonable capacity. One of the best ways to accomplish this is by attending an industry trade show or convention. If this is not possible, try using the phone or e-mail. I would also suggest a little stealth investigation of local concerns that will be your direct competition. Try to determine their strengths and weaknesses, and utilize that information to your advantage when formulating your own business plan.

D.4 Utilizing Your Marketing Research

I would strongly advise researching an industry's failure rate, and avoiding those with the highest failure rates. The Census Bureau estimates the industries with the highest five-year survival rates:

- mining (51.3%)
- manufacturing (48.4%)
- services (47.6%)
- wholesaling and agriculture (47.4%)
- retailing (41.1%)
- finance, insurance, and real estate (39.6%)
- transportation, communications, and utilities (39.4%)
- construction (36.4%)

If you review this list in reverse order, it will tell you which industries are prone to have the highest failure rates. These are broad categories; however, there are some areas of retailing that prove to be much more prone to success than others. There are a multitude of camera enthusiasts starting retail outlets each year for example, and camera stores are near the top of the annual failure rate list.

I would also recommend avoiding highly competitive industries. Again, using our camera store example, you may find there are no camera stores locally to provide direct competition. However, there are many national chains out there that will, in time, also recognize that need. I guarantee that once they move in, you won't be able to compete in price, and you'll be amazed how quickly lower prices can dissuade customer loyalty. And don't underestimate online competition as well.

Ideally, look for a void or a niche to fill, preferably one that is somewhat unique to help dissuade future competition. Look for a segment that can incorporate your past experience and talents. If you can find an industry that incorporates these criteria, you will greatly enhance your chances for success.

Finally, determine which products or services have the best chance for survival in your area. This can be determined by comparing national, state, and local statistical information. Don't just look at product marketability, though. Consider your area's growth rate, employment opportunities and trends, income per capita, and its residents' buying trends. Also take into account the population figures needed to support the type of business you are considering.

E. Chapter Summary

Once you've completed compiling and comparing data, and visiting local information sources, I guarantee you will be able to discern your area's needs with the same assurance a private marketing survey would bring. The one possible exception will be those of you planning to introduce a new product to your area. For those of you in this category, a marketing survey, which will be discussed in chapter 4, will also prove beneficial. As importantly, each of you should be able to discern what type of business best fits into your price range. Remember, proper capitalization is essential to a business's success. Capitalization will be discussed in much greater detail during the remainder of this text.

PART II
THE BUSINESS PLANNING STAGE

BUSINESS PLANNING

CHAPTER 3
Alternative Business Forms

A t some point each of you will have to decide which business format best suits your needs. Before we carry our discussion any further, let's digress a bit to evaluate the three standard business forms: the sole proprietorship, the partnership, and the corporation. The sole proprietorship is by far the most popular format.

Since the 1980s, the number of traditional C corporations has shrunk, while the total number of pass-through businesses such as S corporations, partnerships, and sole proprietorships has tripled. Of the over 32 million businesses in the United States, 23 million are sole proprietorships, 7.4 million are partnerships and S corporations, and only 1.7 million are C corporations. Despite this disproportion, there are distinctive advantages and disadvantages associated with each business form. Let's compare them individually to see which format is best suited to your needs.

A. Proprietorships
Advantages and Disadvantages

The major advantages to the sole proprietorship are the ease of entry, the ease of profit distribution, and the flexibility of distributing assets. A proprietorship is deemed an extension of the owner as opposed to a separate business entity. As such, assets and profits are treated as individual property. Business assets can be bought and sold in the same manner as a house or car. Likewise, business profits are taxed under the same basis as other personal income.

Undoubtedly, the major disadvantage of a proprietorship format is unlimited personal liability. This means that if the business fails or stops paying on its obligations, creditors have the right to attach the owners' personal holding for repayment of debts. Taxation can prove another limitation. Since profits are reported as personal income, they are subject to the personal tax rates. Once your business proves profitable, you could be subject to a higher tax rate than if incorporated.

Additionally, proprietorships are not entitled to many of the same tax deductible expenditures available to corporations such as some types of life insurance and major medical benefit expenditures. Pension and profit-sharing contributions are also not as lucrative as they are for corporations. Finally, unlike a corporation, a proprietorship ceases to exist upon the death of the owner.

A.1 Proprietorship Formation

Again, the sole proprietorship is the simplest and cheapest business format to establish. In many cases the only requirement will be a key to open the front door. Most states do require a fictitious name filing if you use a business name other than your own. In most states this can be accomplished by registering the name with your local County Clerk, and supplementing that registration by public notification in three local newspapers. Those of you who are professionals and those entering regulated businesses will of course have to comply with state and federal licensing regulations.

If you intend to hire employees, you will have to file for a federal tax identification number with the IRS, and payroll tax registration with your state. All of the necessary applications can be obtained online. The sole-proprietorship formation process is quite simple and, in most cases, can be completed without the aid of an attorney.

B. The Partnership
B.1 General Partnerships

Partnerships can come in a variety of formats ranging from a simple two-person venture to complex real-estate syndications. The most common form of partnership is the general partnership, which shares many of the same advantages and disadvantages of the sole proprietorship. Like a proprietorship, general partnerships are easy to form, their profits are as easily withdrawn and their assets are as easy to buy and sell. Similar disadvantages include unlimited personal liability, flow-through of profits or losses to the general partners' personal tax returns, pension and profit-sharing limitations, and the general partnerships dissolution upon a general partner's death.

Unlimited liability can prove a particular disadvantage in the event of unequal personal net worth. Though each general partner is unlimitedly liable in the event of default, creditors have a tendency to attach the holdings of the general partner with the largest net worth. Those of you who may be faced with similar situations should include your risk exposure and your percentage of investment as consideration when destemming ownership percentages and business structure.

Advantages and Disadvantages Unique to the General Partnership

There are several characteristics solely unique to the general partnerships. The major advantage is the ability to pool partners' interests. This could enable enlarging the initial capital investment, increasing the borrowing capacity, spreading the workflow, and enhancing management capabilities. Like the husband and wife team, there is also the option of one or more partners remaining at their present employment until the business is able to support all of those concerned.

There are times the pooling of general partners' interests could prove to be more of a hindrance than an advantage. Many businesses can support one owner well enough, yet are unable to achieve the size necessary to support two or more partners. Additionally, while the overall management could improve through a pooling of talents, most managers differ in their management style and abilities. I've seen the best of friendships, family relationships, and even marriages destroyed over partnership disagreements.

B.2 Limited Partnerships

A form of partnership format that can incorporate all of the advantages of a general partnership, while minimizing many of its disadvantages, is known as a limited partnership. As the name implies, limited partners are limited in the degree of their personal liability to the amount of their investment. Limited partners are also legally restricted from involvement in the day-to-day management of the partnership. This function is reserved for the general partner or partners, of which there needs only to be one.

For those with limited capital resources or borrowing capabilities, the limited partnership can prove a viable alternative for starting a business without bank financing. The best sources for locating limited partners are business associates; bankers, lawyers, and accountants. Many of them will have clients readily available who will usually prove to be reliable investors. Many local investment firms will also have investors readily available, and they can often help in formalizing and structuring the limited partnership.

Be sure to investigate an investment firm's reputation, track record, and fee structures, particularly if they do not come pre-recommended. Remember too, while limited partners' management involvement is limited by law, in reality their involvement is sometimes directly proportional to the percentage of their investment. Finally, though possibly the only alternative for gaining self-employment, the eventual costs of gaining complete ownership control will usually be higher than if a loan had been obtained initially.

B.3 Partnership Formation

A partnership can be formed by drafting a simple partnership agreement, and having it witnessed by two independent observers. In most cases, a fictitious name filing will also be necessary as will a federal tax-identification number. Again, state and federal licensing or regulatory requirements will be applicable for some. Though the assistance of an attorney is by no means a necessity, I would strongly recommend it. This is especially true when questions or discrepancies arise during the formation stage, or when one or more of the partners is previously unknown.

For those of you drafting your own partnership agreement, there are several key components to include. The agreement should clearly state whether the partnership is a general or limited partnership, as well as each partner's individual classification. The agreement should also clearly define each partner's initial contribution, percentage of ownership, and percentage of profits and losses. Management responsibilities should also be defined as should any legally binding restrictions such as who can borrow in the partnership's name.

Arrangements for the buyout of a partner in the event of dissolution, and the requirements for adding or deleting partners should also be detailed. This should include instructions for the disposal of a partner's interests, in the event of death, and should include a proviso for term life insurance in an amount sufficient to buy out his or her interests.

C. The Corporation
Advantages of the Corporation

The third general business form is the corporation. The major advantage to incorporating is the ability to limit your personal liability. Upon formation, the corporation becomes a legal entity. If it were to fail, your personal liability would be limited to the amount of your investment. Many banks and some creditors will, however, circumvent this advantage by requiring major stockholders to sign personal guarantees for corporate obligations. This allows for the attachment of personal assets in the event of corporate default. Most suppliers and less sophisticated creditors haven't reached the stage yet of requiring personal guarantees. Until they do, limited liability will remain a major corporate advantage.

There are additional advantages to incorporate. Corporations have a much wider range of allowable tax deductions, and more lucrative pension and profit-sharing platforms. A corporation can also choose any tax year end, and it may report tax filings on a cash or accrual basis. Corporate losses can be utilized to offset past or future profits to help reduce income-tax liabilities.

Incorporating allows for more than one class of ownership through the use of common and preferred stock offerings. This enables additional alternatives such as stock-option plans, and the ability to raise capital by selling additional shares of common or preferred stock, or bonds, as opposed to borrowing. Finally, the corporation does not cease to exist upon the death of a primary stockholder, and ownership can be easily transferred through the sale of stock rather than the sale of assets.

Disadvantages of the Corporation

The major disadvantage to incorporating is that the decision-making capabilities may not be as flexible since the division of power will be decided by a vote of the stockholders. This disadvantage can be easily overcome, however, if there is only one or just a few stockholders. There is also the possibility of double taxation. By this I mean taxes are paid by the corporation on its profits. If a dividend were declared, the stockholders would also have to pay taxes on the dividend income.

Additionally, an unreasonable accumulation of undistributed profits can also be subject to additional taxation, if the IRS warrants, over and above the initial income-tax liability. Finally, in most cases, incorporating will require involving an attorney, and will cost a minimum of $1,500. This is usually money well spent, and the initial cost will more than be offset by the many advantages of incorporating.

C.1 Subchapter S Corporations

Another form of corporation often used by smaller firms is known as the Subchapter S. To qualify a corporation must have only one class of stock, common, and must operate solely within the United States. A Subchapter S maintains all of the characteristics of a C corporation with the exception of taxation rates. Profits and losses of a Subchapter S corporation are passed through to the owner or owners of record, who then report them as personal income, just as with a sole proprietorship or general partnership. The Subchapter S distinction is often used by firms who intend to pay out most of their profits in owner's salaries.

Limited Liability Company

A limited liability company (LLC) is a hybrid business structure that combines the limited liability features of a corporation and the tax efficiencies and operational flexibility of a partnership. The "owners" of an LLC are referred to as "members," and can consist of a single individual, two or more individuals, corporations, and even other LLCs. An LLC is not considered a separate entity by the federal government, requiring its profits and losses to be "passed through" the business and reported on member's tax returns. Like corporate shareholders, members are protected from personal liability, and they are sheltered from LLC incurred debt. If sued, members' personal assets are usually exempt.

One major disadvantage of the LLC is that it is not being recognized as a separate entity. In many states, when a member leaves an LLC, the business must be closed. The remaining members can decide to continue but, to do so, they must start a new LLC or another form of business entity. Provisions can be included in the original LLC agreement, however, to prolong the life of the LLC in the event a member decides to leave the business. Another disadvantage to some people is that members are considered self-employed and must pay the self-employment tax contributions toward Medicare and Social Security.

Cooperatives

One final form of business that bears mentioning is the cooperative (co-op), which is very common in the agricultural industry. A co-op is a business owned by and operated for the benefit of its members who become part of the co-op by purchasing shares. A co-op is run by an elected board of directors. Officers run the day-to-day operations and the members utilize voting rights to control the direction of the co-op. Profits and losses are distributed among the members for tax-reporting purposes.

C.2 Forming a Corporation

In most cases, incorporating will require the assistance of an attorney to draft the Articles of Incorporation and the appropriate number of common stock certificates. These must then be filed with the appropriate Secretary of State. If the stock is to be sold to the general public, a Security and Exchange Commission filing may also be required. The stock holders must also elect a board of directors, who in turn, must choose corporate officers.

Many of you will be incorporating with one or a just a few stockholders. As such, you will be retaining most, if not all, of the stock ownership and management controls. The few exceptions will be those of you who initially sell stock to the general public to raise capital. Those in this category will have to ensure that ownership and management controls are not significantly diluted by any such stock offering. This subject will be discussed in greater detail later in this text in the public-offering section.

D. Chapter Summary

Each of you will have differing needs and requirements that will need to be weighed against the advantages and disadvantages of the various business forms. Keep in mind, that the form you choose need not be permanent. If it would be best to incorporate, but you don't feel it is economically feasible at this point, choose another form initially, and then incorporate later when it's more economically feasible. You may also find one business form may suit your needs today, but another form may better suit your needs next year or sometime in the future. If and when that time comes, it will be to your advantage to make the change.

CHAPTER 4

New, Used, or Franchise?

I n this chapter we will discuss the possibilities of buying an existing business, starting a new business, or operating a franchise. We will look at each alternative individually, and discuss their advantages and disadvantages. The preowned and franchise section will include discussions on finding the right opportunity, while the start-up discussion will explain how to conduct a marketing survey to further ensure a need exists. I would encourage each of you to read this entire chapter. Though you may have preconceived ideas about which of these alternatives best suits your needs, those conceptions may change after reading this chapter.

A. The Preowned Business
Advantages and Disadvantages
Statistics show that buying an existing business is usually the safest alternative and could greatly improve your chances for success. In most cases, operating systems would have been proven already. These can serve as an ideal base to continue operations, and to base future expansion efforts. Additionally, many of the unforeseen problems that often spell doom to a start-up will have already occurred and been corrected.

In most cases, a healthy customer base will already exist, as will a network of time-tested suppliers and services. The location and floor plan will also have been proven, and you will inherit experienced employees. The existing employees will also be of benefit in helping to learn about the customers, competition, seasonality, and any operational quirks. Finally, the preowned business will usually require a much smaller initial investment, and oftentimes existing owners will help by carrying back some of the initial financing.

There are, of course, instances where the prospective business will not be the well-oiled machine described in the preceding paragraph. There are those who run a business into the ground without proper maintenance, much like an automobile, and then sell it to avoid expensive overhauls. Many of our country's corporate giants are experts in this tactic, preferring to optimize short-term profits at the expense of long-term operations. There are those who are astute at opening a fashionable or trending business, one that can often prove highly profitable in the short term, until the fad begins to fade. These owners will typically sell the business at its peak, just before the trend begins to lose its luster, and about the time it will fetch its highest price.

The chances of purchasing a lemon may have been enhanced by the recent recession, but so too have the chances to find a mismanaged or undercapitalized bargain. It will be up to each of you to discern business and market conditions when evaluating businesses to possibly purchase. We will devote an entire chapter to this process, and those of you who follow its analytical techniques will be assured of avoiding a business lemon. Of course, before conducting this evaluation, we must first identify business prospects.

A.1 Sources for Locating Prospective Businesses

The most common sources for locating business prospects are commercial real-estate brokers, business brokers, attorneys, accountants, newspapers, specialized online sites, and trade publications. Like employment opportunities, however, many of the best prospects never reach these sources. Most owners will offer their businesses to family members, employees, suppliers, and selected business associates, even competitors, before turning to other alternatives.

This is especially true of successful businesses that the owner would be proud to have continued on by someone he or she knows and trusts. The best source for locating a prospective business then, is word of mouth through networking. Ask around, talk to business associates, professional friends and acquaintances, potential suppliers, even existing owners of a company who might be of interest.

Business and Real-Estate Brokers

For small businesses as a general rule of thumb, commercial real-estate brokers will represent those who own real estate, and business brokers will represent those who lease or rent the base of their operation. A reputable broker can prove an invaluable aid in locating the right business opportunity. Many can recommend the best business districts, aid in negotiations, and help arrange financing. Many business brokers specialize in just one industry or carry exclusive listings, so it could prove best to contact more than one to more effectively canvass all of the opportunities in your area. Remember too, the broker will not earn a commission unless the business sells, and that commission will be paid by the seller.

The best sources for locating a reputable broker will be through business associates. Other alternatives are, of course, ads, publications, and online directories. As with every profession, there are disreputable brokers. Be especially careful of those who do not come pre-recommended. Never deal with brokers who require advances or listing fees. Be leery of fast-talking promoters, and don't let a broker's recommendation stop short your investigative process.

Publications

For those of you who must utilize publications and general online sources such as craigslist or specialized websites, be extremely selective. Avoid ads that promise quick riches, solicit partners or investors, and those that fail to mention the type of business for sale. Once you do locate a prospective business, conduct a thorough telephone or e-mail interview first. This will help to ensure that looking at the business will warrant your time. It will also help you to avoid the frustration of being exposed to possible shams, or businesses with little chance for future success.

B. The Start-Up Concern

There are occasions in which starting a new business will be your best alternative, and others in which it will be the only alternative. You may have a new product to the market, or perhaps you're entering an existing market, but have found a better way to sell that good or service than it is currently being utilized by the existing competition. Still another reason might be that your area could support another entry into an existing market, either due to a lack of formative competition or because of population growth.

A Practical Definition

By definition, a start-up is justified if there is a need for a good or service at a sufficient volume and at a high enough price to cover the costs incurred in producing or marketing that good or service, while returning to the business owner a sufficient profit.

B.1 Defining an Unfulfilled Need

Defining an unfulfilled need is best accomplished by studying national trends and new business opportunities. Many of the same publications that we have already discussed can aid in this determination, particularly those that are geared to the independent businessperson. *Fortune, Forbes, Venture, Success, Entrepreneur,* and the *Wall Street Journal* are all great sources for uncovering new trends and business opportunities. The *Wall Street Journal* publishes a business opportunity section every Thursday. You may also want to study urban trends that might be headed for the suburbs. The West Coast is another great source of inspiration. New trends have a history of starting in the west, then spreading east.

Determining Local Adaptability

After identifying compatible needs and trends, you must ascertain which will have the best chance for success in your area. This can best be accomplished by determining what will motivate a person to buy that particular product or service. Most people are driven by the same motivations, though in varying degrees, depending on their level of economic affluence. In most cases, though not necessarily in this order, we all seek prestige among our peers, financial independence, security, comfort, convenience, good health, happiness, and economic value. These needs are, of course, in addition to our basic needs for survival, food, shelter, companionship, and spiritual fulfillment. The more of these needs readily identifiable with your product or service, the better its chances for success.

Additional Capital Requirements

Be forewarned! Consumer identification with a new or unfamiliar product or service will require an extensive marketing and advertising campaign. The initial success of that product or service could in fact depend more on your ability to advertise or create a need for the product, than in the quality of the product itself. The costs to market and advertise a new product or service will greatly increase the initial capital requirements of a new business.

Justifying Entering an Existing Market

For those entering an existing market, your original research materials will provide enough information to prove the need for a start-up concern. Your financial research will verify the business's potential profitability, and your market research will provide the area's population, the number of similar businesses in the area, and the number of people per capita it takes to support this type of business. The census figures can also determine the area's population by age group, their educational and employment backgrounds, their per capita income levels, and their buying preferences.

Justifying Entering a New Market

Justifying the need for a new product or service, or the introduction of one into a new area will prove more difficult, but certainly not impossible. The justification process will be the same as that for entering an existing market, but the decision process will require a more subjective interpretation of your research materials. Additionally, I would suggest conducting a market survey to help corroborate your justification process. A market survey will also provide insight in selecting a location and a marketing strategy.

B.2 A Market Survey

There are firms that specialize in compiling market data, and if you can afford one, feel free to utilize their services. The cost, even for the smallest of businesses, will be a few thousand dollars. Those of you interested in using an outside service should seek recommendations from business associates. Those of you who can't afford this service, or who prefer to utilize the funds elsewhere, can produce your own market survey, provided you're willing to do the leg work yourself.

The first step in structuring the market survey is to define your targeted market. You should already have a potential customer base in mind. Now, further define that base by identifying its educational background, income levels, spending habits, motivational drives, economic and social behaviors, and the geographic boundaries of the market. Those of you whose customer base is other companies should go through a similar identification process. Those of you who have a more general targeted market will have to define several customer bases, and then target traits common to each base. A convenience store, for example, can sell its accessibility to customers of all ages and from all walks of life.

The Questionnaire

The next and possibly most difficult step will be to develop a questionnaire aimed at measuring that targeted market's willingness to accept your product or service. The questionnaire can also be helpful in choosing your location, and for determining distribution methods. For your convenience, I have constructed a sample questionnaire for a hypothetical company by the name of Superior Jewelers, Inc. which is located on the next page.

The questionnaire should include a personal profile to identify the respondent's age, sex, income, and any other factors that can help identify or define your targeted market. Questions should also categorize the participants' willingness or unwillingness to use the product or service, the benefits they would expect to derive from its use and the price they would expect to pay for the product.

Those of you with existing competition, without referring them by name, may wish to include questions regarding competitors' advantages and disadvantages. Individual concerns you may also wish to address are: advertising methods, environmental concerns, consumer identification, and health and safety standards. The particular industry you have chosen will play a part in the development of the questionnaire. Your initial research materials can also prove insightful in formulating your questions.

The results of the questionnaire will prove more meaningful if the questions are structured to require more than a yes or no answer, however, too detail oriented questions could result in an unwillingness to participate. The best format will be a majority of multiple choice questions, particularly in the general identification section, supplemented by short essay-type questions concerning the product or service.

Polling Your Market

Once your questionnaire is completed, you can administer it by phone, mail, e-mail, door-to-door, or a combination thereof. The participants should represent a broad

The Questionnaire

SUPERIOR JEWELERS, INC.
100 Market Street
Santa Fe, California
**QUESTIONNAIRE
MARKETING SURVEY**

Name: Address: Phone:

Age Group:	Education:	Marital Status:
☐ Under 25	☐ Under 8 years	☐ Single
☐ 25-35	☐ 8-12 years	☐ Married
☐ 36-45	☐ 12-16 years	☐ Divorced
☐ 46-55	☐ Over 16 years	☐ Separated
☐ Over 55		

Occupation:

Annual Income:
☐ under $10,000   ☐ $30,000-$40,000
☐ $10,000-$20,000   ☐ $40,000-$50,000
☐ $20,000-$30,000   ☐ Over $50,000

1. How often do you purchase jewelry annually? _____
2. What is the average purchase price? _____
3. Are these purchases for ☐ yourself, ☐ a gift, or ☐ both?
4. Are you more concerned with quality or discount pricing in purchases?
   Please explain:

5. Do you shop around prior to jewelry purchases or deal primarily with
   one jeweler?

6. When are you most likely to purchase?
   ☐ Workday   ☐ Weekend   ☐ Evening
7. Do you feel there is room for another jeweler in the area?_____
8. What do you like about the existing jewelers and jewelry selection in the area?

9. What could a new store provide to improve on the existing competition?

10. Would you consider a quality discount jeweler? _____

cross-section of your targeted market, and the more members of that market you reach, the better the chances for meaningful results. The polling process won't be easy, so don't get discouraged by a few slammed doors or hung-up phone receivers. If conducted thoroughly, the benefits from the final results will far outweigh any minor inconveniences along the way.

Oftentimes local high schools and colleges will be willing to assist with formalizing or conducting marketing surveys as practical assignments for their students. Those of you undertaking a marketing survey would be wise to make inquiries for student assistance. Their help can speed the polling process considerably, while providing the students with valuable experience and insight into the business environment.

Interpreting Your Results

Once the results of your questionnaire are tabulated, you'll find interpreting them will be the easiest part of the process. The marketability of the product or service should in fact become almost self-evident. If for example, you receive a 20% acceptance rate for a retail product, interpolate that rate to your total market. Assuming your total available market is ten thousand consumers, that 20% acceptance rate would translate into two thousand likely customers. Comparing that figure to the total number of customers required to support your type of business should add considerable support as to whether in fact the need exists. Your results will also help in the verification of your targeted market, and how best to reach that market in terms of location, distribution, and marketing.

Some of you may find there is no market for your product or service, or that you have identified the wrong customer base. Be objective when interpreting the survey results. Don't try to rationalize away product or market shortcomings. No matter how painful this discovery might be, it will be better to learn of those shortcomings now rather than after your initial capital outlay. If you are suspicious of the results or desire a second opinion, revise your questionnaire or targeted market and conduct the survey again.

Viewing Existing Businesses

I would strongly recommend that those of you in the start-up category also evaluate similar existing businesses that are for sale. This can prove extremely insightful in justifying and planning your own operation. It will enable you to more closely observe the strengths and weaknesses of others, and pattern your operations more effectively. It will also afford you the opportunity to compare your projected operating figures to actual financial statement data. This can help eliminate much of the guesswork and risk inherent to forecasting the start-up concern.

C. Franchising

The franchising of small businesses has become big business today, thanks in part to companies like McDonald's, Wendy's, KFC, and Subway. These companies originally turned to franchising as a means of expanding their operations despite having limited capital resources. Like some of you, they couldn't afford to expand on their own and lacked the necessary net worth to provide a sufficient borrowing base. Franchising offered them the next best alternative, and I certainly don't have to detail the wisdom in their decisions.

Today there are roughly 785,000 franchise units operating in the United States alone. They employ roughly 8.8 million people, and produce $889 billion in annual revenues. Today's fast-food franchisers were by no means the originator of the franchise concept, however. That distinction falls upon the Singer Corporation, Coca Cola, and International Harvester, who all began franchising in the late nineteenth century.

By definition, a franchise is a license or agreement to operate a local outlet to sell the products or services of a larger organization. In most cases the franchisee is an independent businessperson who operates under the guidelines set by the franchiser. The franchiser benefits by maintaining a network of outlets to distribute its products. The franchisee benefits by association with a nationally known product and, at times, by receiving management, facilities, advertising, and merchandising assistance.

C.1 The Major Types of Franchisers

The Manufacturer

The three most popular franchise formats are the manufacturer sponsored, the wholesale sponsored, and the franchise specialist. The originators of the franchise concept were of course the manufacturer-sponsored franchisers. Examples of this type include today's major oil refiners and automakers. Usually there is no franchise fee involved in this type of franchise, and the franchiser will derive its earnings solely from the products sold to the franchisee. The franchisee in turn agrees to sell only products manufactured by the franchiser under predetermined price and warranty restraints.

The Wholesaler

Wholesale-sponsored franchisers work in much the same fashion as the manufacturer, with the added requirement that franchisees all operate under the same name. Though the wholesale franchisee may carry brand names in addition to the franchisers, these products must be purchased directly from the franchiser's warehouse. The franchisee benefits from volume purchase discounts and the expertise of the franchiser's buying knowledge. The franchiser maintains uniformity among its outlets, and derives additional income from the sale of these products to its franchisees. Examples of this type of franchise include Advance Auto Parts, True Value Hardware, and Ace Hardware.

Specialty Franchisers

The fastest growing segment of franchising is the franchise specialist, which is characterized by today's fast-food chains. Unlike the earlier forms of franchising, today's franchise specialists derive their income as much from services rendered as from the volume of products sold. Specialty franchisers will usually charge an initial franchise fee plus a percentage of gross revenues. In addition, most will derive additional income from the sale of equipment, food products, food containers, paper products, and supplies. The management controls placed upon individual specialty franchisers are also more restrictive. Stringent management policies, quality control tolerances, and merchandising methods are all defined within the terms of the franchise agreement to help ensure the standardization of the product or service.

C.2 The Characteristics of Franchising

The Franchise Agreement

Regardless of the type of franchise, the franchise agreement should contain sections pertaining to the franchisee's rights, including the term of the agreement, the right and conditions of cancellation, territorial rights, management assistance offerings, and requirements for promotional and advertising assistance. Most specialty franchise agreements also include sections pertaining to the amount of the franchise fee, the required initial investment, royalty agreements, operating requirements, and the conditions for termination or sale.

The Advantages and Disadvantages of Franchising

For many of you, especially those with limited business experience, franchising could prove to be a viable alternative. Franchising can help minimize many of the initial risks that can so often bankrupt new businesses. In addition to an association with a nationally advertised brand, most franchisers offer support in selecting a location, construction assistance, equipment leasing, purchasing options, and assistance in arranging finance. The franchisee is, after all, paying for proven operating methods, and most franchisers respond quite admirably, as fewer than 10% of all franchisees fail.

Franchising isn't everyone's idea of a golden opportunity. Few, if any business owners, like giving up a percentage of their revenues, and at least a degree of independence. Then there is the inability to expand product lines. Many franchisers also claim they pay a premium for products and supplies rather than receiving the promised volume discounts. There is also the disadvantage of not having the sole discretion to sell out to whomever you choose, even a family member. Finally, the initial capital and net worth requirements, particularly with the franchise specialist, will be much greater due in part to the cost of the franchise fee and the location and operating specifications.

Minority and Opportunities

In an attempt to make business ownership more accessible, the SBA offers a minority lending program, which will be discussed in our chapter on financing. The program is mentioned here because many of the major franchisers offer additional financial assistance to qualified participants of the SBA program. Those interested in this type of assistance may wish to contact the individual franchiser for details before applying to the SBA.

Choosing the Right Franchiser

Many markets are becoming oversaturated with franchisers, forcing some of the upstarts into lower earnings and even bankruptcy. Be selective when screening potential opportunities. Beware of blind ads and those promising instant success. Also be cautious of newcomers into a field, especially a field with established leaders. Beware too of the hard sell and those who try to force an instantaneous agreement or deposit requirement. All good franchisers will take the time to screen your qualification thoroughly prior to agreeing to a commitment.

Locating Franchise Opportunities

Entrepreneur magazine publishes a listing of the top 500 franchiser each year, complete with operational highlights and minimal capital requirements. The link is **https://www.entrepreneur.com/franchise500**. The International Franchise Association (**http://franchise.org/**) is another great source for franchiser information. One final suggestion is to poll existing franchisees once you have narrowed down your choices. Talking to existing owners can provide a wealth of information including insight into the franchiser itself, and the success and happiness of its franchisees.

D. Chapter Summary

Again, there are certain advantages and disadvantages unique to each of the new, used, or franchise business concepts. Only you can determine which concept best fits your individual needs. Before making that decision, be sure to weigh each concept against your personal qualifications, choice of industries, market area, location needs, and distribution requirements.

PART III
PURCHASING THE GOING CONCERN

CHAPTER 5
The Professional Buying Approach

Looking at potential businesses will prove as exciting as shopping for a new car or any other large-ticket item. You must learn to temper that excitement so that you remain enthusiastic without becoming impulsive. Consider the comparison of a major and minor league baseball player. Quite often what separates the two isn't talent but attitude. At this stage of the game, begin to take the air of a professional buyer. To do this you must leave your emotions behind and deal instead in cold, hard facts. Objectivity is essential. There are hundreds of businesses for sale in most midsized counties and thousands in larger metropolitan areas. So take your time, be selective, and have fun.

A. A Three-Pronged Buying Approach

There are three key interrelated elements in purchasing a going business:

1. Get to know the industry.
2. Be objective when analyzing the business candidate.
3. Gather enough data to confirm your analysis.

A.1 Getting to Know the Industry

The more you know about an industry—its history, products, marketing methods, sales potential, and so on—the better you will be able to recognize where on the success spectrum the prospect falls. This knowledge will certainly broaden and deepen during the remainder of this text, but a basic understanding will be needed to fully grasp the financial analysis that lies ahead.

Again, leave your emotions at the door, and evaluate the business on a purely objective level. This is not to say that a critical analysis will exclude all subjectivity. There must be some heart in the decision, but it must take a back seat to fact. You must persevere in keeping this in mind until your final decision is at hand.

A.2 The Data Needed to Assess the Sale

Though we may not put a lot of credence in the answer, the obvious lead in question is, "Why do you want to sell?" Once you've obtained what you feel to be a satisfactory answer to this question, delve deeper. Ask how long the business had been in existence, how long he or she has owned the business, and how many previous owners, if any, there have been. In short, you are laying the groundwork for developing a history of the prospective business for you to analyze completely.

Developing a History

A business with few ownership changes will usually be a positive sign, as will retirement, or health-related issues as the reason for the sale. These are often pat answers, though; so view your surroundings carefully, both internal and external. Don't limit your discussion just to the owner; ask for permission to talk to the employees as well. Find out if they are happy, and intend to stay after the sale. Find out what they think of the business environment, and its chances for continued success. Find out their views of the present ownership including their strengths and weaknesses. Talk to the owners of neighboring businesses as well, and to suppliers and any business associates that might have knowledge of the business.

Determining what others think about the business and its ownership will provide keen insight in developing a well-rounded history. A variety of input sources will also help to match others' observations against those supplied by the present owner. This can prove vital in determining the accuracy of the statements made by the owner, as well as providing additional insight into his or her management abilities.

Evaluating the Location

The next area of data to collect is information on the location. Evaluating it may require more subjectivity than any other area of your analysis. Just how good is it? Is it free standing, in a mall, a shopping center, or online with no physical location? Is it urban, suburban, or rural? Is it in good condition? Is there room for expansion? Is there adequate parking? Is it easily accessible? Are the traffic patterns conducive to attracting customers? Is the area heavily competitive or conducive to future competition? Is the area on the incline or decline in terms of population and economic affluence?

Evaluating the Product

Hopefully most of you have pre-evaluated the product, but for those who haven't, will there be a continued market for the product or service? Is the market conducive to the present location? Will the area remain conducive to that market? How will future technological advances affect the market? Again, a certain amount of subjectivity will be involved, but don't let your emotions overshadow your subjective analysis.

Evaluating the Present Owners

Next in our evaluation will be the importance of the present owner to the success of the business. This assessment should go far beyond the present owner's management capabilities and should include an evaluation of his or her interaction with the customer base, and involvement in the business community and community at large. How much of the business's success is dependent upon the owner's religious convictions, family connections, social influence, race, or political ties? If you were to buy the business, would a change in any of these relationships prove detrimental to the business's continued success?

Evaluating the Lease

If everything up to this point looks positive and the purchase does not include real estate, the next area of evaluation will be the terms of the lease. When does it expire? Is it transferrable? Is it renewable? Is it payable on a flat rate, a percentage of the gross or a combination of the two? Is the cost in line with the industry's average and with real estate rates in the area? Are there escalations built into the lease such as annual adjustments or for increases to the landlord's expenses? Is it a triple net lease, one in which the lessee pays the taxes, insurance, and repairs?

In a situation where the expiration date is nearing, or the lease terms are not entirely acceptable, it would prove advantageous to negotiate a renewal as one of the conditions of the terms of the sale. It would also prove advantageous to obtain a copy of the existing lease to verify the answers to your questions personally. You may also want to discuss the situation with the building's owner, if someone other than the business's owner, to assure a smooth transition will be possible in the event of the sale.

The Initial Price Inquiry

For those who don't already know it, the next area of concern will be the asking price. Your only consideration at this point will be if the initial price is so far out of line, no amount of negotiation will make the business affordable and reasonable. In those cases, it would be best to say no now rather than waste anymore of your time.

Keep in mind, the initial asking price will be at the top of the owner's price range, and he or she will most likely be willing to negotiate downward from there. The actual price negotiations will not begin until you have had a chance to review the financial statements, and can logically support arguments for price reductions.

The Carry-back Note

Many sellers will be willing to help with the financing by carrying back a note for part of the purchase price. This can prove advantageous for both parties. For the seller it reduces the initial amount on which he or she must pay capital gains; your payments on the note will provide a steady source of income, and the purchase price will be increased by the amount of interest paid on the note.

For the buyer, the note will reduce the initial capital outlay and risk exposure. Usually, the terms of the note can be negotiated at a lower rate and payment amount than at a financial institution, and those sources will remain available for other types of borrowing. Finally, if the current owner is willing to carry back a note, it will provide you with a certain level of assurance that he or she believes the business is capable of supporting the payments.

The minimum amount of down payment the seller will accept, and the rate and terms of a carry-back note are also subject to negotiation. In these areas too, the seller will start at the top of his or her range and negotiate downward. Many sellers will initially ask for rates and terms slightly above those available from financial institutions. Your objective will be to negotiate down to a range that is somewhat below institutional financing. Determine what the owner might obtain as a rate of return on a CD at a local bank, and negotiate a rate somewhere between that and the loan rate you'd pay at a financial institution. A rate somewhere in the middle will provide a win-win for both parties.

B. An Introduction to Financial Statements

This portion of the evaluation may be the most dreaded by both parties. Next to the owner's spouse, the financial records will be his or her most guarded possession. The present owner's willingness to open the financial records will depend, to some extent, on his or her impression of you and how seriously your intent to purchase is viewed. By the same token, if the owner isn't completely open with the financial records, he or she may have something to hide either from you or the IRS, or both. I would strongly urge discontinuing negotiations if faced with a situation where you are not allowed complete access to the financial records.

Confidentiality Agreements

It most cases, you will be asked to sign a confidentiality agreement before being granted access to the financial data or, for that matter, copies of the lease and other business documents. A confidentiality agreement is a good faith document in which you agree to keep any information supplied to you in the strictest confidence, and you will not share it with anyone else not involved in the negotiations. While this step is routine, please read the terms carefully, and consult with your attorney if you find any of the verbiage of concern.

The Extent of Financial Detail

A thorough financial analysis will require the review of the last three and, if possible, the last five fiscal year-end financial statements. If the business has not been in existence for that length of time, you will have to make do with what is available; but the shorter the existence, the more skeptical your approach should be. I would also supplement year-end statements with the most current interim statement, if statements are compiled on more than an annual basis. I would ask for the most recent operating data if they are not. If an outside accountant is used, it would be best to question both the owner and the accountant on all matters of a financial nature.

Your investigation should also include how financial data is reported and accumulated. Are monthly financial statements or income statements prepared internally? If an outside accountant is utilized, is the general ledger configured to submit data on a direct basis? Is payroll handled internally, or by an outside service? What types of management reports are compiled, and how often? Reviewing these reports can significantly aid in your analysis of the business. The extent of management reporting and the owner's knowledge of these functions can also provide keen insight into his or her management abilities.

B.1 The Types of Statements Available

This brief introduction may prove rather basic for those of you familiar with the various financial statement formats. I feel it a necessary inclusion at this point since those who aren't aware of will need to grasp this basic understanding to be able to complete and comprehend the analysis that lies ahead.

There are four basic elements to the financial statement: the Statement of Financial Position or Balance Sheet, the Income Statement, the Cash Flow Statement, and the Statement of Changes in Equity. We will define each of these statements in more detail as we progress. The type of financial statements available for your analysis will depend, in part, upon the size and complexity of the business you are evaluating, and whether or not an outside accountant is utilized.

Tax Returns

At the very least, the owner will have to prepare annual tax returns. These will always include a detailed income statement (Schedule C), which lists revenues, expenses, including the owner's compensation, and profit or loss. All tax returns will also contain a listing of depreciable assets, which can be extremely helpful in establishing equipment values, when negotiating the final sales price. If the business is a partnership or corporation, the tax returns will also contain a balance sheet, which details the company's assets, liabilities, and its net worth. I would strongly advise obtaining copies of a prospect's tax returns in addition to company or accountant-prepared financial statements. The differences between the two can often prove enlightening.

The Compilation

There are three types of externally prepared financial statement: the compilation, the review, and the audit. The compilation is the least comprehensive in scope. To comply with accounting regulations, the compiled statement must contain an introductory letter from the preparer, a balance sheet, and an income statement. Statement of changes to the financial position and footnotes aren't required, but their omission must be acknowledged in the accountant's introductory letter. The accountant must also note whether their inclusion might change the reader's opinion of the data presented. For those of you who receive company-prepared statements in lieu of use of an outside accountant, these will prove similar in reliability, but at least one step below the compilation.

The Review

The reviewed financial statement must contain all of the parts required for the compilation, plus the statements of changes to the financial position and the footnotes. The accountant must also perform certain limited tests to verify the accuracy of the figures being reported. If any material differences are found, they must be noted in the accountant's introductory letter, and they must be detailed in the footnote section. As such, the reviewed statement offers more assurance than the compilation as to the authenticity of the figures being reported.

The Audit

An audited financial statement will contain those same sections required for a review; however, the testing procedures are much more extensive. The audit also requires the accountant to give an opinion of the company's financial position in the introductory letter. In the rare instance, where an accountant misrepresents figures on an audited statement, the accountant and the accounting firm will be legally liable for the misrepresentation, as will the business's owner. Of the three, the audit gives the most assurance as to the accuracy of the figures reported.

B.2 The Accountant's Introductory Letter

The time has come to begin our review of the financial statement. This review will be important for several reasons. First, by evaluating the past operating results, you can determine the company's present financial condition, and its potential for future success. Second, this review will play a vital role in your price negotiations. Finally, the analysis will help to ensure the figures reported on the financial statements have not been misrepresented.

The analysis should begin with a review of the accountant's introductory letter, when applicable. First, review the letterhead and signature to determine if the preparer is a CPA, or a public accountant. Next, review the operating period to determine whether the statement represents twelve months or a shorter interim period. Is the statement properly identified as a compilation, review, or audit? If it is a compilation, are any omissions noted? If it is a review or audit, have all tests been conducted satisfactorily, and have any material differences been noted? If it is an audit, is the accountant's opinion letter qualified or unqualified? If qualified, what are the qualifications? Check also to determine if there has been a change of accountants or a reduction in the scope of the statements during the review period. Either could be an indicator that something is amiss.

B.3 The Footnotes
The Accounting Method
Once you have completed the assessment of the introductory letter, the notes to the financial statements should be examined next. The first footnote will pertain to the accounting methods utilized to prepare the financial statement. The most likely methods will be the cash basis, accrual basis, or modified accrual basis. Under the cash basis, a company doesn't acknowledge a sale until the monies have been received. Under the cash basis, there will be no accounts receivable. By comparison, under the accrual method, a sale is acknowledged when the sale transpires. If the money has not yet changed hands, an account receivable will be generated until the monies have been received. The modified cash basis is a combination of the two methods. It is often used by the contractors who report sales on a percentage of completion basis. The accrual method is by far the most popular today, and it provides the most accurate depiction of a company's financial condition.

The Inventory Valuation
The next footnote will pertain to inventory, where applicable. It will specify whether inventory is valued at LIFO (last in first out) or FIFO (first in first out). Let's define the two methods by way of an example. Suppose you own a retail sporting goods store and you stock one Head Prestige racquet at a cost of $150 and a manufacturer's suggested retail price of $199. Then before you sell the racquet, the manufacturer raises the wholesale cost to $175, and the suggested retail price to $229. Assuming you sell the racquet at $229, your gross profit on this racquet now becomes $79 rather than the $49, right? Well that answer depends on your inventory valuation method.

The LIFO method of inventory valuation allows you to report the cost of the first racquet at the higher price, provided you have purchased a subsequent racquet at the higher cost prior to selling that first racquet. Why? Because under the LIFO method you base the inventory valuation on the last inventory purchased.

Most businesses today prefer the LIFO method. It's particularly beneficial during periods of rising costs since reporting higher inventory costs reduces profits, and subsequently, income-tax liability. The LIFO method also gives a truer picture of current inventory costs, allowing for more accurate budgeting. Don't be overly concerned by a firm using the FIFO method, unless the footnote discloses a recent change from LIFO to FIFO. The change would artificially inflate profits, and could be used by an owner to justify a higher selling price for the business.

Fixed Asset Valuation
The next footnote will be a schedule of fixed assets similar to that found on the tax return. Again, this can be a good starting point for valuing the fixed assets in terms of the selling price. Those of you entering industries requiring heavy investments in fixed assets should also require these valuations be substantiated with current equipment appraisals prior to negotiating the final sales price. Lease obligations if they are capitalized (depreciated) will also appear in this footnote with any corresponding debt listed in the notes payable footnote.

Notes Payable
The next footnote will include a breakdown of all notes and loans outstanding as well as what amounts are deemed current (payable within the next twelve months), and noncurrent. Pay particular attention to notes coming due shortly, particularly those with large balances or balloon payments. In some instances, particularly in the sale of a corporation, the purchase could include the assumption of these obligations.

Subordinated Debt and Contingent Liabilities
Two footnotes that occasionally follow next refer to any subordinated debt or contingent liabilities. Subordinated debts are those that the company has pledged to refrain from paying back until a senior liability has been paid. This happens most frequently when a company owes money to a stockholder, and it pledges not to pay it back until a bank or another creditor has been repaid.

Contingent liabilities are those for which the company is secondarily liable. This would include any debt of the owner or of an affiliate that the company has guaranteed. Contingent liabilities are not listed on the balance sheet, but would still have to be paid if the primary payee defaulted on its obligation. Prior to any purchase, I would suggest you request a listing of any and all contingent liabilities—in writing—or a written affidavit that none exist.

Retained Earnings Reconciliation

This footnote will detail other inclusion or deductions that have been made to the equity account such as dividends or owner's withdrawals. Typically a corporation's retained earnings from the prior year-end plus the current year's net profit will equal the current year's end retained earnings. The same holds true for a proprietorship or a partnership; the beginning owner's or partners' equity account plus the current period's net profit equals the ending equity.

All of you should perform this simple reconciliation, even those whose statements don't include this footnote. Also, if your reconciliation uncovers unexplained withdrawals, require an accounting of the differences. Remember, you won't be able to reconcile the equity or retained earnings account for the first year of operation since there was no prior year's ending balance.

A portion of a company's retained earnings must be retained in the business if it is to continue to grow and prosper. While it's unrealistic to assume that the current owner will leave you all of the business's cash or retained earnings, excessive withdrawals during the years prior to the sale could forewarn of the financial instability of the business itself.

Federal Income Taxes

There may also be a footnote detailing the income tax or deferred tax liability. Normally, deferred taxes are accrued when a company's financial statements are prepared on an accrual basis, and the tax returns are prepared on a cash basis. For a corporation, deferred taxes could also occur if it has chosen different fiscal and tax year ends. In these situations, the deferred tax liability would represent that portion of the tax expense deferred to the following tax year. This footnote will also disclose whether any tax liens exist, or past tax liabilities remain to be paid.

Lease Commitments

Leases that are not capitalized will be listed as a separate footnote, as will the amounts payable under the obligation. Though these obligations will not appear on the balance sheet as liabilities, they are in fact contractual obligations and should be considered as such. The most familiar example would be a lease agreement covering the operating premises. Many companies, however, lease rather than purchase automobiles and equipment. As with continuant liabilities, a statement detailing lease commitments, or lack thereof, should be required from the current owner as part of any sales agreement.

Revaluation and Modifications

The remaining footnotes will pertain to any material differences the accountant may have found or any revaluation of assets. Revaluations will in most cases raise the value of assets from the original cost to the current market value. In turn, this will increase a company's net worth, and could inflate the asking price. As for material differences, they will usually imply an accountant's discrepancy with the figures the company has reported, or with the company's overall financial condition. These should be viewed with great concern, and any questions they raise should be answered prior to continuing negotiations.

C. Chapter Summary

Hopefully, this brief discussion has deepened your understanding of two important, but often overlooked sections of the financial statement. We have only just begun to scratch the surface though in laying the groundwork for analyzing the financial statements themselves. The analysis process will be carried over into the next two chapters. In chapter 6, we will review the most important sections of the financial statements, the balance sheet and the income statement. We will also establish operating trends that will be utilized to determine whether or not a business prospect represents a worthwhile investment. That analysis will be carried over into chapter 7 where we will examine the prospect's ability to generate cash flow, and determine how to establish a fair offering price.

CHAPTER 6

Analyzing Financial Statements

We are now ready to delve into the financial statements. This is an area where most inexperienced buyers—angels or otherwise—fear to tread. But, for the most part, financial statement analysis is just a matter of common sense, and relatively simple once one gets a few basic under his or her belt. This chapter details those basics. Once this portion of the analysis is completed, your ability to understand the operations of the prospective business could very well exceed that of the present owner. We will begin our analysis with a detailed look at the income statement.

A. The Income Statement Work Sheet

I would suggest you construct this work sheet and subsequent work sheets as Excel spreadsheets. This will save you from having to perform tedious financial calculations by hand, and will enable you to use the work sheets to analyze several prospects with ease if need be. For the sake of this exercise, two years' worth of financial statements are included for our sample company, Superior Jewelers, Inc.

The Work Sheet Format

The far-right column of the work sheet contains the corresponding industry averages from RMA. The headings at the top of the page list the dates of the financial statements provided with the oldest statement's figures entered in the farthest left-hand column. Subsequent statements are entered chronologically working toward the right.

Financial Statements

Superior Jeweler's, Inc.
Balance Sheet
For the years ending July 31, 20X1 and 20XX

ASSETS

Current Assets

	7/31/X1	7/31/XX
Cash	$16,565	$10,670
Accounts Receivable-Trade	45,000	25,605
Accounts Receivable-Employees	1,100	1,100
Inventory	141.660	100,010
Prepaid Expenses	2,640	2,790
	$206,965	$140,175

Property and Equipment

	7/31/X1	7/31/XX
Leasehold Improvements	$25,570	$15,500
Fixtures and Furnishings	10,500	5.200
Office Equipment	2,400	2.400
(Accumulated Depreciation)	(11,080)	(4,880)
	$27,390	$18,220

Other Assets

	7/31/X1	7/31/XX
Due From Officers	$4,500	$4,500
Deposits	1,245	1,245
	$5,745	$5,745
TOTAL ASSETS	**$240,100**	**$164,140**

LIABILITIES AND STOCKHOLDER'S EQUITY

Current Liabilities

	7/31/X1	7/31/XX
Notes Payable-Short Term	$24,000	$10,500
Current Portion-Term Debt	3,520	2,765
Accounts Payable-Trade	28,000	17,443
Income Tax Payable	4,875	4,045
Accrued Sales Tax	2,310	2,400
Accrued Payroll Taxes	900	1,500
	$63,605	$38,653

Long Term Liabilities

	7/31/X1	7/31/XX
Loans Payable-Term Portion	$77,107	$53,594
	$77,107	$53,594
TOTAL LIABILITIES	**$140,712**	**$92,247**

Stockholder's Equity

	7/31/X1	7/31/XX
Capital Stock, common, 5,000 shares issued and outstanding with a $5.00 par value	$25,000	$25,000
Paid in Capital	23,988	23,988
Retained Earnings	50,400	22,905
	$99,388	$71,893
TOTAL LIABILITIES AND STOCKHOLDER'S EQUITY	**$240,100**	**$164,140**

SUPERIOR JEWELERS, INC

Statement of Income
For the years ending July 31, 20X1 and 20XX

	July 31, 20X1		July 31, 20XX	
SALES		$390,000		$350,000
COST OF GOODS SOLD				
Beginning Inventory	101,010		75,000	
Purchases 2	46,960		207,010	
(Ending Inventory)	(141,660)		(100,010)	
		206,310		182,000
GROSS PROFIT		183,690		160,000
OPERATING EXPENSES				
Salaries-Officer	30,000		26,000	
Salaries-Other	56,000		52,500	
Payroll Taxes	9,460		8,635	
Rent	16,000		15,000	
Advertising	4,950		4,800	
Depreciation	6,200		4,880	
Insurance	1.250		2,250	
Utilities	6,900		6,490	
Telephone	980		1,240	
Legal & Accounting	2,450		3,200	
Dues & Publications	190		175	
Travel & Entertainment	1,875		1,290	
Interest	13,580		9,240	
Other Operating Expenses	315		1,500	
TOTAL OPERATING EXPENSES		150,150		137,200
NET INCOME FROM OPERATIONS		33,540		30,800
OTHER INCOME & (EXPENSES)				
Interest Income	2,120		1,550	
Bad Debt Expense	(780)		(500)	
Discounts	(2,510)		(4,900)	
		(1,170)		(3,850)
NET INCOME BEFORE INCOME TAXES		32,370		26,950
Provision for State & Federal Income Taxes		4,875		4,045
NET INCOME FOR THE YEAR		**$27,495**		**$22,905**

SUPERIOR JEWELERS, INC.
INCOME STATEMENT WORKSHEET

	7/31/20XX	7/31/20X1				R.M.A. Studies
Sales	$350,000	$390,000				$390,000
Cost of Goods Sold	182,000	206,310				203,580
% of Sales	52.0	52.9				52.2
Gross Profit	168,000	183,690				186,420
% of Sales	48.0	47.1				47.8
Operating Expenses:						
Owners' Salaries	26,000	30,000				29,640
% of Sales	7.4	7.7				7.6
Other Salaries	52,500	56,000				
Payroll Taxes	8.635	9,460				
Employee Benefits						
Rent	15,000	16,000				
Insurance	2,250	1,250				
Utilities	6,490	6,900				
Advertising and Promotion	4.800	4,950				
Professional Services	3,200	2,450				
Travel and Entertainment	1,290	1,875				
Depreciation & Amortization	4,880	6,200				
Interest Expense	9,240	13,580				
Other Operating Expenses	2.915	1,485				
Total Operating Expenses	137,200	150,150				152,100
% of Sales	39.2	38.5				39.0
Operating Profit	30,800	33,540				34,540
% of Sales	8.8	8.6				8.9
Other income (Expense)	(3,850)	(1;170)				(4,680)
Pretax Profit	26,950	32.370				29,860
% of Sales	7.7	8.3				7.7
Income Tax Expense	4,045	4,815				
Net Profit	$22,905	$27,495				
% of Sales	6.5	7.1				

A.1 Inserting the Industry Averages

For those of you who would like to work through the calculations for converting industry percentages into dollars, you'll note we used the prospective business's most current fiscal year-end sales as the industry's sales figure. Then we simply multiply each percentage by that dollar sales figure, and move each answer's decimal point two places to the left. The Income Statement constructed from this exercise represents the industry's median operating results at the business's most recent sales level. This enables the comparison of the prospect's level of success to the median operating results of similar companies with identical sales levels.

The Cost of Goods Sold as a Percent of Sales

The first calculation for our historical information columns, the cost of goods sold as a percent of sales, is derived by dividing the cost of goods sold by total sales, and moving the decimal point two places to the right to convert the answer into a percentage. This tells us the percentage of expenses directly proportional to sales. In most cases, this percentage will remain fairly constant despite any reasonable fluctuation in sales volume. This means that as sales volume goes up or down, the dollar amount for the cost of goods sold will also go up or down in direct proportion. For our example, both years' calculations are fairly representative of the industry median, though the slight increase in year 20X1 could be cause for further analysis.

Don't panic if your prospect's financial statements and RMA materials are void of a cost of goods sold section. Only those businesses that rely on inventory to generate sales will have them. Most service companies and professionals will only have direct operating expenses.

Gross Operating Margins

The gross profit margin is calculated in the same manner, by dividing gross profit by sales and converting the answer into a percentage. Note too, that the gross profit margin will always be the reciprocal of the cost of goods sold to sales percentage. Now make the same calculations and comparisons for operating expenses, operating profit, pretax profit, and net profit. You will notice that these percentages for Superior Jewelers are also in line with the industry's median. We can thus surmise that Superior Jeweler's operating results are a fair representative of the retail jewelry industry.

Uncovering Undisclosed Profits

The net profit reported isn't always a true indication of a company's potential profitability, because most business owners consciously minimize profits to reduce their company's income-tax liability. Let's examine some of the operating expense categories commonly utilized for this practice to see if we can uncover any hidden profits for Superior Jewelers. First, let's examine owners' salaries. Again, our sample is representative but, if for example, owners' salaries were listed at $150,000, we could safely assume the prospect is much more profitable than the industry median.

Let us also look at some forms of indirect compensation. Is there a deduction for pension and profit sharing, owners' insurance payments, auto expenses, publications, or travel and entertainment? Getting the idea? How much is the lease expense? It's quite possible the owner is the landlord too, enabling the ability to substantiate additional withdrawals through rent payments, which can often be offset on personal tax returns through mortgage interest and building depreciation. This technique is also used with equipment leasebacks. Keep in mind also that if these categories are all non-existent, it could be an indication that profits are being artificially inflated to substantiate a higher asking price.

Noncash Expenditures

Depreciation or amortization are also favorite expense groups used to reduce profits since these are noncash deductions. Though deducted from profit just like any other expense, nobody gets paid and no cash leaves the business. Don't automatically consider depreciation as cash in the bank, though. In most cases the monies expensed will eventually have to be reinvested into replacing or repairing depreciated assets.

Other Income and Expenses

Let us now look at interest expense, bad debt expense, and other income or losses. If the interest expense seems high, it could be an indication that the company is overextended. In some cases, there could also be a note due to the owner. Interest payments to the owner are another way to reduce profits, but be cautious because it could also mean the owner is investing his or her own funds to support an underperforming business. These types of relationships should all be detailed in the statement footnotes. If no footnotes are provided, make sure these types of relationships are fully disclosed in some type of documentation from the owners.

Is bad debt expense unusually high? This could be an indication that some of the accounts receivable aren't collectable. How about other income? Is it a major contributor to net profit? If so, maybe the company isn't that profitable from an operational standpoint.

A.2 Establishing Operating Trends

The next step in our Income Statement analysis is to establish operating trends to determine if the operations are growing, stagnant, or declining. Again, the more years we have to compare, the more accurate are trend analysis will be. Three to five years is optimal, but as will be the case for many of you; Superior Jewelers has only been operational for two years.

Begin with sales. For our example, sales increased by 11.4% in 20X1. We determine this by dividing the sales increase of $40,000 by the prior year's sales volume of $350,000. Again, we then move the decimals two places to the right to convert to a percentage. Was this increase due primarily to an increase in the number of products sold or to a price increase? To better understand how price changes can affect and distort sales trends, consider for a moment the operations of a retail gas station. The fluctuation in retail pump prices over the last few years could severely distort any sales-trend analysis that didn't include a comparison of both dollar sales volume and the number of gallons sold.

To fully understand the increase in sales volume for Superior Jewelers, we would need to complete an in-depth analysis of the company's complete sale records. We can, however, interpolate meaningful trend results by also examining the various expense and profit trends. Gross profit by dollars, for example, also increased in 20X1, yet the corresponding gross profit margin declined. Additionally, the reciprocal, the cost of goods sold to sales, increased. From these observations we can safely assume that sales volume increases were due, at least in part, to selling more merchandise by discounting or lowering prices, that is, profit margins.

Operating expenses also increased for 20X1, yet in this instance, operating expenses as a percent of sales decreased. Because of this decrease, we can safely assume that operating expenses remained in line despite increases. From an operating profit standpoint, 20X1 represented a better year. The combination of a tighter rein on operating expenses coupled with the sales increase, more than offset the lower gross profit margin. This is evident by an increase in both pretax profit and the pretax profit margin.

External Variables

Operating trends can often be affected by external variables, and those not directly related to operations. Sometimes a good business may be experiencing operating difficulties because of a recent management change, or trends could slip temporarily because of an employee strike. Maybe a major access road was closed for a period for repairs or operations were impacted by declining economic conditions. The reverse can also be true. Inflation can easily distort sales volume upward. Sales volume must increase by at least the annual inflation rate to maintain the same level of operating efficiency as the prior year.

When you begin to review prospective companies, examine these same types of operating variables. You should now be able to discern a healthy operating condition fairly easily. If you find a prospect's operating trends are stagnant or declining, try to isolate the causes. If they are correctable, you may have found yourself a mismanaged bargain, and find yourself in a position to negotiate a substantially reduced purchase price. On the other hand, if trend declines are not easily correctable, there is no need to carry the analysis any further.

B. An Introduction to the Balance Sheet

For those of you unfamiliar with a balance sheet, we will begin this discussion with a brief introduction. As you can see, Superior Jeweler's Balance Sheet is identical in format to that of the personal financial statement in chapter 2. All balance sheets contain three major sections: the asset section, the liability section, and the equity section. Using the personal statement as a simplified analogy, assets equals what a company owns, and liabilities what is owed against them. Hopefully the value of the assets exceeds the debt. That excess is the company's equity or net worth. In all cases, total assets will be equal to the sum total of liabilities and equity.

The Asset Section

Assets are divided into two general categories: current and noncurrent. Current assets are defined as cash equivalents or accounts that should be converted to cash within the next twelve months, like the accounts receivable and inventory. Noncurrent assets are those that are not expected to be converted into cash within the next twelve months, and those that would be difficult to convert into cash within the next twelve months. A note receivable due in the future would be an example. A note receivable often has a current and a noncurrent component. If payments on the note are being received monthly, for example, that portion due during the next twelve months would be listed as a current asset, while that portion due in later years would be listed as a noncurrent asset.

Fixed assets and intangible assets are also considered noncurrent assets. Fixed assets are any real property holdings or depreciable tangible assets such as land, buildings, and equipment. Intangibles are assets that have no tangible or readily marketable value such as goodwill.

The Liability Section

Liabilities too are divided into current and noncurrent, and the same general definitions apply. Those due within twelve months are current liabilities, and those due later after twelve months are noncurrent liabilities. Examples of current liabilities include accounts payable, accrued taxes, and the current portion of any long-term debt. An example of a long-term liability would be the principle portion of an installment loan due after one year. There are also deferred liabilities, such as the deferred taxes, which were discussed in the preceding chapter. These could be current or noncurrent depending upon the due date.

Larger corporations may also list debentures or bonds in the noncurrent liability section. These are both alternative forms of raising capital, in which the corporation would issue and sell bonds or debenture certificates to the general public. In this manner, a corporation raises or borrows its capital requirement from the general public rather than a financial institution. The holders of these instruments are paid interest during the term of the obligation, but receive no dividends or ownership rights as with a common stock purchase. Depending upon how the issue is written, the instrument can sometimes be converted to common stock at a later date.

The Proprietorship and Partnership Equity Section

The equity section will vary depending upon the business format. If the business is a proprietorship, the equity section could be limited to one line entitled owner's equity. It might also include separate headings for current period's net profits or owner's withdrawals. If the business is a partnership, the equity section could include a capital account for each partner, or separate profit and withdrawal accounts for each partner. These could be further subdivided into general and limited partner accounts depending upon the partnership format.

The Corporate Equity Section

If the business is a corporation, the equity section will include accounts for common stock, retained earnings, and net profit. There could also be accounts for preferred treasury stock or a paid-in capital account. The amount listed for common stock represents the par value of all shares outstanding. If the shares were sold for more than their par value, the excess would be listed as paid-in capital. This account would also include any monies the stockholders have personally injected into the business in the form of capital contributions. The net profit account will only include the current period's net profit. Prior periods' profits that have not been withdrawn or paid out in dividends are accumulated in the retained earnings account.

Very few of you will ever run across preferred or treasury stock accounts. Preferred stock is sold to raise money or capital as another alternative to institution borrowing. In most cases, preferred stockholders are not granted voting rights like common stock holders, but they will usually be granted more attractive dividend programs. Treasury stock is simply common or preferred stock that has been redeemed or repurchased from shareholders by the corporation. It will always be listed as a negative amount.

Suppressing Net Worth

There are times when liabilities will exceed assets resulting in a negative net worth. If you are currently holding such a statement, there is a 99.9% chance you shouldn't buy. The 0.1% chance would occur when the fixed assets are carried at cost, but their actual market value is considerably greater. This could occur if the business had been passed down in a family for generations, a farm for example, and it was advantageous to keep the land values as low as possible for tax purposes. Anyone faced with this situation should substantiate any suppressed fixed asset values with independent appraisals.

C. The Balance Sheet Work Sheet

Let's now review the balance-sheet work sheet, an example of which has been included. As with our prior example, we will start by reviewing the percentages from the RMA statement studies. These too can be converted to cash equivalents, for those who wish, by using a percent of the total assets, total liabilities, or total equity multiplication; just as we did with sales on the income statement work sheet. Again, we input the oldest statement in the furthest left-hand column, and work chronologically to the right.

SUPERIOR JEWELERS, INC.
BALANCE SHEET WORKSHEET

ASSETS	July 31 20XX	July 31 20X1				R.M.A. Statement Studies % of Total
Cash	$10,670	$16,565				6.5
Accounts Receivable (Net)	25,605	45,000				15.6
Inventory	100,010	141,660				61.6
Marketable Securities						
Prepaids	2,790	2,640				
Other Current Assets	1,100	1,100				1.8
TOTAL CURRENT ASSETS	140,175	206,965				85.5
Land and Buildings (Gross)						
Machinery and Equipment	7,600	12,900				
Leasehold Improvements	15,500	25,570				
(Accumulated Depreciation)	(4,880)	(11,080)				
NET FIXED ASSETS	18,220	27,390				9.7
Investments						
Notes Receivable (Officers)	4,500	4,500				
Other Noncurrent Assets	1,245	1,245				3.4
Intangibles						1.4
TOTAL ASSETS	$164,140	$240,100				100.0
LIABILITIES						
Notes Payable - Bank	$10,500	$24,000				9.3
Notes Payable - Other						
Current Portion - LTD	2,765	3,520				3.0
Accounts Payable	17,443	28,000				19.0
Income Taxes Payable	4,045	4,875				
Accrued and Other Current Liab.	3,900	3,210				10.5
TOTAL CURRENT LIABILITIES	38,653	63,605				41.8
Term Debt - Banks	53,594	77,107				14.5
TOTAL LIABILTIES	92,247	140,712				
EQUITY						
Common Stock	25,000	25,000				
Preferred/Paid in Capital	23,988	23,988				
Retained Earnings/Owner's Equity	22,905	50,400		1		
NET WORTH	71,893	99,388				43.7
NET WORTH + LIABILITIES	$164,140	$240,100				100.0

Additional Operating Trends

Let's now begin to establish balance-sheet trends, many of which will further our understanding of the income statement analysis. We will begin with net worth. What correlations can be drawn by comparing the increase in net worth for 20X1 to the net profit reported on the income statement? The net worth reconciliation from the previous chapter applies here as well. The net profit of $27,495 for 20X1 plus the prior year's retained earnings of $22,905 equals the current year's retained earnings amount of $50,400. Additionally, there were no changes to common stock or paid-in capital, so our reconciliation is in balance. This tells us that the entire year's profits were retained in the business and that no unusual or undisclosed withdrawals were recorded—a healthy sign.

What trends can we establish for total asset or liabilities? Again, referring to our example, total assets increased by more than the increase in net worth, requiring an increase in borrowings or liabilities. While this relationship is apparent to fully understand balance sheet changes, their correlation to individual asset and liability accounts necessitate studding the balance sheet in conjunction with our next insert—the ratio analysis work sheet. This work sheet is utilized to measure the effects of balance-sheet changes on the overall operation.

D. The Ratio Analysis Work Sheet

Industry Quartiles

You'll notice the statement studies' ratios are divided into three categories or quartiles. These represent an upper range for the one-third of the companies, whose financial condition is better than the median, a middle quartile for one-third of the companies that fall into or near the median, and a lower quartile for the one-third of the companies whose performance falls below the median.

D.1 The Liquidity Analysis

Though a company's success is measured by profitability, its ability to service operating expenses and pay its debts is as dependent on its ability to generate cash as to generate profits. Liquidity analysis is a series of measures and ratios designed to determine the quality and adequacy of current assets to service current obligations.

Working Capital

The first liquidity measurement, for discussion purposes, is working capital, which is defined as current assets minus current liabilities. This figure, measured in dollars, represents a rough estimate of cash or near cash available after all current liabilities have been serviced. This measurement is vital because it reflects the level of cash available to continue or expand current operations. Current assets aren't always as easily convertible to cash as one might think, however. To make this determination requires studying the level of working capital in conjunction with several key liquidity ratios.

SUPERIOR JEWELERS, INC.
RATIO ANALYSIS
WORKSHEET

		July 31 20XX	July31 20X1				R.M.A. Statement Studies
WORKING CAPITAL		$101,522	$143,460				
LIQUIDITY RATIOS							3.1 2.1
Current Ratio	Current Assets / Current Liab.	3.6	3.3				1.6
Quick Ratio	Cash & Acct. Rec. / Current Liabs.	1.0	1.0				.9 .5 .2
Inventory Turnover	C.G.S. / Inventory	1.8	1.5				1.9 1.2 .8
Day's Supply	360 * / Inv. T.O.	200	240				192 304 456
Accounts Receivable Turnover	Sales / Acct. Rec.	13.7	8.7				30.4 13.8 6.4
Day's Receivable	360 * / A/R T.O.	26	41				12 26 57
Accounts Payable Turnover	C.G.S. / Accts. Pay.	10.4	7.4				N/A
Day's Payable	360 * / A/P T.O.	35	48				N/A
LEVERAGE RATIOS							.6 1.3
Debt/Worth	Total Liabs. / Net Worth	1.28	1.42				2.6
Fixed/Worth	Fixed Assets / Net Worth	.25	.28				.1 .2 .5
ASSET MANAGEMENT RATIOS							1.8 1.4
Sales to Assets	Sales / Total Assets	2.13	1.62				1.1
Return on Assets — %	Net Profit (B4T) / Total Assets	16.4	13.5				16.1 8.9 3.7
Return on Investment — %	Net Profit (B4T) / Net Worth	37.5	32.6				39.8 22.9 10.1

* Or the number of days during the statement period if less than one year.

The Current Ratio

The first of these, the current ratio, is derived by dividing total current assets by total current liabilities and rounding to the nearest hundredth. The current ratio represents the number of dollars of current assets available to cover each dollar of current liabilities. Usually, the higher the ratio, the more liquid the company, and a ratio of at least 1:1 is desirable. As you can see, Superior Jewelers has over $3 in current assets for each $1 in current liabilities, and the median for jeweler of that size is $2.10. Some industries, particularly those requiring heavy investments in fixed assets, may have current ratios that fall below 1:1, so be sure to compare your answer with the statement studies before drawing any conclusions when viewing prospective businesses.

The Effects of Inventory on Liquidity

There are also times when a seemingly healthy working capital or current ratio could prove misleading. An example would be if a large percentage of the current assets were tied up in inventory, that inventory would first have to be sold and possibly converted into a receivable, before it is converted into cash. The time restraints involved in that conversion could prove substantial. If that inventory contained obsolete or slow-moving merchandise, the current ratio could be thrown even more askew.

Inventory Tests

We can measure the effects of inventory on liquidity by two simple calculations. The first is the inventory turnover rate, which is calculated by dividing inventory into the cost of goods sold. This tells us the number of times inventory turned over during the statement period. The inventory turnover rate can then be turned into a daily average by dividing it into the number of days in the statement period. This tells us the average number of days of supply on hand. As you can see from our example, Superior Jewelers turned its inventory one and a half times in the year 20X1, or every 240 days. While that is above the norm, it would still take, on average, eight months to convert a dollar of inventory to cash. These figures do not account for any seasonality though, which might also have to be taken into consideration.

The Quick Ratio

The next ratio we will calculate is called the quick ratio. It too is related to liquidity, and it is often utilized in conjunction with the current ratio. The quick ratio is calculated by taking the sum total of the cash accounts, accounts receivable, and the current portion of any notes receivable divided by total current liabilities. This ratio measures the company's ability to service current liabilities without having to first liquidate inventory. Again, be sure to compare your answer to the statement studies. Don't be surprised if both your answer and the median fall below 1.00, which would imply a dependency to sell inventory to liquidate all current liabilities.

Accounts Receivable Tests

There are times when the quick ratio can also be misleading, the primary example being slow or nonpaying accounts receivable. Two receivable tests are helpful in determining its effect on liquidity. The first test is simply to divide net sales by accounts receivable, which will tell us how many times receivables turned over during the period or the receivables turnover rate. The higher the number, the quicker receivables are turning over. Now divide the number of days in the statement period by the turnover rate. This will tell us the average number of days those receivables were outstanding. Again, these averages don't take into account seasonal trends.

Accounts Payable Turnover

You can also determine the accounts payable turnover rate by dividing the accounts payable figure into the cost of goods sold. Again, this quotient can be divided into the number of days in the period to determine the average number of days required to pay accounts receivable. Though accounts payable measurements are not included in the statement studies, they can serve as a preliminary indication of how relations with suppliers are maintained. These measurements too can be thrown askew by seasonality or special payment arrangements being offered by suppliers as incentives.

Additional Liquidity Measurements

There are several aids that can be used to further your liquidity analysis when the need arises. The first is an accounts receivable aging. An aging lists all receivables due in categories of current, thirty days outstanding, sixty days outstanding, ninety days outstanding, and 120 days and over. An aging gives a more detailed account of the quality and likelihood of repayment of accounts receivable, and it gives valuable insight into customers' paying habits and those with problematic histories.

The second aid is an accounts payable aging, which is detailed in the same manner as the receivables aging. The payables aging will detail how the current owner is paying on his or her accounts with each supplier. If the current owner is not meeting the payment terms, this could indicate underlying financial concerns or problems with merchandise being supplied. At the very least, it will give you an indication of current supplier relationships, and an understanding of how best to maintain and grow those relationships.

The final liquidly aid is an inventory evaluation, which lists all existing inventory by item, date received, cost, and current value. This can be extremely valuable in determining the quality of current inventory, and can shed light on any stale or obsolete inventory. I would suggest requesting all of these aids for prospects under serious contention.

Most good managers will already be producing and utilizing these aids to help optimize operations. If they are not, I'd be questioning the quality of their management abilities.

Superior Jewelers has experienced an increase in both accounts receivable and inventory when comparing 20X1 to 20XX. Both increases should warrant a closer examination. Receivables, in particular, would have heightened my curiosity. I suspect there are a few problematic accounts that need to be addressed prior to the purchase, and possibly even discounted from the final purchase price for the business.

D.2 Leverage Measurements

The next set of calculations we will discuss are commonly known as leverage ratios. These measure the extent of a company's debt in relation to its net worth. The higher a company is leveraged, the more susceptible it is to business downturns.

The Fixed Asset Ratio

The first leverage measurement we will discuss is the fixed-asset-to-net-worth ratio. This is calculated simply by dividing net worth into net fixed assets. This ratio tells us to what extent capital is invested in fixed assets, or the number of dollars invested in fixed assets for each dollar of net worth. The higher this ratio, the less capital there will be available to maintain or expand operations.

The Debt to Worth Ratio

An even more important leverage ratio is the debt-to-worth ratio. This is calculated by dividing total liabilities by total net worth. The lower the ratio, the stronger the company's financial stability, and the greater the availability to increase borrowing if need be. A lower debt-to-worth ratio signifies less dependency on borrowings to maintain operations. Conversely, a higher debt-to-worth ratio, particularly one that falls into the lower quartile, could signify a dependence on increasing borrowings to sustain operations. Too high a debt-to-worth ratio could also disclose financial difficulties or an over-leveraged company.

While Superior Jewelers' leverage ratios are acceptable, they do indicate a slight deterioration. The slowing in receivables and inventory would heighten my concerns enough to request an interim financial statement to help substantiate in which direction this business is trending.

D.3 Management Performance Measurements
Pretax Profit to Net Worth and Total Assets

Two ratios that are considered measurements of management performance are the profit before taxes to net worth, and the pretax profit to total assets ratio. The first is calculated by dividing pretax profit by net worth. The second is calculated by dividing pretax profit by total assets. Both of these ratios are measured in percentages, so we must move the answers decimal point two places to the right. The higher the percentages, the more effective management is at employing capital or assets.

Both of these ratios are subject to a high degree of fallibility and should only be utilized with the statement studies comparison. An undercapitalized business, for example, could look favorable in the pretax profit to net worth ratio, while a company with a high proportion of intangible assets could look favorable in the pretax profit to total assets ratio.

Sales to Total Assets Ratio
The final management performance calculation we will measure is the sales to total assets ratio. This is calculated by dividing sales by total assets. This measures a company's ability to employ its assets to generate sales. This ratio too is subject to a high degree of fallibility, and should only be utilized in conjunction with the statement studies.

D.4 Final Comparisons for Superior Jewelers
In general, Superior Jewelers fares quite well in comparison to the companies included in the statement studies. Liquidity is excellent as evidenced by a current ratio that exceeds the upper quartile. Though typically an inventory-laden industry, the quick ratio also exceeds the upper quartile. Asset management ratios are also quite respectable.

As mentioned previously, there are some trends that bear watching. Notably the slowing in receivables and inventory turns, which may be the reason for a slowing in paying accounts payable. From an owner's standpoint, these areas should be addressed and improved upon before they deteriorate further. From a buyer's standpoint, aging and inventory evaluations should be requested to ensure there is no immediate cause for concern. Additionally, an interim financial statement would be a welcome addition to the analysis to help determine in which direction the company is trending.

E. Chapter Summary
That completes our financial statement analysis. By utilizing and comparing the results of these three work sheets, you should be able to accurately assess a prospect's past performance and financial stability. Again, the work sheets will be most beneficial when compiling the results over a period of several years to establish more accurate operating trends. These trends in turn should be interpreted in conjunction with the industry averages so as not to misconstrue any operational quirks that might be unique to that industry.

CHAPTER 7

The Purchase

A. Making the Decision

For those of you contemplating the purchase of an existing business, the time for making a decision is drawing near. No, I haven't forgotten operating projections. Eventually you will have to do them, especially if you intend to apply for a loan. But when analyzing the purchase decision, the best indication of future performance will come from studying the company's past history. Just as history tends to repeat itself or, as I prefer, run in circles, so too do business cycles. This chapter will illustrate how to evaluate the past history of a business as it relates to future performance, and how to establish a fair purchase price.

At this point, we need to determine whether future performance will be adequate to pay any new debt requirements, provide you with adequate compensation, and provide enough profit to comfortably sustain operations. Again, these questions can be answered in part by studying past performance, and by comparing the prospect's operating trends to the statement studies. However, certainty can only be ascertained through a detailed analysis of cash flow.

A.1 Cash Flow Makes the Business Go

Though a business is measured by its net worth and ability to turn a profit, its life blood is cash flow. Payroll and loan payments aren't paid by net profit; they're paid from the cash generated by operations. Many of today's business owners still operate under the age-old adage that cash flow equals net profit plus depreciation, yet this formula is as outdated as the slide rule.

To measure true cash flow, we must also calculate balance-sheet changes from one period to the next, and determine how these changes affected the overall performance of the business. The reasoning for this is best described by reverting to our original explanation of accrual accounting. As you recall, under the accrual method, a sale is generated at the time a transaction takes place, even if that transaction isn't paid for until a later date.

Let's imagine it's your company's fiscal year-end and the financial statements show a net profit of $100,000, which coincidentally is the best performance in the company's history. You'd like to show your appreciation by paying some key employees small bonuses but, to your surprise, the checking account register is showing a negative balance. Let's examine the balance sheet to see if we can determine why.

Miraculous as it seems, all of the items on this year's balance sheet are identical to the prior year's save three. The new worth has increased by $100,000, the net profit figure, but cash has gone from $25,000 to -$25,000. The third balance-sheet change was to accounts receivable, which increased by $150,000 from $200,000 to $350,000. Could that be the reason you're out of cash? It could be, and is. Though an oversimplification, this analogy accurately demonstrates how balance-sheet changes directly affect the cash position.

A.2 The Cash Summary Work Sheet

We can make the necessary conversion to measure a company's true cash flow by utilizing the cash summary work sheet that follows. The financial statements for our sample company, Superior Jewelers, have also been reinserted for your convenience.

At first glance, this may appear to be the most difficult of our inserts to understand, but bear with me. It's really quite simple, and those of you who fully grasp this concept will be years ahead of your competition in terms of understanding the interworking of a business. To demonstrate my point, cash net of cash flow needs, line twenty-one on the insert, calculates to a negative $19,268 for the year ending July 31, 20X1. This is the figure I would propose as Superior Jeweler's true cash flow for the period. By comparison, its cash flow calculated by conventional means (net profit + depreciation) equals $33,695. Certainly a startling contrast and one that could severely impact your operational planning were you the owner of Superior Jewelers.

Cash Sales

Let's now dissect the various parts of the work sheet to develop a better understanding of the reasons behind the contrast. We begin by inserting the date and number of months covered by the financial statement to be analyzed, in this case, July 31, 20X1 and twelve months.

Next, we list the total sales figure from the corresponding income statement on line 1. Now, look back at the balance sheets and subtract the accounts receivable figure for July 31, 20X1 from that on July 31, 20XX. Place that answer, ($19,395), on line two. As the left-hand column of the work sheet indicates, if receivables increase from one period to the next as in our example, that increase should be subtracted from net sales.

The reasoning should be self-evident. When receivables increase, less cash is generated, since a larger portion of sales has been transferred to accounts receivable.

SUPERIOR JEWELERS, INC.
CASH SUMMARY
WORKSHEET

7/31/X1-12

Inc./Dec.			Date / # Mos.	Date / # Mos.	Date / # Mos.	Date / # Mos
		Net Sales	1) $390,000			
-	+	Change in Accounts Receivable	2) (19,395)			
		CASH SALES	3) **370,605**			
		Cost of Sales	4) 206,310			
+	-	Change in Inventory	5) + 41,650			
-	+	Change in Accounts Payable	6) (10,557)			
		CASH PURCHASES	7) **237,403**			
		GROSS CASH PROFIT	8) **133,202**			
		Operating Expenses	9) 150,150			
		(Depreciation Expense)	10) (6,200)			
		CASH OPERATING EXPENSES	11) **143,950**			
		NET CASH FROM OPERATIONS	12) **(10,748)**			
+	-	Other Income or (Expenses)	13) (1,170)			
		NET CASH BEFORE TAXES	14) **(11,918)**			
		Taxes (Beg Acc + Tax Exp - End Acc)	15) (4,045)			
		NET CASH AFTER TAXES	16) **(15,963)**			

RECONCILIATION OF CASH

Inc./Dec.		Sources (Uses) of Cash				
		Net Cash After Taxes	17) (15,963)			
		Current Portion L.T.D.	18) (2,765)			
		(Last years payable)				
-	+	Change in Prepaids	19) + 150			
+	-	Change in Accruals	20) (690)			
		CASH NET OF CASH FLOW NEEDS	21) **(19,268)**			
-	+	Capital Expenditures (Cur. NFA's + Cur.	22) (15,370)			
		Dep. Exp. - Prior NFA's)				
+	-	Change in Long Term Debt	23) + 27,033			
		(this year CP/ LTD + This year LTD - Last				
		year LTD)				
-	+	Change in Other Short Term Assets	24)			
-	+	Change in Other Long Term Assets	25)			
+	-	Change in Other Short Term Liab.	26) + 13,500			
+	-	Change in Other Long Term Liab.	27)			
+	-	Capital Adjustments	28)			
		Dividends/ Withdrawals	29) -	-	-	-
		CALCULATED CHANGE IN CASH	30) **5,895**			
		BEGINNING CASH	31) **+ 10.670**	+	+	+
		ENDING CASH	32) 16,565			

Financial Statements

Superior Jeweler's, Inc.
Balance Sheet
For the years ending July 31, 20X1 and 20XX

ASSETS

Current Assets

	7/31/X1	7/31/XX
Cash	$16,565	$10,670
Accounts Receivable-Trade	45,000	25,605
Accounts Receivable-Employees	1,100	1,100
Inventory	141.660	100,010
Prepaid Expenses	2,640	2,790
	$206,965	$140,175

Property and Equipment

Leasehold Improvements	$25,570	$15,500
Fixtures and Furnishings	10,500	5.200
Office Equipment	2,400	2.400
(Accumulated Depreciation)	(11,080)	(4,880)
	$27,390	$18,220

Other Assets

Due From Officers	$4,500	$4,500
Deposits	1,245	1,245
	$5,745	$5,745
TOTAL ASSETS	**$240,100**	**$164,140**

LIABILITIES AND STOCKHOLDER'S EQUITY

Current Liabilities

Notes Payable-Short Term	$24,000	$10,500
Current Portion-Term Debt	3,520	2,765
Accounts Payable-Trade	28,000	17,443
Income Tax Payable	4,875	4,045
Accrued Sales Tax	2,310	2,400
Accrued Payroll Taxes	900	1,500
	$63,605	$38,653

Long Term Liabilities

Loans Payable-Term Portion	$77,107	$53,594
	$77,107	$53,594
TOTAL LIABILITIES	**$140,712**	**$92,247**

Stockholder's Equity

Capital Stock, common, 5,000 shares issued and outstanding with a $5.00 par value	$25,000	$25,000
Paid in Capital	23,988	23,988
Retained Earnings	50,400	22,905
	$99,388	$71,893
TOTAL LIABILITIES AND STOCKHOLDER'S EQUITY	**$240,100**	**$164,140**

SUPERIOR JEWELERS, INC

Statement of Income
For the years ending July 31, 20X1 and 20XX

	July 31, 20X1		July 31, 20XX	
SALES		$390,000		$350,000
COST OF GOODS SOLD				
Beginning Inventory	101,010		75,000	
Purchases 2	46,960		207,010	
(Ending Inventory)	(141,660)		(100,010)	
		206,310		182,000
GROSS PROFIT		183,690		160,000
OPERATING EXPENSES				
Salaries-Officer	30,000		26,000	
Salaries-Other	56,000		52,500	
Payroll Taxes	9,460		8,635	
Rent	16,000		15,000	
Advertising	4,950		4,800	
Depreciation	6,200		4,880	
Insurance	1.250		2,250	
Utilities	6,900		6,490	
Telephone	980		1,240	
Legal & Accounting	2,450		3,200	
Dues & Publications	190		175	
Travel & Entertainment	1,875		1,290	
Interest	13,580		9,240	
Other Operating Expenses	315		1,500	
TOTAL OPERATING EXPENSES		150,150		137,200
NET INCOME FROM OPERATIONS		33,540		30,800
OTHER INCOME & (EXPENSES)				
Interest Income	2,120		1,550	
Bad Debt Expense	(780)		(500)	
Discounts	(2,510)		(4,900)	
		(1,170)		(3,850)
NET INCOME BEFORE INCOME TAXES		32,370		26,950
Provision for State & Federal Income Taxes		4,875		4,045
NET INCOME FOR THE YEAR		**$27,495**		**$22,905**

Conversely, when receivables decrease, more cash is generated, not only that generated by cash sales but also that generated from the increase in receivables collections. The cash sales figure from our work sheet will generate the true cash generated from sales during the period by taking into account the changes in accounts receivable.

Cash Purchases

The same analogy holds true for cash purchases. Begin this calculation by listing the cost of goods sold on line four. Now perform the calculation for changes in inventory and accounts payable from the 20XX and 20X1 balance sheets, just as we did with accounts receivable. These answers are placed on lines five and six of the work sheet. As indicated in the left-hand column, increases in inventory are added to the cost of goods sold since those increases require cash to purchase the additional inventory. Conversely, decreases are subtracted since sales costs would be reduced by not having to expend cash to replace the inventory that was sold.

As you might suspect, accounts payable will act inversely to inventory, since an increase in a liability temporarily forestalls a cash use (as in our example), while a liability decrease would require the use of cash. Once you have arrived at the answer for line seven, true cash purchases, subtract that figure from true cash sales to arrive at gross cash profit, line eight. You may also want to compare this figure to the gross profit shown on the income statement for the year 20X1 to get an idea of the variation between the two.

Cash Operating Expenses

Next, we input total operating expenses from the 20X1 income statement onto line nine of the work sheet, and depreciation expense on line ten. Now, subtract the depreciation expense from total operating expenses because it's a noncash item. The result is cash operating expenses, line eleven, which when subtracted from gross cash profit, line eight, will yield net cash from operations, line twelve. Again, compare this figure, ($10,784), to net income from operations on the income statement, $33,540. By now you should be grasping the concept of why changes to the balance sheet affect the true cash flow of a business.

Net Cash after Taxes

Next, we insert other income or expenses on line thirteen of the work sheet. Net cash from operations, line twelve, should then be added or subtracted from it to arrive at net cash before taxes, line fourteen.

To arrive at the true income-tax expenditure, we must add any income tax payable listed on the prior year-end balance sheet, 19XX, to the income tax expense listed on the income statement for the current period 20X1, since both had to be paid during the current period. Next, subtract from that figure any income tax payable from the current balance sheet, 20X!, since that figure represents the current portion of this year's expensed tax liability not yet deducted from cash. That answer is then inserted on line fifteen of the work sheet. The net income-tax expense is then subtracted from net cash before taxes to arrive at the net cash after taxes, line sixteen. This figure ($15,963), represents the true cash generated from operations for 20X1, a much less attractive cash position than first indicated by the net profit of $27,495 listed on the income statement.

Reconciliation of Cash

Again, net cash from operations, though a negative, represents the figure from which the principal portion of term debt must be serviced. Since Superior Jewelers posted negative net cash after taxes on the work sheet, we must assume it wasn't able to service its debt for 20X1, or that debt service was accomplished by generating cash from an alternative means. The next section of the work sheet, the reconciliation of cash, will detail the nonoperational sources and uses of cash.

To begin completion of this section of the work sheet, reinsert the net cash after taxes, line sixteen onto line seventeen. Next, insert the current portion of term debt from the prior year, 20XX, on line eighteen. Why the prior year? This is the portion to be paid out over the next twelve months ending 7/31/20X1 by Superior Jewelers. Next calculate the change in prepaid expenses and accrued liabilities from the balance sheets, and insert those answers on line nineteen and twenty, respectively. Again, looking to the far left-hand column, a decrease in assets in this case, prepaid expenses represents an increase in cash. Conversely, a decrease in liabilities or accruals represents a cash usage or disbursement. Line twenty-one, cash net of cash flow needs, represents the true cash position of Superior Jewelers after it has met its expenses and cash-operating requirements for the year ending 20X1.

Let's now reconcile how those expenditures were paid. Line twenty-two represents increases or decreases to fixed assets. We arrive at this figure by adding the depreciation expense from the current year's income statement, 20X1, to the net fixed assets from the current year's balance sheet. This figure, $33,590, is then subtracted from the prior year's net fixed assets to arrive at the change in fixed assets for 20X1, which is $15,370. This figure represents an increase in fixed assets—that is, capital expenditures for the current year—and must be placed as a negative figure on line twenty-two. That's right; the owner of Superior Jewelers wasn't through spending money in 20X1, and this figure must be deducted from cash net of cash flow needs.

As you may now have surmised, it was necessary to increase borrowings to fund Superior's operations for 20X1. Line twenty-three represents the increase for the year to long-term debt. It is calculated by adding 20X1's current portion of term debt to 20X1's term debt, and then subtracting last year's term debt. The net result represents the increase in long-term debt for 20X1, which is inserted on line twenty-three.

Short-term debt also increased in 20X1, and the increase in notes payable short term of $13,500 must be inserted on line twenty-three. If we add this figure and the increase in long-term debt to cash net of cash flow need, then subtracting out the increase in fixed assets results in a cash increase for the year of $5,895, line thirty. This figure represents the surplus of borrowings over and above the negative cash generated by operations and capital expenditures.

To ensure that our work sheet is in balance, add the change in beginning cash, line thirty-one on the work sheet, which is obtained from the 7/31/20XX balance sheet, to the calculated change in cash, line thirty. The result should be entered on line thirty-two, ending cash. If the work sheet was completed correctly, the figure on line thirty-two will equal the cash balance for the current year as displayed on the balance sheet for 20X1.

What we have learned from this exercise isn't that Superior Jewelers was unprofitable in 20X1, for indeed they earned a profit of $27,497. We've learned that a portion of the cash generated from that profit has yet to be collected as evidenced by the increase in accounts receivable. In addition, we learned that the cash used to increase inventory and reduce payables was more than that generated by profits. The changes in these three areas of the balance sheet produced the negative net cash from operations. This necessitated the need to increase borrowings to both service the current portion of term debt, and to fund the increase in fixed assets. The industry comparisons from our statement studies confirmed the company's operating success. However, our cash summary work sheet uncovered some serious operational flaws, which were most likely caused by a lack of management control and insufficient business planning.

A.3 Arriving at the Decision

Let us assume that Superior's past ability to generate cash flow will be an accurate measurement of future abilities. Then, to arrive at the purchase decision, all that's left is to determine if the cash net of cash flow needs, line twenty-one on the work sheet, will be sufficient to service any new debt, which might be necessitated by the change in ownership.

To determine your particular cash needs, you will have to estimate an approximate borrowing amount and the corresponding monthly payment. Also, if owner's salaries were not included in the operating expenses of your prospect, the cash generated from operations will have to be sufficient to pay your salary in addition to the new debt. There should also be an adequate cash cushion to sustain operations vis-à-vis future fixed asset requirements or increased expenditures for additions to inventory or employees.

By assessing these variables in conjunction with your prior research and historical analysis, the purchase decision will often become self-evident. However, as with our example, you might first have to determine whether deteriorating conditions are correctable. In the case of Superior Jewelers, we have to surmise they are, since profits are sufficient by industry standards, and the major problems are slowing receivables and an inventory buildup, both of which are correctable. Of course, your only decision at this point is whether or not to continue negotiations. A price and the terms of sale must be agreed upon before a final decision can be reached. Either or both could have a determining effect on your final decision.

B. Determining the Price

Most likely, the owner has entered the negotiations with an established asking price. If you feel it is within reason and fairly representative of the business's worth, the next step will be for you to determine how much you are willing to pay for the business. Remember, the present owner may be the worst judge of a company's true value, and most naïve owners will set an unreasonably inflated purchase price. Most owners look beyond the tangibles and factor in too much intrinsic value into their pricing equation, the intangibles.

In their mind, they are the only reason the business succeeded. After all, it took years of trial and error to find the best location, obtain reliable customers and suppliers, train employees, establish a reputation and, in short, build a successful operation.

B.1 A Word about Goodwill

The current owner will probably view you with the same contempt an older middle manager might view a recent MBA graduate. In the owner's eyes, all the work has already been done. He or she anticipates you'll come in and make a fortune without ever having to break a sweat. He or she will have no intention of turning this master creation over to you without being paid handsomely for those past efforts, an intangible commodity commonly referred to as goodwill.

The true value of goodwill will vary by industry and situation, and it will be up to each of you to determine this value as it applies to your particular situation. Unfortunately, the value placed on goodwill will be determined largely by those factors we satirized in the preceding paragraphs. It will also be determined, in part, by the value of the lease, the ease of entry into the market, the risk of starting a new venture, and future profit potential. The list of considerations can be daunting and so too can the numbers of ways to value goodwill. Though difficult, making this determination will become more obvious once we have looked at some of the other factors involved in our pricing decision as well as some of the more popular pricing formulas.

B.2 Pricing Methods

Like goodwill, negotiating the price will vary by situation. Some of you may deal with the current owner directly. Others may work through a broker who may or may not be an aid in negotiations. Still others may use a lawyer, an accountant, or a consultant. For those of you utilizing an outside professional, stay fully aware of all that transpires.

Don't rely upon professional assistance as a crutch. If you don't understand, ask. If you don't agree or have an opinion, voice it. Remember, the final decision rests with you, and so too will paying the bills.

Take the Offensive

There is no better way to begin these negotiations than by asking the seller, or his or her representative just how they established the asking price. This will immediately put them on the defensive. More importantly it will allow you to evaluate the logic behind their pricing method. Don't be surprised if the price was arrived at arbitrarily, especially when dealing directly with the current owner. This is by far the most common method of pricing, although not always admittedly.

Understanding the seller's pricing will better enable you to understand your negotiating position. The less knowledgeable the seller is, the better your chances for negotiating a price reduction. And once you have gained the offensive, keep it that way. Continue to be the one posing the questions when possible. Likewise, be the one with concrete rebuttals supporting your own contentions for price reductions.

The Multiplier Pricing Method

The second most utilized pricing method will involve an earnings ratio or multiplier, usually from two to ten times the gross monthly earnings. Generally, the more attractive the business's appeal, the higher the multiplier. This method surfaces most often with the sale of a retail business, and will usually be supplied either directly or indirectly by a real-estate broker. Most brokers are, after all, primarily real-estate salespeople, and the multiplier is a carryover from investment property valuation methods. At best, it is a crude form of valuation as it fails to take into consideration the complexities and interworking of a business.

There is another glaring disadvantage to the purchaser faced with the multiplier pricing method. Gross earnings figures are easy to manipulate and asking prices are often unrealistically skewed upward as a result. Those encountering this situation have two alternatives. You can try to find an alternative method for establishing a price, or you can appear to go along with the seller's method, establish a fair price on your own, and hope the two prices are reasonably close. Under any circumstance, don't be content to accept a price based solely on a multiplier without first doing your own pricing analysis utilizing a more respected pricing formula.

The Capitalized Earnings Rate

Another common pricing method often proposed by real-estate brokers is the capitalized earnings rate. This method is often used for pricing service companies and professional practices. Past profits are used to determine the asking price in this method, but to avoid possible manipulation; profits are averaged over the past three to five years. Then a capitalized rate, usually between 20% and 59% is divided into that average to determine the selling price.

The exact capitalization rate is determined by such factors as the ease of entry into the business, the degree of management skills required, the size of the business, the length of time it has been in existence, and the number of existing competitors. A retail store for example might use a rate of 25%, while a beauty salon might use a rate as high as 40%. Though more accurate than the multiplier, the capitalization rate is also a flawed method. As our historical analysis has shown, net profit isn't always a true measure of potential success.

Book Value

Most midsized and larger businesses are sold using the actual book value or net worth as a determination of the price. The price will usually be set from one to three times the book value. Oftentimes the price will be stated in terms of price per share, especially if the suitor is interested in purchasing just a controlling interest rather than complete ownership.

Even this method has its flaws. A company could have a terrific net worth and a seemingly secure financial position, but no longer demonstrate the ability to generate a profit. Or the market value of fixed assets could be much lower than their book value causing an inflated net worth. Maybe inventory is obsolete or accounts receivable uncollectable, both of which would inflate net worth. The possibilities are endless.

Why is this formula so popular then? Most acquisitions include an endless amount of research or due diligence as contingencies for closing the sale. It is the responsibility of those conducting the due diligence to test all the variables involved and to either substantiate or arrive at a fair market price. Though the price is stated in terms of book value or price per share, in reality the due diligence personnel are pretty performing an audit and an appraisal and setting an adjusted book value from which the final price is established.

The Adjusted Book Value

The pricing method I would recommend most is the adjusted book value. Once you've completed and studied the balance-sheet work sheet for a prospective company, you should be able to surmise the accuracy of the net worth reported. If for example, you have concerns for the value of accounts receivable because you feel a portion is uncollectable, discount that portion from the stated net worth to arrive at an adjusted net worth and reduce your offering price accordingly.

The same holds true for fixed assets and inventory. What is there true replacement or liquidation value? Are portions either obsolete or outdated? Are there deferred maintenance concerns with regards to fixed assets? If you're knowledgeable enough to make these assessments, do so. If not, hire an appraiser. Most equipment dealers will either have someone on staff that can conduct an appraisal, or will have knowledge of appraisers for referral. Real estate and business appraisers will be discussed in more detail at the end of this section.

Once you've studied the income-statement work sheet in conjunction with the balance-sheet work sheet, you will also be in a good position to assess a prospect's earnings potential. Your initial investigation and analysis, due diligence, will also give you a good indication of the present owner's true value, value of the location, value of the lease, and value of the customer base and suppliers, whether or not the prospect holds any type of competitive edge. Piece this all together, and you will have your interpretation of the true value of goodwill.

Your assessment of the true net worth of the prospect plus the value you place on goodwill, including earnings potential, will represent the maximum amount you should be willing to pay for this business. We will refer to this figure as the adjusted book value.

The Liquidation Method
Simply stated, the liquidation value represents a company's wholesale value or the remaining value, after all of the assets have been liquidated, and all the liabilities paid. In most cases, this value will represent the low end of the pricing range when comparing pricing methods. With the exception of true distress situations, the liquidation value would fall well below the value the current owner would be willing to accept as a purchase price.

Setting Your Offering Price
I would recommend utilizing two valuation methods when setting your initial offering price—the adjusted book value and the liquidation value. From these, I would determine a comfortable price range rather than a fixed purchase price. I would then utilize the support of my due diligence investigation to negotiate a fixed selling price within that initial range that you established.

A Pricing Test
Once you have arrived at an adjusted book value, try this simple pricing test. Choose either last year's profit, or what you project next year's to be. Divide the adjusted book value into that profit figure. Now move the decimal two places to the right to determine what percentage that profit figure represents as a return on your investment. Are there other less risky and time-consuming investments that would pay the same or a higher return? If so, you may want to reconsider your offering price. Keep in mind though, if you are only putting a down payment down on the business, and don't possess the

ability to make the total investment, the use of leverage may need to be factored into your return equation.

B.3 A Word about Appraisers

When in doubt about the asking price or the valuation of fixed assets, hire an independent appraiser. They aren't that expensive, considering the total cost of your potential investment, and in most cases they will be willing to estimate the charge in advance. I would also suggest asking the current owner if any appraisals already exist. Many business owners will conduct an appraisal prior to listing a business both as a means to help establish an asking price and as a way to substantiate that price to potential buyers.

Additionally, oftentimes banks will require a business appraisal in conjunction with a mortgage or loan application, and the owner will receive a copy of that appraisal. Even if it is no longer current, an appraisal update will be less costly than a new appraisal.

A full appraisal utilized three valuation methods: market values, liquidation value, and book value. If possible, they will also include a comparative value by including price comparisons for similar businesses that have sold in the area in the recent past. The appraisal report will include valuations based on each method, followed by a summary that will include a market value derived from the three valuation scenarios.

There are two independent national associations for appraisers: The American Appraisal Institute, whose members are signified by the MAI designation, and the Society of Real Estate Appraisers, whose members will carry the SRA or SRPA designation. In either case, the members have earned their qualifications through a series of classes, sample appraisals, and written tests. With the possible exception of an equipment appraisal, I would strongly suggest only hiring an appraiser from one of these two associations. The best sources for locating a reputable appraiser will be your banker, accountant, or lawyer.

C. Structuring the Buy/Sell Agreement

Once a selling price has been agreed upon, the terms of that sale will also have to be negotiated. The terms too have to be acceptable to both parties. There are several ways to structure a purchase, but in all cases, a buy/sell agreement will be required. For those of you drafting your own buy/sell agreement, sample forms can be over the internet and at most business supply stores. When in doubt for any reason, contact an attorney. Like the appraisal, a few thousand dollars spent at this stage may save tens of thousands in the long run, possibly even the business itself.

The Carry Back Note

Regardless of who drafts the buy/sell agreement, there are several provisions that should be included to protect your rights and investment. Most importantly, the agreement should clearly state the purchase price and the terms for payment. If a note is being carried back, this too should be clearly stated within the terms of the agreement. The note's interest rate and terms for repayment should also be included in the buy/sell agreement as well as in the note itself.

The Encumbrance Provision

The agreement should also specify whether the seller has the right to encumber any of the business assets as collateral for the carry back note. If an encumbrance agreement is going to be included, try to include a provision in which the seller agrees to subordinate his or her debt to borrowings from a bank or finance company. This will prove an important consideration for future borrowing potential.

Purchasing Assets Only

Normally when purchasing a proprietorship or partnership, the buyer will only be purchasing the business's assets as of a given date. The seller will be responsible for all liabilities up to the purchase date. This point should be spelled out clearly within the terms of the buy/sell agreement. There may, however, be some variations in the timing regarding the transfer of some of the assets within the buy/sell agreement. For example, there could be some deviation as to who receives the revenue from accounts receivable billed prior to the transfer date. The same holds true for inventory, cash accounts, and any other current assets. Make sure the agreement clearly lists any assets that are not being transferred with the sale, and make sure their value is deducted from the purchase price.

The Lease Continuation Clause

If you plan on operating under the same trade name, make sure it is permissible under the terms of the buy/sell agreement. If applicable, also include a provision that the sale is subject to the acceptable transfer and renewability of the existing lease. This should offer additional protection in the event of lease cancellation, especially in situations where the lease is close to expiration. At this stage, you should have already reviewed the terms of the lease, and received assurances from the landlord. Nevertheless, documented verification is recommended. There is always the chance you've been given a copy of the original lease but not given subsequent addendums.

The Covenant Not to Compete

A covenant not to compete is the present owner's agreement not to open a similar or competing business nearby, which, in most cases, would undermine your ability to succeed. The agreement not to compete should be spelled out within the terms of the buy/sell agreement, as well as being a separate standalone document like the carry-back note. The covenant not to compete should clearly define the length of the commitment and the geographic area within which it applies.

Sales Including Liability Transfer
There are circumstances when the buyer will be both purchasing asset and assuming liabilities. This happens most often during the sale of a corporation. If, for example, you are purchasing a corporation by purchasing all of its outstanding stock, you are in effect purchasing its assets and its liabilities. This form of purchase, while common, is one of the most dangerous because of the possibility of undisclosed liabilities. To protect yourself from this risk, make sure the buy/sell agreement clearly states that you are only purchasing the liabilities incurred up to the purchase date, and that this assumption is limited to those liabilities disclosed on the financial statement as of that date.

Consulting Provision
Another area you may want to include in the buy/sell agreement is a definition of any management assistance being offered by the seller, and the cost. This proviso can serve as a benefit for many obvious reasons, but it can also serve as a substantial tax shelter as for both parties. If the seller is willing to mask a portion of the purchase price into consulting payments, he or she will be able to defer a portion of the sales proceeds and thereby defer a portion of the capital gains. More importantly, you the buyer will be able to reduce your initial transfer taxes. You will also be able to expense the consulting fees, which will lower your profit, and thereby reduce your future income-tax liability.

The Bulk Transfer
In some states the sale of a business must be accomplished through an escrow agent or notary. They will, in turn, file a notice of bulk transfer with the respective secretary of state, as well as publish the required number of public notifications. The public notifications are meant to inform existing creditors of the pending sale, and it is a good practice to follow even in states that don't require them. The notifications enable creditors to file claims against the seller prior to the business transfer, and disallow claims against you by these same creditors once the sale is transacted.

Miscellaneous Odds and Ends
If you haven't preselected professional assistance for accounting, legal, banking, and insurance, consider transferring the previous owner's relationships, at least temporarily.

In most cases, these professionals will already know the company, and they can prove of vital importance during the transaction. Don't let one minute transpire without insurance coverage. In most cases the prior owner's policies can be transferred, at least temporarily to give you time to evaluate the coverages and cost effectiveness.

D. Chapter Summary

Even the purchase of the most lucrative business must be structured properly if continued success is to be maintained. The decision to purchase is only one of several elements involved in the structuring. Pricing, the terms of sale, and a properly structured buy/sell agreement as well as ancillary documentation are all equally important for the structure and continued success of the ensuing business venture.

PART IV
FINANCING AND OPERATING STAGES

CHAPTER 8

The Operating Projection

The projections model will serve as the operating plan of attack for both the start-up and the existing business. You will use it to chart your business course in the same manner you would use a road map or MapQuest to choose your vacation route. The projection will also act as a gauge to monitor your performance, and it will serve as a diagnostic tool in the event operations begin to falter. There is one other important reason—you won't be able to borrow money without it.

The word "projection" instills even more fear than the phrase "personal financial statement." In fact, many business owners spend more time rationalizing away the need for projections that it would actually take to produce them. The two most common excuses are: I don't have the time, and why take the time they never turn out to be right anyway. Not surprising, but those two answers are usually interrelated. Quite often when projections don't turn out to be right it's because the preparer didn't take the time to do a thorough job. Then, once completed, the projection gets stuck in a drawer or unused computer file, until it's time to complete the following year's projection, again at the lender's request.

A Projection Analogy

You wouldn't hurriedly glance at a road map, and then attempt a cross-country drive, without periodically checking that map to review and update your progress. The same holds true for projection models. As changes occur in operations, the projections need to be revised to reflect those changes. This will give valuable insight into the short and long-range impact of those changes. It will also serve as advance warning of potential operating hazards, or the need for operation changes.

To illustrate our point, imagine that your company's sales growth far exceeds what you had originally anticipated. A simple projection update might signify the need to buy additional inventory or equipment, or possibly to hire additional staff to help meet the increased sales demand. Failure to update the projections could impede this realization process. It's quite possible you would never recognize those needs until your inability to fill the orders forced your customers to buy from a competitor instead. As with natural law, business works on a cause-and-effect principle. The business owner without a plan is forced to react to various causes, while an owner with a plan causes various reactions to happen.

Projection Types

Projection models can be broken into two general categories: short and long term. Short-term projections encompass one year's operations, and they are usually developed on a monthly or quarterly basis. Long-term projections are usually charted for a three- to five-year period, and are most often charted on an annual basis. Though two separate models, the short and long-term projections should be considered together as the main components of one overall business plan. Additionally, what affects one, affects the other, and any revisions or updates need to be incorporated in both.

Personal Expectations

Before beginning the projection process, it will be necessary to develop a set of long-range personal goals and business objectives. Like that cross-country drive, it's much easier to choose the most direct or optimal route when you have a final destination in mind. Certainly that destination will differ for each of you. A small retailer looking to make a comfortable living will choose a completely different path than a wholesaler who is positioning to build a multimillion dollar national sales organization. Recognizing your individual personal goals will be the first step in achieving them.

What level of personal success do you plan to achieve by the end of the first year of operation? What about the second, third, fourth, and fifth years? Be as detailed and as imaginative as you wish in formulating your goals, but also be realistic. Goals and objectives will prove of little value if they are unobtainable.

Business Expectations

Once you have defined your personal goals, consider longer range objectives for the business. Now that you know where you want to be, let's determine how the business can get you there. Will it take a 15% annual sales growth rate? Provided that growth rate is obtainable, how will it affect operating expenses? Will additional employees and equipment be needed to sustain the growth? What effect will the growth rate have on gross profit margins? As you can see, the objectives develop rather quickly and lead to additional short and long-term operational questions.

External factors will also have to be taken into consideration. The local, state, national, and international economies may all have a considerable effect on your operating performance. So too could other local competitors or new competitive technologies. By examining the possible effects of these external variables, you will gain valuable insight in how best to utilize changing market conditions to your advantage, or at least to minimize their negative impact.

Keep it Realistic

By now you have probably raised more questions than you can effectively answer, and you realize that defining business objectives will require completing the projection models. As in the formation of your personal goals, business projections can be easily compiled to display whatever results an inflated ego or an excited imagination can conjure up. Projections will be of little value, quite possibly even point you onto a harmful course, if they are unrealistic. This isn't to say that projections should be so conservative that they're easy to obtain, only that human and financial limitations should be taken into consideration during the formation stage.

Let's assume that Harry P. Sample, our prospective buyer from the second chapter, has successfully negotiated the purchase of Superior Jewelers under the following conditions.

1. An $80,000 purchase price.
2. The seller has agreed to carry back a note for the entire purchase price at a 10% interest rate for a term of five years.
3. Mr. Sample will assume the existing bank debt of the corporation as listed on the 7/31/X1 balance sheet. This includes the $24,000 short-term note, and the short and long-term portions of the term note, which equals $80,000. These will be combined into one term loan to be fully over fifteen years at an interest rate of 14%. The loan will be secured by a second deed of trust on Mr. Sample's home.
4. The seller will receive the proceeds from the collection of all accounts receivable as of the 7/31/X1 balance sheet.
5. The seller will draw down the cash account to $1,100, the amount of the employee advance account as of 7/31/X1.
6. Mr. Sample has agreed to the revaluation of fixed assets to $35,000: $10,000 for equipment and $25,000 for leasehold improvements.
7. The seller will sublet the operating premise for the remainder of the lease, 3.2 years, for $18,000 per annum.
8. The transfer of the business will take effect on 8/1/X1.

A pro forma balance sheet is provided in the next chapter under our balance-sheet projection model. In essence, Mr. Sample has agreed to purchase $41,408 of net worth, consisting primarily of inventory and fixed assets as well as $43,763 in goodwill. If this seems exorbitant, consider our pricing test from the previous chapter: expected profits divided by book value multiplied by 100 equals the expected return as a percentage. If we include 7/31/X1 earnings of $27,495 as the expected profit, and divide that by the purchase price, the expected first year return on Mr. Sample's investment will be 34.4%. Not bad for no money down.

A. The Projected Income Statement

We will begin the actual projection process by completing a projected income statement for Mr. Sample's first year of operation. We will again utilize the income statement work sheet. We will also include the two prior years' operating figures for your convenience, since many of the projection assumptions will be based on the previous owner's past performance.

SUPERIOR JEWELERS, INC,
PROJECTED INCOME STATEMENT WORKSHEET

	July,31 20XX	July,31 20X1	19___	July,31 20X2			R.M.A. Statement Studies
Sales	$350,000	$390,000		$448,500	+	15%	$390,000
Cost of Goods Sold	182,000	206,310		237,705	+	15%	203,580
% of Sales	52.0	52.9		53.0			52.2
Gross Profit	168,000	183,690		210,795	+	15%	186,420
% of Sales	48.0	47.1		47.0			47.8
Operating Expenses :							
Owners' Salaries	26,000	30,000		30,000			29,640
% of Sales	7.4	7.7		6.7			7.6
Other Salaries	52,500	56,000		57,200	+	1,200	
Payroll Taxes	8,635	9,460		9,592			
Employee Benefits							
Rent	15,000	16,000		18,000	+	2,000	
Insurance	2,250	1,250		1,500	+	20%	
Utilities	6,490	6,900		7,590	+	10%	
Advertising and Promotion	4,800	4,950		5,500	+	11%	
Professional Services	3,200	2,450		1,750	(29%)		
Travel and Entertainment	1,290	1,875		1,875			
Depreciation & Amortization	4,880	6,200		9,960			
Interest Expense	9,240	13,580		21,580			
Other Operating Expenses	2,915	1,485		9,250			
Total Operating Expenses	137,200	150,150		173,797	+	16%	152,100
% of Sales	39.2	38.5		38.8			39.0
Operating Profit	30,800	33,540		36,998	+	10%	34,540
% of Sales	8.8	8.6		8.2			8.8
Other Income (Expense)	(3,850)	(1,170)		(1,591)			(4,680)
Pretax Profit	26,950	32,370		35,407	+	9%	29,860
% of Sales	7.7	8.3		7.9			7.6
Income Tax Expense	4,045	4,875		4,249			
Net Profit	$22,905	$27,495		$31,158	+	13%	
% of Sales	6.5	7.1		6.9			

Estimating the Operating Expenses

Since operating expenses are for the most part fixed, and thereby unaffected by sales, this will be the easiest area to begin the projected income statement. When estimating operating expenses, it will be important to consider the operating trends from past years for each expense category, and to reflect those changes in your projections, if for example, utilities have been increasing at a rate of 5% a year, it would be safe to assume that the projections should also reflect a 5% increase. Again, percentage increases can be measured by subtracting the current year's expense figure from the preceding year's expense figure, and then dividing your answer by the preceding year's expense figure. The decimal point must then be moved two places to the right to convert your answer into a percentage.

Owners' Salaries

The first operating expense listed on the work sheet is owners' salaries. How do you decide on a figure? Incorporate your existing living expenses, your past salary history, and the salary level of the previous owner or owners of similar businesses from the statement studies. It's anyone's bet as to when those in the start-up phase can actually begin to draw a salary, but let's accrue them regardless. You have personal living expenses too, and aren't this just for the fun of it. For our example, we assumed last year's salary level will meet with our expectations for the first year.

Employee Expenses

The next three operating expense categories are employee related. All of you, even those in the start-up phase, should have an idea of the number of employees you will require during the first year, and you should be able to estimate their pay rates or salary levels. For our sample company, we are assuming no additional employees, but $1,200 in additional employee salary expense to cover incremental pay increases. If you're in a situation where you'll be adding employees during the year, estimate their salaries based upon the number of months under your employment during the first year. Those of you in wholesaling or manufacturing will also have to determine which employee salaries, such as warehouse or shop personnel, belong under the category of cost of goods sold.

For our example we have estimated payroll taxes at 11% of total salaries, including the owners. As of this writing, the social security tax rate is 6.25%, Medicare is 1.45%. Local taxes vary by state and local, and three states, Pennsylvania, New Jersey, and Alaska require employees to pay an unemployment tax. The employee-benefit category includes pension and profit-sharing contributions and possibly union benefits. Most of you can ignore this category for the time being, unless you are purchasing a business that is unionized or has an existing pension or profit-sharing program.

Rent

Those of you purchasing existing businesses will already know your actual lease or mortgage expense. Those in the start-up phase who have yet to sign a lease, should survey local occupancy costs prior to estimating this figure as rents will vary greatly by locale. Local realtors and bankers can both be valuable resources for estimating local rental costs. For our example we have utilized a $2,000 annual rental increase, which is based on the information provided regarding the sublease.

Insurance

Those of you purchasing an existing business should already know your actual insurance costs. Those in the start-up phase should first determine or estimate your insurance needs, and then obtain quotes based upon those needs. I would obtain at least three quotes before binding any coverage. Insurance costs can vary greatly from company to company, and when agents know you are soliciting other bids, they will normally respond with their most competitive rate. For our example we utilized a 20% annual increase due to some inadequacies in the prior owner's coverage.

Telephone and Utilities

It's safe to assume utility bills will be on the rise. Year to year historical percentage increases will be the best estimate for this expense category. If you are in the start-up phase and need additional assistance, contact the service provider directly for help in estimating service costs. For Superior Jewelers, we are estimating a 10% annual increase.

Advertising and Promotion

When you have past historical performance as a guide, you can calculate year to year changes to estimate this category. For those with no accurate comparison, it would be best to estimate this expense as a percent of sales or cost of goods sold based upon industry comparisons, then convert that percentage to a dollar amount. Mr. Sample has allotted an 11% increase in advertising expense in a planned effort to advertise more in hopes of generating additional sales.

Professional Services

This category encompasses legal, accounting, and consulting fees. Again, comparisons to past operating statements for existing businesses or industry guidelines for start-ups are the best means for estimating this category. For our example we have estimated a $700 or 29% decrease in professional fees as Mr. Sample intends to do much of the accounting himself.

Travel and Entertainment

This category will vary greatly depending upon the industry and your personal preferences. This is one of the easiest expense categories to reduce or inflate depending upon your needs. Let your conscience be your guide. For our example, we have budgeted no change.

Depreciation and Amortization

Any tangible fixed assets except land can be depreciated. There are several methods for calculating depreciation. For this exercise, we have used the straight-line method. Annual depreciation under the straight-line method is determined by dividing the value of the asset by the number of years to be depreciated based on the IRS's useful life guideline. We used a five-year depreciation scale for office equipment for our example.

Leasehold improvements can only be depreciated if they aren't deductible from rental payments, and then only for a term equal to the remainder of the lease. For our example, leasehold improvements are depreciable over the 3.2 years that remain on the lease.

We are not amortizing or impairing goodwill for our example company. There are situations in which goodwill can be amortized over a ten-year period, provided certain IRS testing requirements are met. I would urge those of you in this category to consult an independent accountant to aid in this determination.

Some of you will also have to designate a portion of your depreciation as a cost of goods sold rather than as an operating expense. The depreciation of the machinery a manufacturer uses to produce a product is considered a cost of goods sold item, while the depreciation of office equipment would be considered an operating expense.

Lease Expense

Fixed asset needs may require further analysis in conjunction with projected sales increases. If additional equipment or other fixed assets will be needed to meet sales targets, these expenditures too should be included in your projection analysis. Many of you, particularly those in the start-up phase with limited capital resources, may prefer to lease rather than purchase new equipment. Leasing requirements are typically less stringent than loan approval requirements, and a lease can often be entered into with little or no down payment.

Leases in which you become the legal owner at the end of the lease for an incidental buyout fee can be capitalized and depreciated just like any other fixed asset. Leases that do not qualify, or those that you prefer not to capitalize, would be treated as an operating expense.

Interest Expense

The interest expense category will include the interest on all existing obligations plus the interest on any anticipated debt. Most of you should have at least a rough estimate of borrowing needs, capabilities, and interest rates at this point, although it could be necessary to revise this estimate when actual borrowing arrangements have been finalized. For our example we have used a 10% interest rate on the carry-back note, and a 14% interest rate on the existing debt. At some point in the not too distant future, Mr. Sample may want to renegotiate or refinance the existing debt to lower the interest rate.

Other Operating Expenses and Other Income

Other operating expense is a general category, and should include any remaining expense categories unique to your industry. I would also recommend including a contingency factor within this category, as we have with our example, since unforeseen expenses tend to have a nasty habit of occurring.

Other income will include any income from non-operating sources such as interest income. Those of you without historical performance measures will find this area difficult to estimate and may wish to leave this field blank. For our example, we have included $500 in bad debt expense, $2,691 in sales discounts, which represents an arbitrary 0.6% of sales, and $1,600 in interest income.

The Cost of Goods Sold

The cost of goods sold is best estimated as a percent of sales. This percentage too can best be determined by studying past performance or financial statement trends from the research materials from our statement studies. Though we can decide on the percentage now, it will be necessary to set a projected dollar-sales volume prior to converting this percentage into a dollar amount.

Income Tax Expense

Assume a tax rate of 15% for the first $50,000 in pretax profit, 25% for the next $25,000, 35% for the next $25,000, and 40% thereafter. This is an area we wish to minimize, and for our example, we are forecasting a tax liability equal to 12% of pretax profit. To make this possible, Mr. Sample has elected to report taxes on a cash basis rather than accrual. This will enable him to forestall reporting credit sales for July until the next taxable year.

A.1 A Break-Even Analysis

Before we calculate the first year's sales projection, let's conduct one extremely beneficial exercise. Few business owners know their true break-even sales figure. Fewer still know what effect increasing sales will have on their operation. Yet, determining both break-even sales figure and an optimal sales volume can prove invaluable in projecting and planning future growth, especially during the start-up phase.

Possibly the largest fallacy associated with operating a business is that increased sales automatically translate into increased profits. This isn't always the case. Eventually a point of diminished returns will be reached, whereby sales increases will be outpaced by expense increases. This will result in diminished profitability. An example would be when increased sales volume necessitates additions to staffing or equipment.

There are three variables involved in determining the break-even sales figure: the variable expense ratio, fixed expenses, and the gross or adjusted gross profit margin. First let's look at variable expenses, those directly proportional to sales. In most cases these will equal the cost of goods sold and the variable expense ratio the cost of goods sold to sales percentage. In a few instances, such as with a commission sales force, you may also have to add semifixed operating to the cost of goods sold to arrive at the true variable expense total. For our sample, this wasn't applicable.

Once you have determined the variable expense ratio, the adjusted gross profit margin will also be known. Since we know that sales will always equal 100%, the adjusted gross profit margin will be the reciprocal of the variable expense ratio. If variable costs equal 53% of sales, the remainder, or 47%, will be the adjusted gross profit margin. We already know the dollar amount of fixed costs. In most cases, these will equal our operating expenses. If we divide the adjusted gross profit margin into those total costs, we will arrive at the break-even sales figures.

A Break-Even Example

The break-even formula looks like this: total fixed costs divided by the adjusted gross profit margin equals break-even sales. To follow our example through, the fixed costs for Superior Jewelers are projected to total $173,797 for its first year under new ownership. Dividing that figure by the adjusted gross profit marking 0.47 results in a break-even sales figure of $369,781 ($173,797/0.47 = $369,781).

To verify our answer, simply multiply the break-even sales figure by the variable cost margin ($369,781 × 0.53 = $195,984). This represents the variable cost figure or cost of goods sold at the break-even sales level. When this amount is subtracted from the break-even sales figures, the result is the break-even adjusted gross profit in dollars, $173,797. Subtracting this figure from our total projected fixed costs, also $173,797, leaves us a pretax operating profit of 0, thereby proving our equation. For those of you entering an industry without cost of goods sold or variable expenses, your break-even sales figure will equal your total fixed costs.

Measuring Projected Profits

As you can see, calculating the break-even sales figure is a simple yet effective management tool. Since none of you are going into business to break even, let's examine a variation of this formula, which will prove beneficial in determining sales requirements at various profit levels. We can utilize the break-even formula to determine the sales volume required to obtain a projected profit figure simply by adding that profit amount to our fixed costs.

Say you've chosen a $30,000 pretax profit figure for the first year. We can amend our break-even analogy as follows: $173,797 + $30,000/0.47 = $433,611, to arrive at the sales figure requirement. As you can see, increasing sales volume to produce more profit isn't a dollar for dollar proposition. Due to ever increasing variable costs, it's necessary to increase sales by $63,830 to realize a $30,000 pretax profit.

Again, we can prove our formula by subtracting the sales figure from the two expense figures. First, since sales increased so too did variable costs ($433,611 × 0.53 = $229,814). Fixed costs will remain unchanged at $173,797. Subtracting the two expense figures from the new sales figure equals the anticipated pretax profit figure ($433,611 – $229,814 – $173,797 = $30,000).

Estimating Sales

While the break-even analysis is a worthwhile management tool, it's a theoretical application and does not take into consideration economic and market conditions. Projecting sales volume for an existing business will best be accomplished by studying past percentage changes and basing your estimates on those trends. If possible study the past unit sales as well as dollar volume. This will help determine the effects of price increases on total sales. Inflation is another key variable. Sales increased must at least equal the inflation rate just to keep pace with past performance.

For those of you in the start-up phase don't necessarily assume you can match the sales of an existing business during the first year of operation. Remember, you will be starting with a sales base of zero, and it could easily take six months to a year to reach the break-even point. Though projected sales volume for a start-up could prove more inaccurate, at least you will know the sales volume required to break even, the sales volume needed to return your anticipated profit, and the costs involved to obtain that profit. This will enable you to plan your operations to meet those projections, and to know when and where to make adjustments should actual sales vary from those projections.

A.2 The Long-Term Income Projection

For our example, we have projected a 15% first-year sales increase. Once you've completed your own first-year income statement projection, you should also project forward to arrive at a three- to five-year income plan. To do so, simply calculate your expected sales volume increases or decreases for the remaining years, and then carry through the various expense category analogies just as we have done for the first year. You will also find it helpful to list the assumptions used to formulate your projections, so you won't have to search or second-guess your assumption process, when it comes time to review or revise your projections.

B. The Short-Term Projection Model

It would be best to complete the short-term or monthly operating projection before completing the balance-sheet portion of the long-term projection. The monthly operating projection will in turn be utilized to more accurately project the first fiscal year-end balance-sheet requirements. An example of the short-term projection model for Superior Jewelers is as follows:

SHORT TERM PROJECTION

SUPERIOR JEWELERS, INC.	AUGUST	SEPT.	OCT	NOV.
PROFORMA INCOME STATEMENT				
Sales	25,000	42,000	45,000	68,000
Cost of Goods Sold	13,250	22,260	23,850	36,040
Gross Profit	11,750	19,740	21,150	31,960
Less: Salaries	8,500	9,500	9,502	10,500
Rent	1,500	1,500	1,500	1,500
Utilities	632	633	632	633
Insurance		375		
Depreciation	830	830	830	830
Interest	1,798	1,798	1,798	1,798
Other Operating Exps.	1,100	1,500	1,600	2,705
Total Operating Expenses	14,360	16,136	15,862	17,966
Operating Profit	(2,610)	3,604	5,288	13,994
Other Income (Expense)	(132)	(132)	(132)	(132)
Net Profit Before Taxes	(2,742)	3,472	5,156	13,862
Less: Income Tax Expense			(1,062)	
Net Profit	(2,742)	3,472	4,094	13,862
PROFORMA CASH BUDGET				
Beginning Cash Balance	16,100	7,487	6,746	9,707
Plus: A/R Collection and Cash Sales	6,250	29,250	42,750	50,750
Other Income (Exps.)	(58)	(160)	(160)	(316)
Total Cash Available	22,292	36,577	49,336	60,141
Less: A/P Disbursements		13,250	22,260	23,850
Operating Expenses	14,360	16,136	15,862	17,966
Building Improvements				
Equipment Purchases				
Inventory Increases (Decreases)				
Tax Payments			1,062	
Other				
Total Disbursements	14,360	29,386	39,184	41,816
Cash Surplus (Deficit)	7,932	7,191	10,152	18,325
Minimum Cash Desired				
Short Term Borrowing Requirement				
Short Term Borrowing Repayment				5,000
Long Term Borrowing Requirement				
Long Term Borrowing Repayment	445	445	445	445
Cash Balance Ending	7,487	6,746	9,707	12,880
Short Term Borrowing Balance	24,000	24,000	24,000	19,000
Long Term Borrowing Balance	159,555	159,110	158,665	158,220

8/1/X1 thru 7/31/X2

DEC.	JAN.	FEB.	MAR	APRIL	MAY	JUNE	JULY	TOTAL
76,000	25,000	45,000	20,000	22,000	36,000	22,000	22,500	448,500
40,280	13,250	23,850	10,600	11,660	19,080	11,660	11,925	237,705
35,720	11,750	21,150	9,400	10,340	16,920	10,340	10,575	210,795
13,290	8,500	8,500	5,500	5,500	6,500	5,500	5,500	96,792
1,500	1,500	1,500	1,500	1,500	1,500	1,500	1,500	18,000
632	633	632	633	632	633	632	633	7,590
375			375			375		1,500
830	830	830	830	830	830	830	830	9,960
1,802	1,798	1,798	1,798	1,798	1,798	1,798	1,798	21,580
2,770	1,100	1,600	1,100	1,100	1,600	1,100	1,100	18,375
21,199	14,361	14,860	11,736	11,360	12,861	11,735	11,361	173,797
14,521	(2,611)	6,290	(2,336)	(1,020)	4,059	(1,395)	(786)	36,998
(139)	(132)	(132)	(132)	(132)	(132)	(132)	(132)	(1,591)
14,382	(2,743)	6,158	(2,468)	(1,152)	3,927	(1,527)	(918)	35,407
	(1,062)			(1,063)			(1,062)	4,249
14,382	(3,805)	6,158	(2,468)	(2,215)	3,927	(1,527)	(1,980)	31,158
12,880	15,832	12,876	14,161	26,852	23,844	28,017	29,217	
70,000	63,250	30,000	38,750	20,500	25,500	32,500	22,125	
(364)	(58)	(160)	(28)	(40)	(124)	(40)	(83)	
82,516	79,024	42,716	52,883	47,312	49,220	60,477	51,259	
36,040	40,280	13,250	23,850	10,600	11,660	19,080	11,660	
21,199	14,361	14,860	11,736	11,360	12,861	11,735	11,361	
			(10,000)		(3,763)			
	1,062			1,063			1,062	
57,239	55,703	28,110	25,586	23,023	20,758	30,815	24,083	
25,277	23,321	14,606	27,297	24,289	28,462	29,662	27,176	
9,000	10,000							
445	445	445	445	445	445	445	16,440	
15,832	12,876	14,161	26,852	23,844	28,017	29,217	10,736	
10,000								
157,775	157,330	156,885	156,440	155,995	155,550	155,105	138,665	

B.1 The Monthly Income Projection

As you can see the top portion of the short-term projection is merely a monthly recalculation of the first year's income statement projection. When it's completed correctly, the total column will match your first year's income statement projection. In our example we begin with the month of August, since Superior Jewelers' fiscal year-end is July 31.

Few, if any, businesses have constant operating cycles. Rather, operations will fluctuate according to such variables as seasonality or changing economic conditions. By breaking the income statement down on a monthly basis, we can more accurately determine month-to-month operating requirements. As with our road-map analogy, though we have determined our destination, this will not necessarily prepare us for the day-to-day events that will occur along the way. The short-term projection will help us plan our operating procedures on a daily, weekly, and monthly basis to better guide us in reaching our final destination.

Monthly Sales Volume

Sales and consequently the cost of goods sold, line one and two of our work sheet, will fluctuate more than any other income statement item. Again, those of you in the start-up phase will need to project lower sales volume during the initial months of operation. Don't be surprised or discouraged if your short-term projections reveal it will take six months to a year to reach the break-even point. That's about normal for the small and midsized start-up.

Even those of you buying an existing business will have to put some thought into projecting monthly sales volume. Most businesses fluctuate somewhat on a seasonal basis. Possibly your sales will be higher during the Christmas season and lower during the summer months as with our example, or maybe spring and summer will be your busiest periods. Determining seasonality or short-term sales trends will be an important element in planning and scaling operating procedures accordingly.

Monthly Cost of Goods Sold

Once monthly sales figures have been projected, simply multiply each by the percentage equivalent for the cost of goods sold, in this case 53%, to arrive at their corresponding dollar amount. Then each of these figures can be deducted from the monthly sales figure to determine gross profit on a monthly basis.

Monthly Operating Expenses

Many of the operating expense categories, line four through eleven, will be fixed and can be divided by twelve to arrive at a monthly figure. A few categories may need further analysis, however. You may begin with fewer employees, and then add to staff as sales volume increases, in which case your payroll expenses would be graduated. Possibly insurance payments are made on a quarterly or semiannual basis. This type of analogy should be carried through for all of your operating expense categories to arrive at the various monthly levels.

For Superior Jewelers, we assumed salaries would be graduated and increase in direct proportion to holidays, primarily Christmas. Other operating expenses, line ten, were based on that same assumption. We also assumed that insurance and income tax expense would be paid on a quarterly basis. All remaining operating expense categories were based on a level twelve-month expectation.

Once you've tabulated the monthly operating expenses, monthly operating profit, line twelve, can be derived by deducting total operating expenses from gross profit, Then, of course, other income is added (other expenses deducted) to arrive at the monthly pretax profit figure, line fourteen. Income tax expense, line fifteen, is then deducted to arrive at net profit on a monthly basis, line sixteen. Again, you can check your accuracy by totaling each row, and entering that figure in the total column to the right. The totals will match the first year's income statement projection. Let's now determine how monthly operating levels will affect our operating cash position.

B.2 The Pro Forma Cash Budget

Though the monthly income statement projection is a useful tool, it has some inadequacies, which will become evident as we complete the cash budget, the second portion of our short-term projection model. We need to be most concerned with the ability to generate cash in the short term, since this is the substance used to pay our bills. By varying the monthly income statement slightly, we can create a true cash-flow measurement tool to determine the required cash-flow levels. This cash-flow model is known as the pro forma cash budget.

Cash Receipts

The first step in completing the cash budget will be to enter the beginning cash balance for the first month under the August column. This figure will be your opening checking account balance, which for our example is $16,100. This figure consists of the $1,100 at the business transfer date plus a $15,000 capital injection by Mr. Sample.

Next we calculate the true projected cash receipts for the first month of operation. For our example, we projected first month sales of $25,000, but we are assuming only 25% of those sales will be on a cash basis. Based upon this assumption, the true cash inflow from the first month's sales will only be $6,250, which is entered on the A/R collection and cash sales line for August. The remaining $18,750 will be uncollected accounts receivable.

Accounts Receivable and Payable

When will Superior Jewelers receive the rest of the proceeds from the first month's sales? Take a look at your historical financial statement analysis or the statement studies to determine the average day's receivable. Mr. Sample, however, believes he can speed the receivables turn from forty-one to thirty days, so we have projected that the remaining $18,750 will be collected in September. That figure then is added to September's cash sales to arrive at the A/R and cash sales line item for September ($42,000 × 25% = $10,500 + $18,750 = $29,250). This same analogy can be carried through to calculate the line item amount for A/R and cash sales for the remaining ten months.

Other Income

Other income fluctuates in this example because we are including the effects of a 0.6% sales discount based upon our monthly sales volume. We've also included $500 a month in bad debt expense and $1,600 in interest income spread evenly throughout the year. By comparison, we've included the same total dollar amount under other income (expense) in the monthly income statement projection. The differences help to highlight the variances between cash (income statement) and accrual (pro forma cash budget) accounting.

Total Cash Available

Total cash available can be determined for the month of August by adding beginning cash to our A/R collection and cash sales figure, and then adding our figure for other income (expense). At this point, we cannot determine the total cash available beyond the first month, since we have yet to define the beginning cash balance for the subsequent months.

Cash Disbursements

Superior's suppliers give them thirty-day terms on purchases, so jewelry received in August will not have to be paid for until September. To arrive at the accounts payable disbursements (A/P disbursements) total, we simply insert our cost of goods sold figure for the preceding month. August is left blank since there were no prior month's purchases by Mr. Sample.

Operating expenses will remain constant to the projected income statement so that number can simply be transposed. Building improvements and equipment purchases do not come into play for our example, so those line items are purposefully left blank. For those of you with either simply list the cash disbursement in the month or appropriate months. Again, we are allotting for taxes to be paid quarterly. Other expenses are also purposefully left blank since they have already been accounted for under other income (expense).

Inventory Requirements

The final cash disbursement item, inventory increases (decreases) will require additional analysis. This area could also have a significant impact on your monthly cash flow.

Say for example, your busiest season is Christmas, and it takes approximately ninety days to receive inventory purchases. You would have to order that inventory as early as June to have it in stock for the beginning of the Christmas season, which starts in late September. Assuming thirty-day payment terms, those orders would have to be paid for in October, but the majority of Christmas sales won't take place until December. To make matters worse, only 25% of your sales are cash, and the remaining 75% of December's sales proceeds will become accounts receivable. That money won't be received until the end of January. Though the normal lag between paying for inventory and collecting receivables is usual thirty days, that lag can stretch considerably during busier seasons—in this case up to ninety days.

This analogy is not uncommon to true business seasonality, and it may require additional seasonal operating adjustments, most likely in the form of an operating line of credit from your bank. Again, can you imagine the surprise of the owner who hasn't planned for this kind of occurrence, and finds that he or she has no money to pay for inventory in October, or salaries in December or January. That owner could easily spend three months of sleepless nights without even a clue as to what has happened. This presumes he or she had the foresight to order Christmas inventory in June and was still in business in January.

Monthly Cash Surplus or Deficit

For our example we have assumed there will be no unusual inventory buildups, and that purchases can be received within thirty days. We are also going to bring about inventory reductions to lower the inventory levels to reflect the upper quartile of the industry. These reductions will occur in March and May.

Now that the monthly expenditures are determined, we can total the monthly disbursements (Total Disbursements). For the first month, August, the available cash was $22,292, while cash disbursements were $14,360. By subtracting total disbursements from total cash available, we arrive at the cash surplus (deficit) of $7,932.

The next line item can be used to input a minimum cash requirement as defined by an owner or creditor. If for example, the bank had required Superior to maintain a $10,000 minimum checking account balance as a condition of its term loan, that figure would be inputted here. The line item could then be used as a handy cross-check to alert the owner to an immediate borrowing need any time the cash surplus (deficit) falls below $10,000.

Borrowing Requirements

The cash surplus (deficit) is the cash available before debt service, that is, the principal reduction for existing term loans, line item long-term borrowing repayment. Conversely, the cash surplus is also the cash available before adding any new loan proceeds, line items short-term borrowing requirements, and long-term borrowing requirements.

For Superior, we are budgeting a $445 monthly principal reduction on its existing term loan. We are also budgeting the $16,000 annual principal reduction for the carryback note in one lump sum in July. Mr. Sample has also assumed a $24,000 short-term note, which is payable within one year. He has scheduled repayment of this note in three equal installments to occur in November, December, and January. Mr. Sample has purposefully chosen these three months to take advantage of cash surpluses he is expecting during his busiest selling season.

Fortunately, Mr. Sample has not projected the need to increase short or long-term borrowings during the year. If he had, or if he needs to revise the projections at a later date to include borrowings, line items exist for both categories. These items would, of course, represent a cash inflow, and they would be added to rather than deducted from the cash surplus line, when calculating the cash balance ending line item.

The final two lines on the work sheet, short-term and long-term borrowing balances, are used to keep a running total of the respective loan accounts. The beginning balances are inputted from the corresponding balance sheet, and then each month's principal reduction is deducted to arrive at the next month's balance. Again, any increases in borrowing would be added to the borrowing balance line. Like the minimum cash-balance line item, the borrowing balances are listed primarily for reference purposes.

We are now in a position to complete the cash budget for the month of August. We simply deduct the loan payment of $445 from the cash surplus of $7,932, to arrive at our cash-balance ending of $7,487. That ending cash balance is, of course, also our beginning cash balance for the month of September.

Now, let's carry this analogy through for September. The beginning cash balance of $7,487 is added to September's A/R and cash-sales line item of $29,250, and to arrive at cash available of $36,577. Likewise, to arrive at September's cash disbursements, we add the A/P disbursements of $13,250 to the operating expenses of $16,136 for a total of $29,386. Again, the difference between cash available for September and cash disbursed becomes our cash surplus of $7,191. The loan principal reduction for the month of $445 is then deducted to arrive at the cash balance ending for September of $6,746. This figure becomes the beginning cash balance for October. The remaining month's cash budgets are calculated in the same manner.

The short-term projection model does require considerable time and mental energy, however, the operational insight it provides more than makes up for any inconvenience. This tool can identify many of the causes that bankrupt new businesses in time, to either avert them, or to make operational plans to help minimize their impact. For Superior Jewelers, the projection has alerted us to the fact that there could be six unprofitable months during the year, but that cash balances should be sufficient throughout the year to maintain operations and meet all scheduled debt service.

C. The Balance Sheet Projection

The final step in completing the long-term business plan will be to prepare pro forma and projected balance sheets. Some of you may wish to complete the pro forma or opening balance sheet prior to completing the short-term projection. This will enable you to determine the opening balances for such items as cash and accounts receivable. In either case, these figures will have to be known to complete the short-term projection model correctly. For this exercise, we will again utilize the balance-sheet and ratio-analysis work sheets.

SUPERIOR JEWELERS, INC.
PROJECTED BALANCE SHEET
WORKSHEET

ASSETS			August 1, 20X1	July 31, 20X2		R.M.A. Statement Studies % of Total
Cash			16,100	20,696		6.5
Accounts Receivable (Net)				16,875		15.6
Inventory			141,660	127,897		61.6
Marketable Securities						
Prepaids			2,640	2,640		
Other Current Assets						1.8
TOTAL CURRENT ASSETS			160,400	168,108		85.5
Land and Buildings (Gross)						
Machinery and Equipment			10,000	10,000		
Leasehold Improvements			25,000	25,000		
(Accumulated Depreciation)				(9,960)		
NET FIXED ASSETS			35,000	25,040		9.7
Investments						
Notes Receivable						
Other Noncurrent Assets - Deposits			1,245	1,245		3.4
Intangibles			43,763	43,763		1.4
TOTAL ASSETS			240,408	238,156		100.0
LIABILITIES						
Notes Payable - Bank			24,000			9.3
Notes Payable - Other						
Current Portion - LTD			21,335	21,335		3.0
Accounts Payable				11,925		19.0
Income Taxes Payable						
Accrued and Other Current Liab.						10.5
TOTAL CURRENT LIABILITIES			45,335	33,260		41.8
Term Debt - Banks			74,665	69,330		14.5
Term Debt - Former Owner			64,000	48,000		
TOTAL LIABILTIES			184,000	150,590		
EQUITY						
Common Stock			25,000	25,000		
Preferred/Paid in Capital			15,000	15,000		
Retained Earnings/Owner's Equity			16,408	47,566		
NET WORTH			56,408	87,566		43.7
NET WORTH + LIABILITIES			240,408	238,156		100.0

SUPERIOR JEWELERS, INC.
PROJECTED RATIO ANALYSIS
WORKSHEET

		August 1, 20X1	July 31, 20X2	R.M.A. Statement Studies
WORKING CAPITAL		$115,065	$134,848	
LIQUIDITY RATIOS				3.1
Current Ratio	Current Assets / Current Liab.	3.5	5.1	2.1 / 1.6
Quick Ratio	Cash & Acct. Rec. / Current Liabs.	.4	1.1	.9 / .5 / .2
Inventory Turnover	C.G.S. / Inventory	N/A	1.86	1.9 / 1.2 / .8
Day's Supply	360 * / Inv. T.O.	N/A	194	192 / 304 / 456
Accounts Receivable Turnover	Sales / Acct. Rec.	N/A	26.6	30.4 / 13.8 / 6.4
Day's Receivable	360 * / A/R T.O.	N/A	14	12 / 26 / 57
Accounts Payable Turnover	C.G.S. / Accts. Pay.	N/A	19.9	N/A
Day's Payable	360 * / A/P T.O.	N/A	18	N/A
LEVERAGE RATIOS				.6
Debt/Worth	Total Liabs. / Net Worth	3.3	1.7	1.3 / 2.6
Fixed/Worth	Fixed Assets / Net Worth	.6	.3	.1 / .2 / .5
ASSET MANAGEMENT RATIOS				1.8 / 1.4
Sales to Assets	Sales / Total Assets	N/A	1.9	1.1
Return on Assets — %	Net Profit (B4T) / Total Assets	N/A	13.1	16.1 / 8.9 / 3.7
Return on Investment — %	Net Profit (B4T) / Net Worth	N/A	35.6	39.8 / 22.9 / 10.1

* Or the number of days during the statement period if less than one year.

The Pro Forma Balance Sheet Asset Section

The pro forma balance sheet will be the balance sheet on the date the business is trans-ferred, in this case August 1, 20X1. It will be compiled before any sales transpire. Assets will most likely include cash, whatever inventory you've purchased, any fixed assets (at this point there will be no accumulated depreciation), prepaid expenses or deposits, and any intangibles such as goodwill. For our example, the opening assets consist of

$141,660 in purchased inventory, $35,000 in purchased fixed assets ($10,000 in lease-hold improvements and $25,000 in machinery and equipment), $1,245 in prepaid deposits, and $43,763 in goodwill. Additionally, Mr. Sample has injected $15,000 of his own money, which is reflected in both the cash and the paid-in capital accounts.

The Pro Forma Balance Sheet Liability Section

Liabilities on the pro forma balance sheet will be limited to accounts payable if you purchased any initial inventory on credit, and any borrowings that you may have already incurred including any loans that you may have made to the company or that the previous owner has carried back. For our example, there is no accounts payable yet, since the entire inventory was included with the purchase. The only beginning liabilities are the assumed loans. Again, these include a $24,000 short-term note, an $80,000 term loan, and the $80,000 carry back, not from the previous owner. Those portions of the term debts payable during the first twelve months are combined and included as current portion-LTD in the current liability section.

The Pro Forma Balance Sheet Equity Section

The beginning net worth will be the equal to the amount by which total assets exceed total liabilities. In the event total liabilities exceed total assets, that net worth would be a negative number. If a proprietorship or partnership, the net worth would include any capital injected into a start-up, or any equity purchased for an existing firm. If a corporation, the net worth would consist of the amount paid for all outstanding common and preferred stock. If that amount exceeds the par value, the excess would be included in paid-in capital. The paid-in capital account would also include any capital injected by the new shareholders. The net worth for an existing corporation would also include any retained earnings that were transferred as part of the sale. For Superior Jewelers, the beginning net worth consists of $25,000 of par value common stock, $16,408 in transferred retained earnings, and $15,000 in paid-in capital, which represents the monies that Mr. Sample injected.

The Percent of Sales Method

Many balance-sheet projection models simply recalculate asset and liability items as a percent of sales. Past year-end statements or statement study comparisons would be used as the basis for determining the percentages. Each percentage equivalent would then be multiplied by the total sales projection for the year to arrive at the projected balance sheet. In this type of modeling, short-term borrowings are used as a plug figure to balance the statement. It is assumed if the remaining items are projected accurately, short-term borrowings in an amount approximating the plugged figure will be needed to maintain the projected sales volume.

Incorporating the Cash Budget

The percent of sales modeling method utilizes little operational analysis and takes no consideration for changes you may wish to effect to the balance sheet. You can develop a much more accurate balance-sheet model by utilizing the cash budget, which we've already completed to help analyze and project balance-sheet items. The July 31, 20X2, projected balance sheet included on our work sheet insert is an example of this process.

Projecting the Fiscal Year-end Asset Section

There are several known line items that can be transferred directly from our cash budget model. First, the cash balance as of July 31, 20X1 will be $20,696. This consists of $10,736, the ending cash balance from the short-term projection, plus any noncash expenditure (expensed items not deducted from cash) from the first year's income statement. In this case, the depreciation expense of $9,960 would be added as noncash expenditure.

Accounts receivable is another known item. Since we are assuming a thirty-day collection period, July's credit sales will become the month-end accounts receivable. Again, assuming 75% credit sales, the calculation for determining accounts receivable would be: $22,500 × 0.75 = $16,875.

Inventory isn't always a known item, and may at times have to be projected by the percent of sales method or through other assumptions. In this case, we are effecting an inventory decrease of $13,763 as depicted on the short-term projection. Therefore, beginning inventory of $146,660 minus the decrease of $13,763 equals $127,897; the balance-sheet entry for projected inventory as of 7/31/X2. For our example, prepaid expenses remain unchanged, so total current assets equal $168,108 for the first year-end.

We have also assumed there will be no fixed asset purchases or deductions during the year. Net fixed assets will, however, decrease by the increase in accumulated depreciation, in this case the depreciation expense of $9,960. We are also assuming no changes in deposits for the year, so our total projected assets as of July 31, 20X2 will equal $238,156.

Projecting the Fiscal Year-end Liability Section

For our example, first year-end liabilities are also easily distinguishable. We know there is no additional short-term borrowing needs being projected, and that the $24,000 short-term note is expected to be paid back in full. We are also not projecting any additions to long-term borrowings, and that the current portion of term debt will remain unchanged at $21,335.

The only remaining current liability is account payable. Again, since supplier terms are thirty days, the cost of goods sold for July of $11,925 as shown on the short-term projection, will equal the accounts payable balance for 7/31/X2. Since there were no additions to long-term borrowings projected, the ending balance of $138,665 from our short-term projection will become our long-term debt for the 7/31/X2 balance sheet. Remember, $21,335 of the $138,665 has already been accounted for as the current portion of term debt. The remaining $117,330 becomes this year's term debt. Since the note to the former owner is payable at $16,000 annually, that term portion is $48,000. The bank loan is payable at $5,335 annually so that term portion becomes $69,330. Total projected liabilities add to $150,590 for the 7/31/2X projected balance sheet.

Accrued Liabilities

We have yet to discuss accrued liabilities to any extent, but some of you may wish to include a few in your own projections. An accrued liability is one that has been expensed on the income statement, but has yet to be disbursed from cash. The most prevalent would be taxes that are usually accrued monthly but paid out quarterly. Had we decided to accrue the last quarter's income-tax expense for our example, an accrued tax liability would be listed as a current liability on our balance sheet in the amount of $1,062. Total current liabilities and total liabilities would both increase by a like amount. Conversely, the cash account, total current assets, and total assets would increase too by $1,062. Net worth would remain unchanged.

Net Worth Calculations

In most cases net worth at the end of the first year will consist of the beginning net worth plus or minus any net profit (loss) for the year. This is true for our example. There can be exceptions, though. A corporation might pay dividends that would reduce net worth by the amount of the dividend. Or stockholders could inject additional capital or sell more shares of stock as a means of increasing net worth. Any anticipated variances should be taken into consideration when determining the projected net worth for your own prospective companies to better plan the impact on operations.

D. Chapter Summary

Few projected balance sheets will work out as easily as our example. In most cases, once all the known items have been transferred from the cash budget, it will be necessary to utilize the percent of sales method for a few remaining items. Under these circumstances, I would suggest utilizing cash as the plug figure rather than short-term borrowings. If by chance, cash becomes negative, I would suggest first increasing accruals if possible and increasing borrowings as a last resort.

Since a short-term projection is usually just completed in one-year increments, it will most likely be necessary to use the percent of sales method to project out the balance sheet for a three- to five-year period. Long-term projections do not need to be revised as often as short-term projections, but they should be reviewed at least semiannually.

Again, consider the projection of your road map to the future. It's one of the most important, though often neglected, management tools available. The successful business owner plans for tomorrow as well as today. The most effective decision-making process involves projecting the effects of short and long-range decisions on present and future operations. The importance of operating projections cannot be overemphasized.

CHAPTER 9

Bank Financing and the Loan Package

Most of you will have to borrow money to start or purchase your business. Unlike Mr. Sample who borrowed from the owner, the majority of you will be borrowing from a commercial bank. The advantages of bank financing are many. In most instances, interest rate and loan terms will be more favorable than with other sources of financing. Additionally, problem situations, should they arise, are generally handled in a more professional and accommodating manner. Finally, banks provide a host of ancillary services, which will prove a necessity to operating and growing your business.

To reemphasize an earlier point, most banks are in business to lend money. Nothing gives a commercial lender more pleasure than to lend, advice, and share in the successful development of a new or growing business. Your banker can prove to be your most ardent supporter. All you need to do to win this support is take the initial step to demonstrate your management capabilities and the soundness of your business proposal.

Your progress to date has amounted to proving to yourself the soundness and feasibility of your concept. Now the time has come to package that concept and to sell it to your banker. Before we begin to outline that process, let's briefly discuss capital requirements and the various types of loans available.

A. Defining Your Capital Requirements

By now you should be able to define your capital requirements. Those of you with term loan needs, such as for a portion of the capital to start or purchase a business or to purchase of equipment, will have defined those needs on the long-term projections. Operating needs, such as a line of credit should also have been easily defined, since they have already been clearly determined on your initial cash budget, under short-term borrowing requirements. Your initial capital requirements, whether in the form of a capital injection, short or long-term loans, or a combination thereof, will have to be sufficient to meet all of these identifiable needs plus provide an adequate level of working capital.

As an added level of caution, I would suggest your initial capital base be sufficient to carry your operations at least six months past your projected break-even point.

Short vs. Long-Term Loan Requirements

As previously discussed, loan requests can be divided into two general categories, short-term and long-term loans. Short-term loans are payable within a twelve-month period, while long-term loans are those with payback terms that exceed twelve months. The importance of understanding this concept is two-fold. One, it will help to identify repayment sources for the loan package. Two and perhaps more importantly, understanding the concept will add to your cash budgeting and management planning skills.

Identifying Repayment Sources

The repayment sources are distinctively different for short and long-term loans. If you think back to any of the income statements we've worked with, you'll recall there are no expense line items titled loan payments. There were accounts for interest expenses, which includes the interest paid on loans but, at least for accounting purposes, principal reductions are an after-profit deduction. Short-term loans are typically paid through operational changes such as the collection of accounts receivable. Long-term loans are repaid from the cash flow generated by the business.

Short-Term Repayment Sources

Again, referring back to the cash budget, you'll recall that short-term borrowing needs are created by cash shortages and repaid by cash excesses. The causes of both the shortage and excess could be the buildup and repayment of accounts receivable. The same is true of temporary inventory needs such as the Christmas buildup in our previous analogy. A short-term loan could provide the funds to purchase that additional inventory, while the sale of that inventory could provide the eventual cash to repay that loan. Those three months of sleepless nights would have been avoided, as the cash from operations would have been retained to fund operations, including employee salaries, rather than used to purchase the additional inventory.

Long-Term Repayment Sources

Term loan obligations are, of course, repaid over a scheduled period of time. The current portion of long-term debt is the principal reduction to be paid back within one year. It's repaid from current year cash flow. Again, this cash is generated from net profit plus depreciation plus or minus any other cash inflows or outflows. It would not be practical or advisable to repay terms from short-term sources as this would drain the company of the cash needed to fuel current operations.

Asset and Liability Management

Recognizing the differences between short and long-term needs and planning accordingly are the foundations for proper asset and liability management. This concept affects every type of business, regardless of size. Your understanding and utilization of this rather simple concept will be one of the keys to incorporating larger corporations' management techniques into your own operating system. These operational procedures will be discussed in upcoming chapters.

A.1 The Types of Loans Available

At this stage, borrowing needs can be divided into three general categories: seasonal lines of credit, start-up or purchase financing, and fixed asset financing. Seasonal needs are those previously defined as short-term needs on our cash budget. Most often this will take the form of accounts receivable or inventory financing and is sometimes referred to as a working capital line of credit. Expect to pay between 2% and 4% above prime on a variable rate for this type of financing, and to pledge both inventory and accounts receivable as collateral. The actual loanable amount will be anywhere between 50% and 80% of the corresponding assets value, depending upon the collectability of the receivables or the liquidation value of the inventory. It will be up to each of you to help establish the true value of the underlying assets based upon aging and inventory evaluations.

Purchase and Start-up Financing

Start-up financing will normally be utilized as a permanent working capital injection to supplement initial capitalization, or to help purchase an existing business. This form of financing will usually take the form of a term loan. The term will usually be between three to five years, and the rate could be either variable or fixed at 3% to 5% over prime. This type of loan could also necessitate the encumbrance of receivables and inventory in some instances, and fixed and personal assets in most others.

As a working capital injection, this type of financing could be used to buy the initial inventory or finance the initial receivables of a start-up. While both of these examples appear to be short-term needs, most businesses will have a base inventory and receivables requirement. Seasonal levels will fluctuate above those base levels giving the initial base a degree of permanency. It would be best to finance and repay these base levels on a long-term basis for those in this situation.

Fixed Asset Financing

Equipment or facilities financing will also take the form of a term loan. Normally the asset financed will also be utilized as collateral, and the maximum loan amount will not exceed 80% of its cost. Expect to pay between 2% and 4% over prime for equipment financing on either a variable or fixed rate basis, with a term not exceeding five years in most cases. Facility financing will be at a more favorable rate, approximately 2% over prime, with a term of up to fifteen years.

B. Preparing the Loan Package

Most commercial banks have standardized criteria by which they evaluate loan requests. This standardization can be utilized to your advantage by addressing the most critical areas within the context of your loan proposal. Let's identify each of these critical areas, and then structure a loan request designed to address each concern with a minimum amount of effort and confusion.

The lending officer will first evaluate the soundness of your loan request in terms of its overall need and cost effectiveness. Next, he or she will evaluate the ability to repay the request from operating sources and available collateral, in the event those operating sources don't materialize. Finally, the loan officer will evaluate the strengths and weaknesses of the business or proposed business, and the management capabilities of its owners.

Correlate your request to the designing of a marketing brochure. Next to you, the loan package will be the most important tool in selling your business or idea. In most cases, the lender will have little or no advanced knowledge of your proposal, and it will be up to you and the loan package to provide the assurance necessary for its approval. The proposal should tell an introductory story substantiated by facts and proven research materials. The reading should prove interesting, and though the package will encompass many pages, it should be kept as concise and fast moving as possible.

The loan package will be subdivided into five general sections as listed below:

1. <u>The Request</u>
   a. Introduction
   b. Purpose
   c. Amount requested
   d. Terms Requested
   e. Repayment sources
   f. Available collateral
2. <u>Financial History and Projections</u>
   a. Copies of the financial statements and analysis for the existing business
   b. Copies of the projections and analysis for both the start-up and existing business
   c. Any research materials that might supplement to projections

3. The Business History or Plan
   a. A brief narrative paralleling the financial history if applicable
   b. Mention of operating strengths and weaknesses and how you intend to capitalize or correct them
   c. Discussion of your operating plan
   d. Discussion of how the requested loan ties into this plan
4. Management Qualifications
   a. Personal financial statements of all active owners
   b. Résumés of all active owners and any other key personnel
   c. A listing of directors if a corporation
5. General Information
   a. A narrative about the products or services rendered
   b. Seasonal trends
   c. Sales and distribution methods
   d. Production methods for the manufacturer
   e. Market survey information
   f. Aging and inventory valuations if applicable
   g. Articles of incorporation, partnership agreement or franchise agreement when applicable
   h. A copy of the buy/sell agreement if applicable
   e. A copy of the lease agreement.

The Cover Letter

Each section of the proposal should be indexed to make it easier to follow. The package should also be presented with a brief cover letter summarizing your needs, the business or proposed business, and your personal profile. The cover letter will give the package a more professional appearance, and will start the lender's educational process. The reader will be much less apt to get confused or overwhelmed by the package as a result.

B.1 The Request

The loan request should begin with a short introduction of the need as summarized in the cover letter. More importantly this section should contain the purpose for the loan, the amount requested, the term of that request, the source of repayment, and the available collateral. You could very well have multiple requests at this phase such as a receivables line and the need to purchase equipment. Just remember to separate each request and to identify it as a short or long-term need.

The Primary Source of Repayment

The source of repayment is so critical to the lender's approval process that internally they will try to identify at least two sources of repayment—a primary source and a secondary or backup source. You can stay one step ahead of the game by clearly defining those sources within your proposal. If you have multiple requests, be sure to segregate and list the repayment sources for each.

The primary source of repayment will be the most likely operating sources such as the sale of inventory for inventory financing, or cash flow for equipment financing. Don't just state the source though, substantiate it with figures. Provide the markup and historical turn for inventory. Provide the historical or projected cash flow available for term financing, both of which can be identified from your original cash budgets that have been supplied for supporting documentation. List the source even if it is a projected rather than historical source, but be sure to label it as such.

The Secondary Source of Repayment

The secondary source of repayment will usually be tied to available forms of collateral. For a short-term request it might be a blanket assignment of receivables or inventory. For a long-term request such as an equipment purchase, it might be the liquidation of the equipment itself. When listing the secondary source, state and, if possible, substantiate the value by referring to the quality and speed of receivables' turns, or the wholesale valuation of the equipment. In the event there isn't adequate value, include additional collateral such as a secondary piece of equipment to increase the collateral value, or list another income source if one is available. Again, every situation will differ, so learn to identify and utilize your strengths.

Personal Net Worth as a Secondary Source

If the business assets are not adequate to collateralize the loan request, you may at this point wish to list personal assets or income sources available to serve as a secondary source of repayment. These could take the form of liquid assets or real property holdings, and the listing should include the liquidation value. The potential creditor will examine your personal financial statement in much the same manner as we discussed previously.

B.2 Financial History and Projections

The financial history and projection section will be devoted to the facts and figures necessary to substantiate your request, and they should be arranged in the most logical progression to supplement your proposal. If you are purchasing an existing business, you will include copies of the past three fiscal year-end financial statements or tax returns, as well as the most current interim statement. You will also submit a copy of your pro forma balance sheet, your projected income statement, and your ratio analysis. This section should also contain copies of your short and long-term projection. Those in the start-up phase may also wish to include information from the statement studies or other financial research materials in support of your projections in lieu of historical data.

B.3 The Business History or Plan

The business history section will parallel the financial history. For those purchasing an existing business, it will begin with your reasons for wanting to purchase the business. Next will be a brief narrative detailing the company's operating history, including any operating highlights or deficiencies. This will be followed with a brief discussion detailing your operating plan, including any changes you intend to implement and the reasoning behind those changes. For example, you may wish to detail your need for a particular piece of equipment and how its purchase will benefit the overall operation.

Those in the start-up phase will be at a disadvantage since there is no historical financial statement to help substantiate your request. You will need to rely almost exclusively on your projections to support your request. The narrative will have to incorporate your basis for reaching the projection's conclusions from your initial research data and market analysis. It would also be helpful to include any supporting historical data that may have been acquired from studying competing businesses without naming the companies or their principals.

B.4 Management Qualifications

This section will be devoted to familiarizing the potential lender with your qualifications, as well as the qualifications of any other owners or key personnel. This section will include personal financial statements for everyone with an ownership interest and the résumés of all active owners and, possibly, key personnel. Those of you incorporating may wish to include a listing of the board of directors, and a short summary of each member's qualification. You may also wish to intersperse short narratives whenever necessary to provide additional insight, or to tie together any loose ends.

B.5 The General Information Section

The general information section will be utilized for any additional information needed to further substantiate your request. It could include a brief narrative about the products or services rendered, the product or services sales mix, and any seasonal trends. Sales and distribution methods might be defined here as well, and those involved in manufacturing may wish to summarize production methods.

Those of you in the start-up phase should include any marketing surveys in this section that might substantiate the need, or prove the market for your product or service. You may also wish to include any general industry information that might further enhance your request. Those of you who have developed information about your competitors and feel you hold operating advantages such as a superior product line, better qualified management, better selling techniques, or other competitive edges, should discuss them here.

Customer Relations

If customer relationships already exist, it would be advisable to include contact information for each major account in this section for verification purposes. Be sure to advise your customers beforehand to assure they are ready and willing to assist. For those of you applying for receivables financing or wishing to utilize receivables as collateral, this section should be supplemented with a current accounts receivable aging. This will give a more detailed assessment of the receivables' collectability, and the time restrains involved in their payment.

For those whose customer base is made up of only a few major clients, it would be important to stress the strength of those relationships, and to provide copies of any written contract in this section. This could prove vital to your request since just as those few customers can ensure your success, the loss of one or more of those customers could easily result in your failure. Lenders will be fully aware of this condition, and failure to substantiate these relationships will most likely result in your loan request being denied.

Supplier Relations

Those of you entering businesses relying on the sale of inventory should include a list of all major suppliers along with their contact information in this section. For those subject to supplier volatility, this section should also include a summary of supplier relationships, supply availabilities, and cost volatility. Be truthful in detailing those relationships or potential relationships, because in most instances the suppliers will also be contacted to discuss them.

Inventory and Fixed Asset Valuations

Those wishing to utilize inventory as collateral or those seeking inventory financing, should include an inventory listing in this section to substantiate its value. Those wishing to purchase or use fixed assets for collateral purposes should also substantiate their values here. A fixed-asset valuation should include the age, useful life, the initial cost, the current market value if not new, the liquidation value, as well as the appraisal certification if applicable.

Miscellaneous Information Section

Those of you purchasing an existing business should also include a copy of the buy/sell agreement in this section. Those of you involved in a partnership or corporation should include a copy of the partnership or articles of incorporation, as well as a partnership or corporate authorization, which grants you the power to borrow in the company's behalf. Those purchasing a franchise should also include a copy of the franchise agreement. You should also include information regarding the terms of any lease or real property purchase with copies of any agreements or documentation. Finally, include a brief summary of the insurance coverages on both the business and the owners.

C. Chapter Summary

While the format of the loan package will very rarely, if ever, be altered, the contents of each individual section will differ slightly, depending on the industry, company size and format, and whether or not the proposal is for an existing or start-up concern. Once again, following this loan packaging format will greatly enhance your chances for obtaining bank financing, as long as you have detailed the soundness of the request and substantiated the sources of repayment. Earning the lender's trust throughout each of the sections of the proposal will all but assure the approval of your loan request.

CHAPTER 10

Alternative Sources of Financing

To date, our financing discussion has been limited to commercial banks. Today, these institutions are receiving increased competition from brokerage firms, investment bankers, insurance companies, private investors, and finance companies. Though most of these sources will charge a higher interest rate, possibly even an equity position, their lending criteria is often less restrictive. The lending programs offered by these sources could prove better suited to some of you, and a necessity for others.

This chapter will be devoted to discussing these alternative sources and the lending programs they offer. It will also include a discussion of governmental lending and assistance programs such as those offered by the Small Business Administration (SBA). This will include information about specialty programs for veterans, members of minorities, the handicapped, and those with low incomes. It should also be mentioned that the loan-packaging format detailed in the preceding chapter will work equally well for most of these sources. The exception will be government agencies. Though the same format will apply, preparation on government-supplied forms will be required.

A. Public and Private Financing Alternatives
A.1 Factoring
Some finance companies and private specialty firms specialize in factoring—a form of accounts receivable in financing. The factor will either buy your existing receivables at a discount or collect them for a fee. They will also lend equivalent cash against a percentage of the receivables in much the same manner as a commercial bank.

You will find factoring to be an extremely expensive form of financing, but one some of you may be forced to use as a means of supplementing cash flow. Discounts can run as high as 30% for receivables purchased outright, and interest rates on factoring lines of credit run from 4% to 6% over prime plus monthly servicing fees.

Factoring will only be an alternative to those currently in business or those purchasing a business with receivables with which to finance. Those interested in this type of financing should first approach their bank as most major banks have factoring divisions.

Though these divisions will be more expensive than direct bank financing, they will still prove cheaper and more reliable than most direct-factoring companies.

A.2 Sales Contracts

For those of you selling retail goods, another similar but far less expensive form of raising cash is to sell retail sales contracts. Those of you selling automobiles, appliances, stereo equipment, furniture, jewelry, or any other large ticket items can make arrangements to sell the contract or receivable to a bank or finance company like GMAC or General Electric Credit Corporation. These institutions will provide immediate cash for the transaction, and often the only fee will be the installment interest charged directly to the customer.

A.3 Floor Planning

Inventory financing is of course available through most major banks, but many private firms such as GMAC and General Electric Credit Corporation also offer inventory financing or floor planning. So too do most manufacturers of larger ticket items, either directly or through a subsidiary. Those of you with large investments in retail inventory will find this type of financing extremely attractive. Interest rates will normally run from 1% to 3% over prime for floor plan lines.

A.4 Equipment Suppliers

When purchasing equipment, check first with the seller. Many manufacturers also provide financing for their sales outlets, which is how GMAC, Ford Motor Credit, and General Electric Credit Corporation got their starts before expanding their product offerings. In effect you would become the customer from the sales contract category. Oftentimes suppliers offer incentives as a means of selling its products such as price discounts or low-interest financing. It pays to shop rates and terms when making equipment purchase decisions.

A.5 Finance Companies

Finance companies such as HSBC or OneMain Financial may be another source of financing for the small start-up concern. These institutions are more willing than a commercial bank to lend on an unsecured basis or against personal property. Many also have divisions that lend against commercial equipment. In most cases, finance companies lending limits and credit criteria will be much lower. Interest rates, however, will be higher than those charged by a commercial bank.

A.6 Savings and Loan Associations

Savings and loans have traditionally specialized in residential mortgages. They too will lend against your personal residence as well some forms of commercial property, and at rates comparable to commercial banks. Some federally chartered savings and loans offer a full range of commercial lending and depository services.

A.7 Venture Capitalists

Every locale has venture capitalists, ranging from individual investors to international conglomerates. They can even take the form of government supported SBICs and MESBICs and affiliates of major banks and investment firms. Venture capital firms will be most attractive for those of you who have exhaustive appetites for capital, including those with expansive manufacturing or research and development requirements.

Interest rates and fees will vary significantly with venture capital financing. Typically, direct capital injections are provided by means of stock purchases or through convertible debentures. While this can provide capital with favorable repayment terms, it can also provide an unwanted partner who could be expensive to remove at a later date.

Those of you interested in venture capital financing should try to match your individual needs with a like-sized investment firm. If, for example, you're opening a small retail store, an individual limited partner, might best suit your needs. If you are planning to open a manufacturing firm requiring a multimillion dollar investment, a larger venture capital firm might be your only alternative.

Your attorney, banker, or accountant will be the best source of referral for those wishing to explore this alternative. A simple Google search can also provide you with a directory of venture capitalists, as can the National Venture Capital Association (nvca.org).

A.8 Investment Bankers

Many investment banking firms also provide venture capital support, and many investment bankers also serve as brokers for alternative capital sources. This can include private investors, limited partners, and loans from public corporations. These public sources often include companies seeking to invest excess cash, or companies, or unions seeking to invest pension funds.

This type of financing typically works best for those seeking real-estate financing with minimum needs of $500,000. Although a brokerage fee of between 2% and 3% will be charged to arrange the transaction, the underlying interest rate will usually be competitive with those charged by commercial banks.

A.9 Insurance Companies

Another source for placing private loans is the insurance industry. Like investment bankers, they are rarely interested in loans of less than $500,000, and always secured by real estate. Locating this type of financing is best accomplished by contacting regional rather than local representatives. Most insurance company lending programs will closely parallel commercial bank real-estate programs with regards to credit criteria, interest rates, and loan terms.

Loan Packagers

Guard against companies that advertise strictly as loan packagers specializing in arranging bank or SBA financing. Some may even claim to guarantee loan approval, and most will require a fee up front. Be forewarned, there are no guarantees, and the vast majority of firms with up-front end costs are not legitimate. Most seasoned commercial lenders and SBA loan officers can relate dozens of horror stories about those who have been duped by these types of firms.

B. Government Assistance Programs

There are several agencies within the federal government that lend money directly to small businesses or assist with financing arrangements. Some of these agencies will provide longer terms and lower rates than commercial institutions. Others will provide guarantees to assist in obtaining financing from commercial banks. This section will detail the programs currently available. Your business's needs and personal qualifications will determine which, if any, of these programs are suited to your capital requirements.

B.1 The Small Business Administration

The Small Business Administration (SBA) is the best-known and most often utilized government small-business assistance agency. There are actually two types of SBA lending programs available—direct and indirect financing. Direct loans refer to the SBA acting as the lender, and indirect loans refer to the SBA providing a partial guarantee on your behalf to a lending institution. In the 1980s and 1990s, it was not uncommon for the SBA to be the direct lender in instances where at least three banks had turned down an indirect application beforehand. That program ended in September 2011. Today, direct lending only exists within the SBA's disaster loan program. The SBA's indirect lending program provide the underlying lender with a guarantee of up to 85% of the loan proceeds of a loan under $150,000, and up to 75% of a loan in excess of $150,000.

Meeting SBA Qualifications

There are certain restrictions firms must meet to qualify for SBA assistance. The first is to be a small business as defined by the SBA. To qualify as a small business, a company must have fewer than five hundred employees, average under $7.5 million in revenues for the past three years, average net profit after taxes of under $5 million, and have a tangible net worth under $15 million. In addition, applicants must be a for-profit business with at least one location in the United States, and operate primarily within the United States. Applicants must also prove a need for the loan, exhausted alternative financial resources including personal property, have no defaults or bankruptcies on previous SBA loans, and not be delinquent on existing debt obligations to the US government. Finally, applicants must prove credit worthiness and possess a minimum credit score of 680.

There are a few industries that are not eligible for SBA financing. They include financial businesses primarily engaged in lending, developers, and landlords who do not occupy the asset being acquired or improved, life insurers, businesses engaged in pyramid-style distribution schemes, businesses primarily engaged in gambling activities, religious organizations, private clubs, cooperatives, loan packagers, lobbyists, speculative businesses like oil and gas exploration, and businesses that engage in activities of an indecent sexual nature or other illegal activities.

If all this sounds confusing, you have to realize the SBA is a part of the federal government. For those who do qualify, you're not out of the woods yet. The SBA also has restrictions on the use of the loan proceeds. Acceptable purposes include the purchase of real estate, equipment, machinery, furniture, fixtures, supplies, working capital, refinancing existing debt, establishing a new business, and purchasing an existing business.

Though the SBA approval process is predicated on the soundness of the request and the ability to pay back the loan, consideration is also given to those who will expand employment, particularly in economically depressed areas. Again, the SBA loan application is identical in format to the loan package discussed in the preceding chapter, but it must be completed on SBA-supplied forms. I would strongly urge those considering SBA financing first discuss the option with your banker or a representative of the SBA prior to completing a formal application.

B.2 The SBA Financing Programs

SBA 7(a) Loans

There are six types of SBA loans. The most common is 7 (a) General Small Business Loan. This category also includes the SBA Express and the SBA Advantage programs, which are intended to speed the approval process. The 7 (a) loan cannot exceed $5 million and is typically used for working capital, refinancing, starting or purchasing a business, real estate, or equipment. Currently, interest rates are between 5.75% and 8.25%

(8% to 10% for SBA Express). Loan terms are up to ten years for general purposes, and twenty-five years for commercial real estate.

CDC/SBA 504 Loans

CDC/SBA 504 loans combine a loan from a nonprofit CDC with a loan from a bank to create a long-term, low-interest rate loan. The program is designed to provide afford-able, long-term financing for businesses seeking to buy or build their operating facilities as well as to outfit those facilities equipment. The program actually pairs two lenders together to fund the project. A bank, credit union or nonbank lender provides up to 50% of the project cost. A community development corporation (CDC) lends up to 40% of the project cost. The borrower must provide at least 10% of the project's costs.

An SBA 504 loan is actually two loans with differing rates, terms, and limits. The SBA does not set limits on the rates and terms of the lending institutions portion, but typi-cally the interest rate will fall between 4% and 8% with a term of between five and ten years, amortized over twenty to twenty-five years. The SBA does set limits on the CDC portion. This portion must have a term of either ten or twenty years, and the interest rate is pegged to the five and ten-year US Treasury rate. Currently, CDC ten-year loans carry an interest rate of 3.2%, and twenty-year loans carry an interest rate of 3.7%. Combined, the two loans cannot exceed $14 million. Borrowers can take out multiple SBA 504 loans for different projects, however, up to a maximum of $20 million.

To qualify, the borrower must meet the SBA standard criteria as well as provide at least 10% of the project's cost and occupy at least 51% of the building. The SBA has also set rules to promote job creation, community development, and other pub-lic policy goals. Applicants must create or retain at least one job per every $65,000 loaned ($100,000 for manufacturers). Community development goals include promot-ing business district revitalization, expansion of exports, expansion of minority, women, or veteran-owned businesses, rural development, energy efficiency, and clean energy production.

SBA CapLines of Credit

CAPLines are lines of credit meant to help small businesses meet short-term and sea-sonal working-capital needs and to fulfill purchase orders and contracts. There are several different line types available depending upon the need and type of business. The seasonal line is the most popular used to finance seasonal receivables or inventory buildups, or for seasonal labor costs. The next is a contracts line used to pay for the materials and labor for assignable contracts. The next is a builder's line used by contrac-tors for the materials, labor, equipment, and permission for residential and commercial building projects. Finally, there are standard and small asset-based lines used to convert short-term assets like invoices into cash.

All of the lines carry a maximum amount of $5 million, with the exception of the small asset-based line that cannot exceed $200,000. SBA CAPLines can be issued as standalone products, but are typically only offered to borrowers in conjunction with a traditional SBA 7(a) loan or a CDC/SBA 504 loan.

SBA Export Loans

Export loans are designed to help small businesses fund new exporting operations, and to offer short-term cash flow solutions to enable more flexible payment terms to international customers. There are three types of export loans available. The first is the SBA Express Export loan, which streamlines approval for up to $500,000 in working capital needs with up to a seven-year payback term. The second is the Export Working Capital loan with funding of up to $5 million. Terms are typically twelve months, but can extend to three years. The third is the International Trade loan with funding of up to $5 million for working capital or fixed-asset purchases and terms up to twenty-five years. Applicants for the International Trade loans can be both exporters and businesses that have been negatively impacted by imports.

SBA Microloan Program

The SBA Microloan program provides loans to nonprofit intermediary lenders who then relend the monies to for-profit small businesses and nonprofit child care centers. The SBA does not guarantee any portion of the loans made under the SBA Microloan program. Microloans have terms up to six years and must be for less than $50,000. The partner institutions set their own credit criteria and interest rates. On average, the interest rates range from 8% to 13%; the average size loan is about $14,000. The non-profit intermediaries can borrow up to $750,000 from the SBA in its first year, and up to $1.25 million each year thereafter. The intermediary cannot have more the $5 million borrowed at any one time.

SBA Disaster Loan Program

In general, SBA disaster loans are used to recover from a declared disaster or, in the case of the MREIDL, the loss of a key employee. The proceeds can be used to repair or replace real estate, machinery and equipment, furniture and fixtures, inventory, and supplies. You cannot borrow to repair or replace things that are fully covered under insurance policies. Only uninsured and uncompensated disaster items are included.

There are three types of disaster loans available. The first is a business physical disaster loan (BPDL), which is a long-term, low-interest loan designed to help businesses that suffered physical losses and damages not covered by insurance. The second is an economic injury disaster loan (EIDL), which is a short or midterm working capital loan, to help meet normal operating expenses. Both of these are also available to nonprofits. The third type of disaster loan is a military reservist economic injury loan (MREIDL), which is a short or midterm working capital loan to help businesses that have lost an essential employee from being recalled for active military service.

The maximum amount you can borrow for a disaster loan is $2 million, with repayment terms of up to thirty years, determined on a case-by-case basis. Interest rates vary between 4% and 8% depending upon the type of disaster loan. Businesses can apply for multiple types of SBA disaster loans at the same time, and the proceeds can be utilized to relocate the business with prior approval from the SBA.

B.3 Programs Assisted by the SBA
SBA 8 (a) Business Development Program
The SBA no longer offers separate loan programs for minority-owned or women-owned businesses, but it does offer business assistance to firms owned or controlled at least 51% by socially and economically disadvantaged individuals. The program aims to help minority-owned businesses gain a foothold in government contracting. Participation in the program is divided into two phases over nine years: a four-year developmental stage and a five-year transition stage. Please contact the SBA directly for more information on this program.

SBIC
The SBA also helps finance Small Business Investment Companies (SBIC), which are privately-owned investment companies that lend to small businesses for start-up, modernization, or expansion. The size of a loan available from an SBIC is dependent on the size of the SBIC itself. Though privately owned, SBICs are licensed and regulated by the SBA. SBICs provide capital in the form of loans and debt securities, and they typically target more mature businesses with sufficient cash flow similar to venture capitalists. Their fee structures too are just as prohibitive. I would recommend only using them as a last resort for firms with unquenchable capital requirements. For more information on SBICs, including a directory, go to **https://www.sba.gov/sbic**.

B.4 Additional Federal Lending Programs
The Farmers Home Administration
The Department of Agriculture administers the Farmers Home Administration (FSA), which guarantees loans to purchase farms and agricultural businesses, purchase equipment, and provide working capital. FSA's programs offer opportunities to existing farmers and ranchers, beginning farmers, racial and ethnic minority farmers, and women producers. They also have programs available for urban farmers and roof-top

producers, and to those using alternative farming methods like hydroponics. In addition, the FSA administers programs for Native Americans and for emergency funding for disaster relief. Those interested in FSA programs should contact the nearest field office or inquire online at **https://www.fsa.usda.gov/programs-and-services/ farm-loan-programs/**.

The Federal Housing Authority

The Federal Housing Authority (FHA) is also indirectly involved in lending by insuring mortgages to builders and developers for constructing 5+ rental unit buildings through the HUD FHA 223 (f) program. This program is available both for market rate rental housing and for properties accepting rental assistance, either tenant based or project based. The minimum loan amount is $1 million, and there is no maximum. Those interested in learning more about this program can inquire online at **https://portal.hud. gov/hudportal/HUD?src=/program_offices/housing/mfh/progdesc/purchrefi223f**.

C. Equipment Leasing

One final alternative is not to borrow at all, but to lease. Though usually a bit more costly overall, leasing does have its advantages. Leasing can be accomplished with no or a minimal down payment. Monthly payments are typically lower too. Both can prove real lifesavers to those with minimal capital. Many long-term leases can now be capitalized and depreciated affording the same tax advantages as an outright purchase. All that's required is for the lessor to transfer ownership to the lessee at the end of the lease. As a rule, lease if you can't afford to purchase, but you can ill afford to do without.

Most banks and finance companies have leasing divisions, as do many machinery and equipment manufacturers. Their representatives are normally very informative about the advantages and disadvantages, and can advise you as to which might work best with your individual situation.

D. Chapter Summary

There are a multitude of financing sources and programs available. Try to adopt the programs that best fit your needs and repayment abilities, and don't rule out using a combination of sources to arrive at the optimum combination of funding. Your aim, of course, will be to obtain funding at the lowest cost and most favorable terms, while pledging the least possible collateral. The following table capsulizes what we discussed in the two preceding chapters, and should prove a handy reference guide.

Small Business Borrowing and Source Guide

FUNDS USAGE	FINANCING STRUCTURE	SOURCE OF FUNDS	TYPE OF FINANCING
I) Business start-up or purchase	Long term loans	Banks	Term loans- unsecured
		Savings & Loans	Real Estate secured loans
		Commercial Credit Co.	Equipment secured loans
2) Permanent working capital.		Consumer Credit Co.	Personal Property loans
		Life Insurance Co.	Policy loans
			Real Estate secured loans
3) Sustained growth		SBA	Term loan guarantees
		FSA	Term loan guarantees
		SBICs	Term loans
	Equity	Individual Investors	Partnership formations
			Stock issues/sales
		Venture Capital Firms	Stock issues/ sales
		SBICs	Bonds/ Debentures
Seasonal Requirements	Lines of Credit or Short term loans	Banks	Lines of credit-unsecured
		Savings & Loans	Accounts Receivable lines
		Commercial Credit Co.	Inventory Lines of credit
			Floor planning
			Factoring
			Sales contracts
		SBA	Line of credit-guarantees
		Suppliers	Floor planning
			Dating terms/credit terms
Equipment or facility financing	Long term loans	Banks	Real Estate loans
		Savings & Loans	Equipment loans
		Commercial Credit Co.	Equipment leases
		Life Insurance Co.	Real Estate loans
		Manufacturers	Equipment loans
			Equipment leases
		Leasing Companies	Equipment leases
		CDCs	Facility loans
		FSA	Facility loans
		SBIC	Term loans

CHAPTER 11
Choosing a Location

The next logical step for starting a new business or relocating an existing business will be the choice of location, a decision with major consequences. A good location can often spell success, even for a poorly managed business or an inexperienced owner, while a poor location could mean years of struggle and possible failure, even for the most earnest individual. While this chapter is geared primarily to the start-up concern, it will also provide valuable insight in evaluating the quality of an existing business location. Those of you that will be relying exclusively or heavily on Internet sales will also find this chapter helpful since you will need to validate proximity to suppliers and shipping alternatives, and variables like the ease of supplier's deliveries and the concerns of inventory storage, safety, and repackaging.

A. Determining the Best Geographic Region
The Local Advantage
Most of you will probably locate in an area near your home. This can prove beneficial for several reasons. First, obtaining credit will be easier when you are dealing with people who already know you and your abilities. Second, you will be much more familiar with real estate in the area, and with the community's buying habits and buying potential. Third, family and friends nearby can serve as the beginning of a customer base, provide professional contacts and offer moral support. Don't rely too heavily on this group, though. You'll find it will take much more than their support to ensure success, and even that support could wane over time. Finally, the money you save by not relocating your home can be utilized to support the success of your business venture.

The Out of Area Location
Some of you will prefer to relocate to another area. Possibly you want to pursue a rural or suburban lifestyle. Or maybe your best chance of success will be in an area closer to your suppliers or a particular customer base. You might prefer a particular geographic

region, or wish to achieve success on your own merit away from family interference. These are all viable reasons to relocate, and while relocation might prove a benefit in the long run, remember that it will place additional hardships upon you and your family initially.

Risk Reduction for the Out of Area Location

The risks of relocating can be substantially reduced by laying the initial groundwork ahead of time. Your original research will play a vital role in this decision. Since census figures are compiled by region, state, city and county, you can narrow your choice of locales mainly by evaluating these figures. As we stated earlier, emphasis should be placed on such variables as an area's population base, growth rate, consumer buying power, and economic trends.

Once you have sufficiently narrowed your choices, travel to those areas, if possible, with your family. Try to determine suitability, both personal and professional. Look at potential locations, talk to local banks, and contact local trade associations. A little investigative homework at this juncture will help to ensure the correct decision as well as relieve many of the burdens of starting a business and relocating a family.

B. Narrowing the Choice of Locales

Once a general geographic area has been decided upon, it will be time to pinpoint the ideal locale within that chosen area. Again, the narrowing process will be defined at a large extent by compatibility with your initial market research. Specific locations should also be judged in terms of the surrounding population, their buying habits and abilities, the stability of the major industries or employment sources, and the ability to support another entrant into the marketplace.

Your Clientele

Your targeted customer base will also play a major role in choosing the best locale. Are they professionals or their families' blue-collar workers, students, retirees, or a mixture thereof? Will they be purchasing your products or services during working hours, on their way to or from work, in the evening or weekends? Will they identify your product with a freestanding location, mall, urban, or light industrial setting?

Understandably, the best location will be one that is near your clientele and conducive to their purchasing patterns. Keep in mind too, areas are constantly evolving and as they do, the makeup of their populace also changes. When evaluating a location, you can anticipate how the area is evolving by studying its new construction. Pay particular attention to the types of businesses or residents moving into an area, as well as those moving out and those being displaced.

Examining Existing Competition

The next determination will be whether or not to locate near your existing competition. If this concept sounds absurd, think about that cluster of fast-food restaurants nearby. They purposefully locate next to each other for a reason. Their research indicates that although their clientele allocates a percentage of its dollar to fast foods, the choice of which fast food often isn't made until driving past that cluster. In a sense, their clustering serves as a form of advertising, and for them locating near the competition actually improves sales volume. The same rationale applies to clustering car dealerships.

Many businesses do best when located near the right type of competition. Retail stores that sell general merchandise fare better when located in a shopping center or shopping district rather than in a standalone location. A specialty grocer can improve sales by locating near an outlet for a grocery chain, while a convenience store would be doomed by choosing that same location. As a general rule, locating near your competition will be desirable if it proves more conducive to attracting customers, but gives neither competitor a decided competitive advantage.

There are also location concerns unique to each industry. The consideration of these concerns mandates subdividing the remainder of this chapter into discussions of each general category. Though adapting the location will vary greatly for the retailer, servicer, and professional, all three will choose their location using similar considerations and requirements. Therefore, we will discuss these three industry types as one. Wholesalers and manufacturers will be discussed separately. For those servicers whose business includes a manufacturing component, you may wish to incorporate any applicable elements of the light manufacturing discussion. Likewise, the wholesaler with a retailing component may wish to incorporate the retailer discussion.

C. The Retailer, Servicer, or Professional
C.1 The Urban Location

Major department stores, which have always been the main attraction for downtown shopping districts, have been exiting to the suburbs for decades. As a result, many urban shopping areas have been in a state of decline. Those hit hardest are the smaller and midsized cities whose past success had been based more on the ability to attract the surrounding populace than office workers and urban residents. As such, those considering an inner-city location should think over the decision through carefully, and your customer base and its availability should weigh heavily in your final decision.

There is a growing trend toward redevelopment in many larger urban areas, and a focus to attract residents and smaller businesses back from the suburbs. Certain inner city locations could prove ideal for the specialty shop, restaurant, servicer, or professional, geared to attracting the office worker and urban resident, or businesses that require the patronage of the resident companies themselves. If you are considering an urban location, you should analyse the makeup of its daily populace (evenings and weekends as well), its evolutionary pattern, and the compatibility of your business to both. Also, study the parking availability, traffic patterns, and mass transit systems.

Government Incentives

In some instances there will be added incentives to locating in a city with a designated redevelopment program. Many cities are offering federal, state, and local incentives. These include lower rents or building costs, low-interest loans, and lower tax bases. A surprising number of urban areas have also remodelled or replaced older buildings, providing attractive and unique business settings. For additional information on redevelopment programs, contact your state's commerce department or your local city government.

C.2 The Urban District Location

Every large city is bordered by smaller districts, most often centered around a factory, a college, a hospital or a combination thereof. Each district will have its own neighbourhoods and business district. Quite often these are a microcosm of the larger city, though the shopping areas are usually categorized by smaller, less sophisticated merchants. In many cases, a district will be made up of one predominant ethnic group or social class, and the merchants will cater to that particular market segment.

The district location could prove to be the most dangerous of setting for the new business. They are often economically depressed, particularly those centered around industrial plants. Frequently they will be characterized by higher unemployment, increasing crime rates, and a general population decay. Even those districts with a seemingly stable economy quite often are stagnating because of an older populous or declining population. Those considering this type of location should again look to trends such as new construction or redevelopment, stability and growth in the employer base, and an influx of younger residents.

C.3 Towns and Rural Locations

The reader who is considering a small town or rural location must also weigh the consequences. Many towns, which for our purposes will include cities of up to one hundred thousand residents, have much in common with the urban district. They too must draw customers primarily from the surrounding populace, and many are economically dependent upon one or a few major employers. Depending upon the stability of the employment base, the small city may also suffer from the same higher unemployment, increasing crime rates, and decaying economic affluence as the larger urban areas. You'll find this situation too lends to a loss of the younger population.

For those who live in a small town or rural paradise where none of these problems exist, beware of the shopping center or mall, and big-box retailers. Many seemingly affluent small towns are suffering from the same shopping district decay. The same relocated department stores and retailers that are keeping suburbanites out of the city are oftentimes also keeping the ruralites out of the small town.

C.4 Malls and Shopping Centers

Possibly the most common location today, particularly for the new retailer or servicer, is the mall or shopping center. These come in a variety of shapes and sizes, and most share a common operating structure. Oftentimes, they'll charge a base rent plus a percentage of gross sales for which they will provide maintenance and a limited amount of advertising. Though most merchants prefer this type of location, even here there can be drawbacks that should be noted.

When considering any type of shopping center, study the makeup of its major tenants. Are they department stores, discount merchandisers, or grocery stores? You can pretty much guess which type of retailer and servicer will cluster around each of these categories of major tenants. The predominant tenants will dictate customer types, traffic patterns, and shopping hours. How will this affect your business? There is also the added impact of Internet shoppers, and their effect on those major tenants. Many suburban malls and shopping centers are experiencing the same difficulties as those that plague urban business districts.

If the location is an older shopping center, is it still accessible and viable to major traffic arteries? Is there adequate parking? Is the exterior dated or has it been recently renovated? What is the occupancy? Is it thriving or are there vacancies? Are there new, larger centers that might prove more attractive to your customer base? Are there restrictions for the type of business or the number of each type permitted as tenants? If so, will this help or hinder attracting your targeted audience? All of these questions should be answered before you make your final decision.

An excellent source for many of these answers will be the existing tenants. Don't be afraid to ask. Experience has shown they are willing and frequently anxious to share information as to their satisfaction or dissatisfaction, both about the location and the landlord. As a general rule, a business with a higher priced product, a rapid inventory turnover, or the need for extensive window displays, will best be suited to the more glamorous and expensive malls and shopping centers. A merchant with a lower markup, a slower moving inventory, or the need for a large amount of floor space, will be better suited to a less expensive mall or shopping center.

C.5 Freestanding Locations

Freestanding locations are best suited to large volume "solo" type businesses that can pretty much make it on their own. Discount stores, furniture stores, and grocery stores are all good examples. Freestanding locations are generally less expensive, but don't forget our earlier conversation about inaccessible locations requiring more advertising. Also consider traffic patterns, not only heavy traffic, but willing traffic. Don't find yourself next to a freeway full of unconcerned commuters. Though you may not want to locate within a mall or shopping center, don't necessarily consider them the opposition. What better way to realize the benefits of clustering than by locating next to a shopping center or mall?

C.6 The Cottage Industry

Many professionals, servicers, Internet based and some types of wholesalers and retailers prefer to work from their homes. When considering this alternative, conduct the same patterns of analysis utilized for other locations. Your product or service must indeed be conducive to an in-home location if you are to be successful. For those whose customers and clients must come to you, will it be? Will there be ample storage and display areas? How about parking availability and zoning restrictions?

For those who must visit or call upon your clientele, will most be within driving distance? Will visitation require extensive travel that could be avoided by a more centralized location? Though working from home can prove both convenience and a real money saver, make sure it's not at the expense of your business's success.

D. Locating the Wholesaler

The small wholesaler shares many of the same concerns as the retailer, and often derives income both from wholesaling and retailing. Those wholesalers involved in retailing must define what percentage of their total revenue will be derived from retailing and choose a location that is compatible to the entire operation. Even for those whose general operation will be geared primarily to wholesaling, the best chance for success will be in an area where the economic climate is conducive to the retail consumer. Excluding other variables, a plumbing supplier servicing contractors in the Tampa Bay, Florida area, for example, will have a much better chance for success than one located in the Youngstown, Ohio area.

The Wholesale District

In many larger urban areas, a complete wholesale district exists. Generally these will be occupied by older, established businesses, and most often locating nearby will prove a mistake. Usually these locations will be highly competitive and expensive, and many of the buildings will be dated and highly inefficient. Many will suffer from poor lighting, inadequate ventilation, insufficient insulation, outdated heating systems, and offer little or no room for expansion. Parking and transportation requirements could also be problematic since most of these districts were established during prior transportation eras.

The Suburban Industrial Complex

Most wholesalers will find it best to join their clientele and the retailer by locating in the suburbs. Choosing a freestanding or light industrial complex in a suburban location will most likely be more cost-effective and provide a more pleasant work environment. Transportation and parking will be better, and buildings will be newer and more energy efficient. Accessibility will also be easier both for commercial and retail clientele.

Specialty Considerations

There are a few occasions when a wholesaler would be best suited to locate near his or her suppliers. This occurs when the wholesaler needs to visit the suppliers frequently, or vice versa. Those wholesalers with a delivery component may want to look for a location near the center of their trading area. Local and city ordinances will also be a factor. Are there building, transportation, or environmental restrictions that could hinder your growth? Are there any government incentives available to reduce the cost of entry?

E. Locating the Small Manufacturer

Though the manufacturing industry's era of dominance is coming to a close, our transition to the information age hasn't brought an end to manufacturing, only its dominance. Though relatively immobile in comparison to other industry types, manufacturing has also entered a migratory period. For large manufacturers, the trend is overseas. For smaller manufacturers, the trend is to the Sunbelt. There are a host of underlying reasons for this geographic shift. Manufacturing is sensitive to shifts in economic, technological, and environmental conditions. The present migration is a direct result of this sensitivity fuelled by factors such as cheaper labor, lower building costs, lower taxes, and less state government restrictions. The small manufacturer would do well to examine each of these issues before choosing a location. Additional considerations should include nearness to customers and suppliers, operating costs such as utilities and insurance, availability of waste disposal, resident attitudes, building and operating restrictions, future expansion requirements, and transportation needs.

Government Incentives

Many states and local governments are offering a host of incentives to prospective manufacturers, both those who locate or relocate to the Sunbelt, and those who locate within an older industrial area. These incentives include tax-reduction programs and low interest loans. Many of the owners of these facilities will offer further incentives to fill underutilized buildings or liquidate used equipment. Those of you wishing to explore these incentive programs should contact the respective state commerce department as well as the local government entity.

When evaluating these incentives, particularly for an older industrial area, be sure to consider the long-term consequences for your business. Once again the effects of deteriorating roads and transportation systems, eroding economic conditions, and a declining population base must be taken into account. Any and all of these factors could result in higher incidents of vandalism, increased insurance and utility costs, increased building maintenance costs, and the inability to attract qualified employees. Additionally, any industrial area in a state of decline is an area badly in need of additional tax revenues. Those incentives that now appear so attractive could disappear before they are ever realized.

F. To Buy or Lease

Most existing businesses are sold excluding real estate, either by choice or because the current owner also leases. Only a few of you will have the opportunity to purchase your location, and fewer still will have the financial resources available to do so. While there are certain tax advantages to depreciating a building, buying real property can substantially increase your initial investment costs as well as the potential for loss. Additionally, the money that would be utilized for the down payment could oftentimes be used more effectively for working capital. For those with limited resources, it would be best to lease your initial location. If, however, a lease purchase option is available, jump on it.

There will be a select few with the opportunity and the financial resources to purchase your location from the outset. For those buying an existing business with a successful track record and those starting a new business, if the site is easily leasable and convertible, most of the initial risks of purchase will be minimized. There are however several additional factors to consider before making the final decision.

F.1 Evaluating the Purchase
A Building Appraisal

First and foremost, make sure there is an accurate and independent appraisal to verify the property's worth. If there are additional tenants for whom you will be the landlord, review their leases in terms of expiration dates, renewal clauses, payment history, lease costs and escalators, and their length of time in the building. Are the leases triple net, meaning our property taxes and maintenance costs passed through to the tenant? Make sure you are aware of any cash needs that may be required to keep the building in top operating condition. This information will be included in a good appraisal, and confirmed by your own physical inspection.

Keep in mind too that in a situation where there are good tenants, the income generated by their leases can be used to help qualify for a mortgage as well as increase your borrowing capacity. I know countless business owners whose business premises is housed in a small strip center that they own. In most cases, the rent they receive from other tenants pays for the mortgage, and their business is basically rent free.

Terms of Sale

Next consider the terms of sale. Most commercial real-estate mortgages today are amortized over fifteen, twenty or twenty-five year periods, but many are due and payable in five to ten years. This is done to keep the monthly payment lower and to minimize the length of time the creditor is at risk. In this situation, you will be at best barely covering interest costs. At the mortgages maturity, you could owe as much or more as you initially borrowed.

There are as nearly as many mortgage products available today as there are lending institutions, so shop around, including Internet searches, in addition to soliciting your now trusted banker. Most good lenders are offering fifteen-year, fully amortized mortgages for commercial clients. In most cases, the monthly payment will not be much higher than the balloon payment alternative, and your overall interest expense will be cut in half.

As for interest rates, expect to pay between 1% and 3% above the institution's base real-estate rate on a floating basis. If you can find an attractive fixed rate, again, jump on it. Most institutions also charge loan fees. Expect to pay up to two points, but beware, many private lenders charge as many as five or more points. Avoid their services at all costs!

A Real Estate Agent or Broker

Many commercial real-estate sales can be negotiated between the buyer and seller, and transacted by both parties' attorneys. In a situation where a real-estate agent or broker is involved and he or she is the listing agent, I would strongly recommend that you find independent representation for yourself. The listing agent may try to convince you that they can represent both parties equally. Possibly they can, but their real motivation is to retain the entire commission for themselves. Again, the seller will be paying the real-estate commission; better to have your own representation, especially when the seller is footing the bill.

Structuring the Purchase

Each of you will have differing personal and tax situations that will impact how you title the property you are about to purchase. Your attorney will be the best source of guidance in this situation. In all likelihood, he or she will suggest you purchase the property either individually or under another self-owned business entity, and then lease it or the portion your business will occupy back to that business.

F.2 Evaluating the Lease

For those of you entering into a lease agreement, evaluate the terms of that lease just as we did during our initial lease evaluation. The first consideration will be the length of the lease. Five to ten years with renewal options would be ideal. Be leery of leases for less than three years, especially if there is no renewal provision. This could open the door for the owner to escalate renewal costs or refuse renewal altogether. Having to relocate a business is at least as difficult as changing residences, and there's the additional concern of the effect on the business itself.

The next area of consideration is the payment terms. Is it a flat rate, or does it include a percent of sales escalator? Is there a cost-of-living adjustment clause or scheduled annual increases? Again, is the lease triple net? Will you be responsible for the taxes, utilities, maintenance, and property insurance? Is the landlord providing any marketing or advertising support? Are there signage restrictions? Who pays for the initial leasehold improvements, and are future improvements allowable? Is subleasing permitted? This can be an important consideration if you eventually sell the business or a helpful escape clause if the business were to falter.

Lease terms and conditions will differ somewhat in every situation, and it will be your responsibility to understand the terms and conditions thoroughly. If you have questions, seek professional guidance. In most cases, your attorney, banker, and accountant are going to want to review the terms regardless. Also for those of you with borrowing requirements, most banks and lenders won't structure a loan term beyond the expiration date of the lease, so this too needs to be factored into your lease negotiations. For those in situations where the lease is being negotiated by a real-estate agent or broker, the same rules apply as were just discussed in the purchase section. It would be advisable to use independent representation.

G. Chapter Summary

Regardless of which type of location you're considering, talk to business associates, suppliers, and neighboring business owners. If an existing location, try to develop a history to determine how past tenants have fared. Don't find yourself as one of a string of unsuccessful businesses tied to a building with a stigma as a poor location. Also be sure to review local ordinances that might directly or indirectly affect your business.

I hope that I haven't painted too bleak a picture by playing devil's advocate during much of our discussion on choosing a location. There are, of course, ideal locations within each of the setting we've discussed for the right business. It will be up to you to weigh the advantages and disadvantages of each scenario, and then decide which location is best suited to your needs. Finding the right location is only the first half of the battle, the second half will be adapting it.

CHAPTER 12
Adapting the Facility

This chapter will be devoted to adapting the location. While obviously of the utmost importance to the start-up concern, this discussion should prove equally insightful to those of you purchasing an existing business. The layout and design of a facility are always critical to the success and efficiency of any business. However, those of you purchasing an existing business should take the time to study the effectiveness of the current floor plan before enacting wholesale changes.

A. Sources for Assistance

For those with hidden artistic talents, this area will be a welcome challenge. If you are like me, however, you may feel that you have no flair for designing building fronts or interiors. For us there are two alternatives: design firms for those who can afford assistance, and any number of free information sources for those who'd rather spend their money elsewhere. For those seeking professional assistance, local interior design firms will prove the best alternative. If you are midsized wholesaler or manufacturer, you may wish to utilize an architect or engineering firm. Again, talk to your professional associates for recommendation, and be sure to follow up with references from prospective firms.

There are a number of informational sources available for those seeking free advice, as well as several free and low-cost interior design software programs, which some of you may find helpful. Information on lighting, heating, and cooling can be obtained from utility company representatives. They can provide both cost-effectiveness analyses and suggestions for designing optimal lighting configurations and heating and cooling systems. Interior design assistance such as color coordination can be obtained from paint supply store representatives and painting contactors. Effective and emotionally appealing office configurations can be assisted by most office furniture suppliers. Equipment and fixture suppliers can provide assistance as to optimal installation configurations. Additionally, there are a number of books on the subject that can spark ideas, so too can creative spouses, family members, and friends.

The design process should be geared to creating a location, which, though possibly intangible, will become one of your most valued business assets. Treat it as a form of self-expression, let your inhibitions go and have fun with it.

The Written Design

One final suggestion before we subdivide our discussion into the general categories of retailing, wholesaling, and manufacturing. The physical layout, though certainly not as detailed as your operating plan, should be relegated to computer modeling or paper drawings. It's much easier, less expensive, and certainly less time consuming to erase or cut and paste a portion of a sketch than to move counter locations or reconfigure equipment and machinery after the fact.

B. The Retail Shop

The Exterior Appeal

It goes without saying that the attractiveness of a location's exterior and its ability to entice the customer to come inside will have a major impact on the initial success of any retailer. This is equally true for most servicers and professionals. We've already discussed accessibility, but getting the customer in the door will take more than just an optimal location. The company's name and any exterior advertising must be displayed in an appealing and eye-catching manner. Window displays too are an integral design element, and must also be appealing and eye-catching. The impression they leave will translate into a perception of the store's itself. Just as the exterior of your home is a reflection on you, so is your storefront a reflection of your business.

Creating Interior Atmosphere

The eye-appeal of a store's interior is equally important. You'll want the feelings presented in your window displays to extend to the sales floor, so that when the customer opens the door, he or she will experience a sense of continuity. This leads us directly to the consideration of atmosphere, specifically determining the most appealing interior design, to attract and motivate your targeted audience. Certainly merchandise displays will be the most critical element, but there are a number of underlying variables that must also be taken into consideration.

Interior Lighting

One frequently overlooked consideration is lighting. Yet this will have a dynamic as well as subliminal impact on your business's atmosphere. Is there natural lighting, and if so, how will it change during the day? What type of artificial lighting is there? Is it uniform or are there sharp contrasts? What type or types of lighting combined with natural lighting if applicable will be most appealing to your customers?

Color Coordination

Color coordination will play an equally important role. Pastels can help intensify lighting, while wallpaper can add warmth. Physical dimensions can also be maximized or minimized by well-thought-out color schemes to help impact lighting configurations. A white or mirrored wall will have a deepening or enlarging effect on a small narrow space, while darker colors will make an overly large room appear more intimate. Each of you will have differing needs based on your type of business and location's configuration, but the deductive reasoning process will be the same for all.

Counter Displays

Before designing the counter layout, or for restaurants the seating arrangement, we must consider a few interrelated variables. How many entrances are there? Are you gearing to self-service or sales assistance? What percentage of your business will be by phone or Internet? Is there a drive-through feature? Which of these will require separate sales personnel? Would it be better to locate telephones or computers near or away from cash registers and POS systems? Will pilferage be a problem and, if so, how can sales stations or computer displays be organized to minimize theft? Will any merchandise need to be displayed under lock and key or refrigerated? For a restaurant, what seating arrangement will provide the highest seating capacity while still preserving comfort atmosphere and ambience? Finally, and most importantly, what configuration will maximize sales?

The answer to this last question will differ depending on the type of retailer. A clothing store, for example, will want to draw customers through various parts of the store, but this same type of networking would prove costly and counterproductive for a retail butcher. The butcher's sales would be maximized by limiting customer's movement and segregating the customers from the employees by means of the counter display cases themselves.

While fixture and equipment salespeople can be helpful in determining needs and layouts, they work on a commission basis and may have a tendency to oversell. Store fixtures and equipment also have a very limited resale value. You can easily save 50% of the cost of new fixtures by buying used ones. Most areas have fixtures and equipment outlets that are used ones. Many manufacturers sell refurbished products. Check local newspapers and craigslist for those quitting business sales and those disposing of used furnishings.

B.1 Anticipating Customer Traffic Patterns

A retailer's most valuable floor space will be immediately inside and to either side of the main entrance, because these areas will receive the most customer traffic. Floor space will decrease in value as you move toward the back of the store due to a corresponding decrease in customer traffic. Anticipate traffic flows and design displays to maximize merchandise accessibility to those flows. A customer-service area, for example, would be best suited for the back of the store, where traffic patterns are lower rather than in a highly accessible area.

To some extent, you can also try to direct customers' traffic patterns to maximize sales potential. Large ticket retails, for example, normally place high-priced electronics or appliance displays toward the back of a store. They know customers looking for those items will seek them out. Forcing those customers to walk past display areas with more general sales items quite often leads to additional purchases of ancillary products.

Again, the retailer's interior design must incorporate many elements, and the optimal design will differ for each of you. Try to utilize as many input sources as are available, including suppliers, competitors, and research aids during the initial design process. Don't be afraid to experiment after you've opened the doors as well. Put a slower moving item next to a bestseller and see what happens. Just be sure not to get too carried away. Over manipulation discourage the best of shoppers.

Grocery stores are notorious for this. They purposely reconfigure isles on a regular basis to confuse shoppers in hopes that the customer will buy more impulse items. This forces the customer to walk more isles in search of the items they came for. While this tactic might work for a grocer who we are somewhat dependent on, it would prove disastrous for a retailer of discretionary merchandise.

C. The Servicer

Designing the exterior of a service location will necessitate most of the same basic considerations already mentioned. The interior design, however, will vary dramatically depending upon the type of services being rendered and could include a number of dissimilar functions. A dry-cleaner, for example, would find it best to simulate a manufacturer when designing the processing area, while simulating a retailer in the customer pickup and drop area.

Imitating the Retailer

In this example, the customer contact area would be arranged like a small retail shop with a counter register and clerk. In most cases, the counter would separate the clerk and possibly the processing area from the customer. A portion of the counter or customer contact area might also include display stands to sell ancillary items like ties, clothing lint removers, and so on. A drive-through or delivery service would provide additional routing concerns. Again, optimal efficiency and customer satisfaction will be the ultimate goals in the design process.

Imitating the Manufacturer
The processing portion of the dry-cleaning facility would require a completely different design perspective. Where to situate equipment and employee workstations would best be determined by using a workflow chart similar to a manufacturer. If a conveyer system is used, there may even be a little warehousing involved in the design process. In the crossover situations, it would be best to design each element independently, and then combine them into one functioning and interdependent operational design.

The Restaurant
Similar problems will arise when designing the interior of a restaurant. Again, the dining area must be arranged to ensure optimal seating capacity, comfort, and possibly view considerations. The ease of movement for servers must also be considered. There's also the need to place workstations in optimal locations. The kitchen will have its own equipment, counter space, workflow, and safety requirements. A takeout or pickup area, drive-through, or delivery service may also need to be factored in. Here too, a workflow chart is suggested to optimize the design process. As with the dry-cleaner, it would be best to separate and plan each function independently, then overlap the plans into one functional design.

The Professional
Those of you in the legal, medical, or accounting professions are probably wondering what the two previous examples have to do with the service industry. The dry-cleaner and restaurant owner are of course a part of the servicing industry, yet they are as far removed from the aforementioned professions as they are from each other. Or are they?

I've seen numerous medical practices set up to resemble a factory. You probably have too. There's a reception and waiting area where you may spend an hour or two before being ushered to a weigh station to measure your weight and temperature. Then you're conveyed to one of five examination rooms for an equally long wait before a practical nurse comes in to update your chart and take your blood pressure. Then you're conveyed again to a technician for x-rays, or another nurse for a blood test and urinalysis. Then you're taken back to the examining room where the doctor stops for a brief visit and to suggest that you come back in two weeks to review the test results. All this for a cold.

I won't bother to note the specific procedural steps, but you can see how this fictionalized example quite accurately resembles an assembly line. As for optimal operating efficiency, this dramatization makes good sense, in part, and those in the medical profession would do well to follow a similar pattern. As with the small manufacturer, there are equipment and placement needs to be determined as well as optimal configurations for workstations and examination rooms. Then there is the check-in and waiting area that must present a relaxing and comfortable atmosphere for patients. All of these functions lend themselves well to a workflow chart.

Accountants and lawyers face similar design elements. Configuring the reception area, clerical stations, offices, employee lounge, and conference room optimally requires the consideration of factors such as lighting, privacy, comfort, employee interaction and oversight. Again, each situation is unique, and there can be elements of the design process that are best optimized by emulating the manufacturing process.

D. The Cottage or Home-based Business

Many of you in the service industry will be engaged in home or cottage-type endeavors. You too should define your work flow and arrange your office or organization to maximize output. For some this might be a simple as organizing an office. For those with direct customer involvement, you will need to consider parking, the best means for entering your home, a reception area, possibly even a conference area. Separation from other home and family functions will also be an important consideration.

If retailing is a function, you will doubtless need a display area and storage area. Space considerations must also factor in the potential for pilferage and protecting any inventory from outside elements. Though working from home can prove advantages for many, it can also be a counterproductive trap with continual distractions. Self-discipline becomes a critical component. A design that isolates your work area and enables you to function within a separated business environment is optimal.

E. The Wholesale Enterprise

Designing the Exterior

The exterior design for the wholesaler will be less of a consideration than for a retailer or servicer. It should, however, be designed to be as appealing as possible. This is especially true for those with a combination of retail and wholesale customers. As with the home example, the exterior is an extension of you, and your business. Signage should be designed with an advertising slant as well as to serve as a reference point for those visiting for the first time. The appearance of the building and grounds needs to convey a well carried for environment so as to serve as a positive reflection on the business itself.

Designing the Interior

Unlike the retailer the interior design for the wholesaler will be geared less to the customer and more to workflow. The first order of business will be shipping and receiving. The size of the business will dictate whether these functions should be separated or combined. The same holds true for unpacking and repacking. These functions could be small enough to combine with shipping and receiving, or they could warrant segregating into separate functions. The number of employees involved in each function and the amount of floor space required will be the determining factors. These functions will most likely be located nearest to the shipping and receiving docks, and bordered on the other side by inventory.

Inventory Requirements

The majority of a wholesaler's floor space will be utilized for warehousing inventory. Here, optimal flow will be the main consideration. Faster moving items should be in convenient locations enabling easy access. Slower moving inventory, though out of the way, should not be forgotten. It's better to sell these items at a reduced price than to let them accumulate on valuable floor space, slowing your cash-flow turn in the process.

Depending on the products, forklifts and pallets may also need to be taken into consideration. So too might gravity chutes or conveyor systems. The most effective design will be one that allows for the fewest number of employees, yet affords the quickest, safest, and most comfortable working environment.

Retail and Office Functions

Those with retail display areas should separate this function from the rest of the operation. It should be designed to present the look and feel of a retail store. The office function too should be separated. Providing a professional environment for administrative personnel will result in happier and more productive administrative employees. Again, you may find it best to start with up to three separate design elements, one for each major function, and then incorporate the elements into one interdependent design.

F. The Manufacturer

The manufacturing location will be the most difficult to design, and it will be subject to more local, state, and federal regulations than all of the other industry categories combined. The design must also be functional from an operational standpoint. There will be shipping and receiving considerations, both raw materials and finished goods. There will be added parking concerns because more employees will be required to fulfill the manufacturing process. There could also be an outdoor area for raw materials that could bring its own set of storage and environmental issues. This could be amplified if waste storage and removal is a consideration.

Designing the Exterior

Like the wholesaler the exterior design will be less of a consideration than for a retailer or servicer. It too, however, should be designed to be as appealing as possible. Create an environment you and your employees can take pride in. Signage should be designed both to advertise as well as to serve as a reference point. The appearance of the building and grounds should convey a well carried for facility that serves as a safe and environmentally conscious setting. Employee and visitor parking should be safe and secure, and allow for easy access into the facility. Entry is also a concern for incoming and outgoing truck traffic, possibly even for rail or barge traffic. Any outdoor storage or waste containment areas need to be out of site if at all possible.

Designing the Interior

There will be a variety of interrelated functions inside the plant, many of which will be unique to each type of manufacturer. There will be safety, environmental, and employee working condition issues to consider. There will be electrical and plumbing requirements. There will be lighting, ventilation, and pollution-control issues. Any and all of these variables will have to be taken into consideration in conjunction with equipment placement and defining the optimal workflow pattern.

Inventory Requirements

Individual department needs like shipping and receiving will have to be optimized. So too will the storage environment for raw materials and finished goods, and their transfer to and from the manufacturing process. Again, each of your needs will differ. Study your own organization and location, design each function independently, and then combine them into one integrated plan.

The Job Shop

Many small manufacturers are of the "job shop" variety. Rather than manufacture one or more standard products, they manufacture variations of a products according to each customer's contract specifications. As a result, actual work flow patterns will differ by contract. In this environment, flexibility is a key consideration in determining equipment placement. The design needs to allow for workflow and product-specification changes, without having to constantly reconfigure the equipment. A rectangular or horseshoe pattern is generally optimal, allowing for easy transfer from machine to machine as identified by each individual contract.

The Production Line

For those engaged in the manufacture of one or a few standardized products, it would be better to layout the equipment in a straight-line pattern resembling an assembly line. The workflow is designed to begin the process at one end, and conclude with a finished product at the other end. Keep in mind, while this design will optimize output, it will severely limit flexibility should product design changes occur.

The Office Design

The manufacturer will typically have a fairly complex administrative structure that could include sales and marketing, accounting, human resources, and senior administrators. Each function needs to be departmentalized in a way that promotes productive workflows within and between departments, and allows for easy communication with personnel in the plant. A separate administrative area will work best where a more typical office environment can be created and more easily controlled.

Larger manufacturers may even wish to separate and segregate this function, locating production managers at the plant, and the remaining administrative staff at an offsite location closer to the customer base. The most effective means of interacting with your customer base and your employees will be the determining factor for such an arrangement.

G. Chapter Summary

Regardless of the industry, the effectiveness of the final design will be a critical element in the success of your business. For the retailer and servicer, the design will provide the first and possibly most lasting impression to the customer. For the wholesaler and manufacturer, the effectiveness of the design will prove a major determination in the overall efficiency and cost-effectiveness of the operation. Either could spell the difference between a profit or loss situation.

PART V

ESTABLISHING MAINTENANCE AND OPERATING CONTROLS

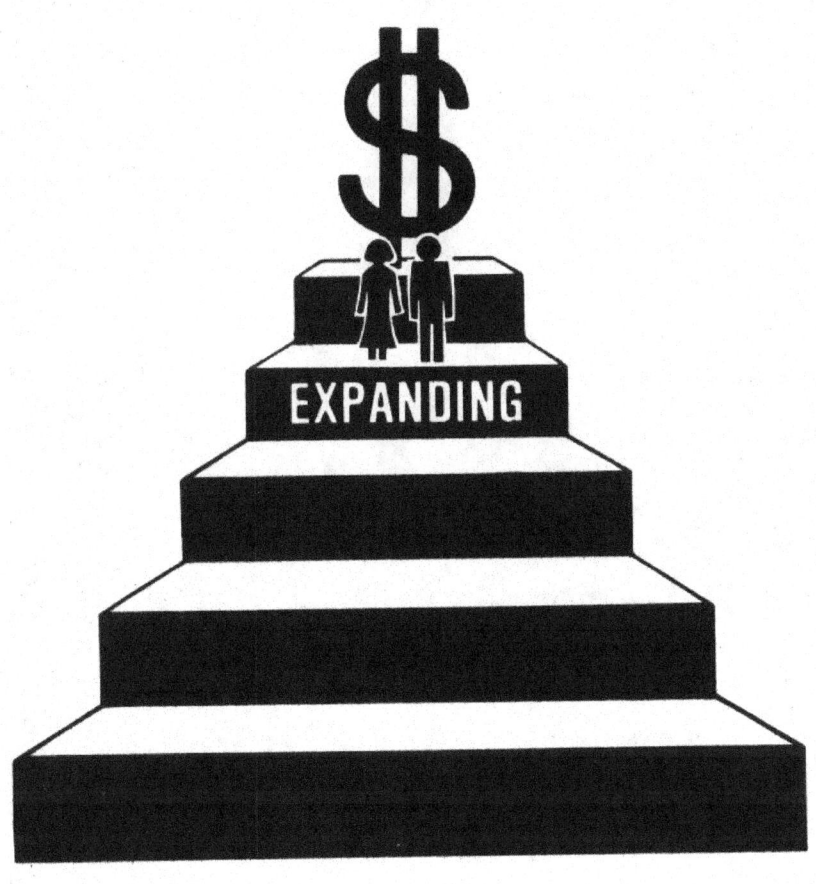

CHAPTER 13
The Organization

A. The Improper Planner, an Analogy

We have all experienced the nervousness of meeting a deadline. Owning your own business can rapidly become a never-ending series of nerve-racking deadlines. You'll have sales to generate, suppliers to deal with, inventory to turn, receivables to collect, customers to keep happy, employees to supervise and keep happy, a husband or wife who rarely sees you, kids who are misbehaving to reattract your attention, and in-laws who are boisterous distractions. You can all too quickly, often without realizing it, create an environment that is even more hectic and dreadful than the one from that you came.

This situation isn't as hypothetical as you might think. The number-one gripe voiced to me by customers and clients alike is, "There just aren't enough hours in the day to get all of my work done, let alone have time to spend with my family." Business owners regularly malign the average employee's nine to five work day, while complaining about putting in upwards of fourteen hours themselves. Yet, more often than not, this workaholic syndrome is created by the business owner him or herself, and it is most often a direct result of improper planning.

The emotional stress of playing catch-up or reacting to effects rather than causing reactions is a situation we have previously discussed. There is an alternative procedural planning. Though we have created operating projections to define and gauge a business's performance, we have yet to consider procedural steps to set that plan in motion. Just as projections guide the operating performance, organizational polices and operating procedures guide the employees to the fulfillment of those projections.

B. Fulfilling Staffing Requirements

During our projection modeling and facilities adaptation discussions, we defined staffing needs. Now let's define specific employee duties and job functions. Then we'll move on and examine the hiring process, employee orientation, and training. We will conclude this chapter by discussing wage and incentive packages and the formation of personnel policies.

B.1 Establishing an Organizational Chart

We will begin by defining the organizational structure. Whether you're beginning with just a few employees or a departmentalized staff, the organizational chart is an important procedural foundation. Those of you purchasing existing businesses may or may not be entering a situation where these organizational needs have been defined. If they have, take some time to study their effectiveness before enacting wholesale changes. If they have not, take some time to study the existing operation to help you in formalizing your own organizational chart. Those of you in the start-up phase have the luxury of starting business with an organizational chart already in hand. Two examples of an organizational chart are listed on the next page.

The Chain of Command

The main purpose of the organizational chart is to identify and simplify the chain of command. Like links in a chain, the strength of your entire organization will hinge on the interaction of the sum of its parts. The optimal organization will be one with a minimum of cross supervision, while still assuring a uniform chain of command from top to bottom and back.

Those of you with larger organizations may wish to subdivide your charts into two functional areas, line and staff. This simply identifies which functions are directly related to making or distributing a product (line functions), and those who are in support of that production (staff functions). This can be beneficial when defining specific departmental duties or the means by which to evaluate a department's performance.

Upon completion, the organizational chart should direct your thoughts to staffing. The next procedural step should be to formulize job descriptions for all employees, including you. This is a critical function for any size business as a job description will define your expectation for a position, help the employee to better understand and perform the duties of that position, and it will aid in evaluating an employee's performance review.

B.2 The Job Description

A job description is simply a one or two-page list detailing responsibilities for a particular position. It should also list specific educational or experience prerequisites, and any supervisory responsibilities. If the position requires certain physical skills, computer skills, or knowledge of machinery, these too should be identified. A sample job description is provided on the following page for your convenience.

Some of you may wish to include instructions for work hours, vacation policies, pay scales, and promotional opportunities directly on the job description. For those of you with larger staffs, it would be best to define these areas in a separate personnel manual or handbook. Hopefully, those of you in this position will have at least one human-resources employee to whom you can delegate this responsibility.

ORGANIZATIONAL CHART
Retailer

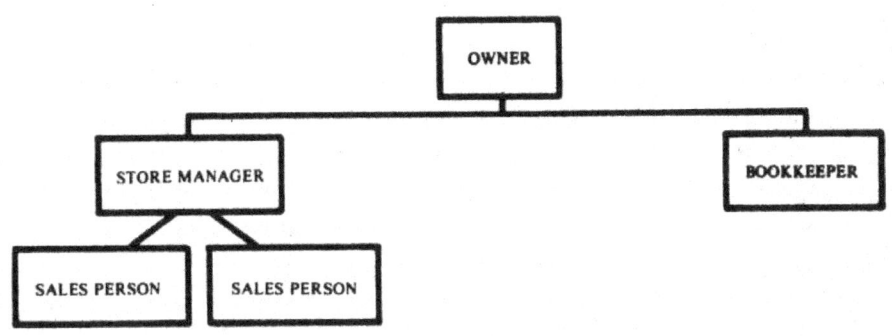

ORGANIZATIONAL CHART
Small Manufacturer

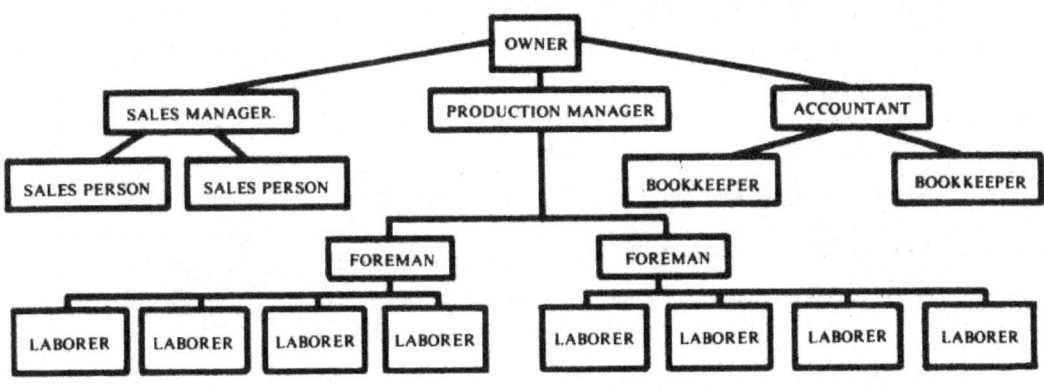

B.3 Initial Staffing Considerations
Reviewing Existing Employee Qualifications

Those purchasing an existing business should study the educational backgrounds or skill levels of all current employees. If possible, discuss employment histories with the previous owner. It would be nice if personnel files existed to help document past performance but, in most cases, this will only happen when there is an existing human-resources person or staff. Next, assess the current staff against the job description requirements. Then add, adjust, replace, or cut back on staff as needed, taking into consideration how any changes might affect the employee morale.

JOB DESCRIPTION

(Sample)

Date: _____

Position: Secretary   Salary Range:_____

Job Function: To perform general secretarial duties including typing reports and routine correspondence, mail distribution, answering the telephone and scheduling appointments. To report directly to the Sales Manager though duties may also be performed for Sales people.

Responsibilities: To transcribe and distribute memos, letters, and reports.

To attend departmental meeting, take minutes, and transcribe into final form. Set up and maintain customer files.

Answer the telephone and schedule the Sales Departments appointments. Greet visitors, and inform the necessary personnel.

Sort and distribute the incoming mail.

Sort and arrange the outgoing mail.

Arrange travel and promotional reservations.

Maintain Sales Departmental personnel's time sheets.

Compile routine Sales reports.

Maintain general office supply levels.

Perform general office duties as deemed appropriate by the Sales Manager.

Requirements: High School graduate, typing skill of at least 60 error free words a minute. Must maintain a cordial attitude towards customers and fellow employees. A general knowledge of office functions.

Office Machinery: Must be proficient with Microsoft Office, a typewriter, calculator, fax machine and photo copier.

Promoting from Within

Whether starting up or purchasing an existing business, I would strongly recommend that you establish a policy to consider existing employees first when promotional opportunities arise. Establishing a policy of promoting from within, whenever possible, will help maintain employee morale and improve overall job performance.

B.4 Fulfilling Employment Needs

Employee Advertisement

Once you've outlined positions and responsibilities, you may need to find employees who meet those qualifications. There are a variety of ways at your disposal to accomplish this task. The most obvious is to advertise in newspapers, periodicals, and trade journals. Ads should be kept short and to the point. Specify the position available, its primary responsibilities, and the skills and educational requirements needed. You may also wish to list the salary range and any benefit packages associated with the position. All of the sources will have an online posting option to their websites. Today, this is a much more effective tool for employment searches. I would urge you to use it, possibly even exclude the print edition depending on the cost.

Online Services

Employment-sourcing websites like Indeed, Glassdoor, and Monster have revolutionized the job-search market. They provide portholes for employers to post job listings, and for candidates to upload résumés for review by employers. From the employer's perspective, there are analytical tools to help track, evaluate and respond to candidates, as well as to conduct preliminary evaluation. These sites also enable you to conduct searches in complete or partial autonomy if you would like. Best of all, many of their services are free.

Competitors' Employees

Two additional and often overlooked sources for employees are competitors and associated companies. Hiring away employees who are looking to improve their situations can be of great benefit in structuring your own organization. These candidates will already possess knowledge about the industry and position, typically have a network of clients and associates to pool from, and will have in-depth knowledge of your competitions' organizational structure, which can often be utilized to help build your business. Be sure to consider the consequences of possibly damaging relationships with these other companies. Also, make sure you know the employee and his or her qualifications well to ensure that their current dissatisfaction isn't the result of their own personal shortcomings.

Employee Referrals

Another good source for locating employees is through employee-referral programs. Good employees usually know others with similar traits. Many larger companies even enact monetary rewards for employees who refer a successful candidate, typically payable after ninety days or more of service. Complications can arise, however, if family members or friends work in close proximity to each other, or when an employee's spouse, boyfriend or girlfriend is hired. I can relay numerous incidents where disciplinary action for one resulted in having to replace two employees. This situation can be easily avoided with one simple personnel policy restricting spouses and boy/girl friends from employment.

Educational Institutions

Educational institutions are another excellent source for locating personnel. Most colleges, universities, and trade schools offer career days for potential employers, and have job posting sites available. Internships for current students are another avenue to explore with educational institutions. Schools are also an excellent source for part-time employees for those in this category.

Professional Placement Services

Professional employment placement services are another option. Generally, the cost for utilizing a placement service will approximate the equivalent of six months' salary for the available position. As an employer, I would find these costs exorbitant but, as an employee, I have utilized their services on more than one occasion. Because of the expense involved, I would limit using the option to middle and senior management positions.

Unions

Some of you may also have to deal with unions, which often dictate hiring practices. I mention the subject for those who must consider it, but will limit the discussion, since each situation will differ dramatically depending on the industry and the union. I do believe, however, that unions should not be considered the enemy, but rather as allies working toward the same end: a profitable company that ensures safe and fair working conditions, and properly rewards its employees for their efforts.

B.5 The Selection Process

Employee Applications

All of you should utilize employee application forms for all applicants selected to be interviewed. The application can be of great benefit in establishing knowledge of the applicant and his or her qualifications. It is a good policy to keep all applications on file for at least six months both in the event of hiring grievances, and as a source in the event of subsequent employment needs. For those who are hired, the application should serve as the initial input into the employee's personnel file. Application can be downloaded from a multitude of sites both with a fee and free, and they can also be purchased from most office supply stores. A sample is provided for your convenience on the next page.

Preparing for the Initial Interview

Screening résumés beforehand can be a daunting task than can be eased by using screening tools provided by most online services. Online questionnaires and tests can also be utilized to reduce large candidate pools further. In instances where there are still too many qualified candidates to personally interview, telephone interviews can provide a quicker solution. Many employers will reduce the candidate pool to say ten qualified candidates, and then conduct telephone or Skype interviews to narrow that pool to three or four candidates to be invited in for face-to-face interviews.

The résumé and application will provide the best source for formulating your initial interview questions. In addition to questions to determine the applicant's qualifications, try to determine the applicant's reasons for wanting to leave his or her present employer and why they think your company would be a better fit. Keep in mind too applicants will often answer with what they believe you want to hear, rather than with their own true feelings. Structure your questions so that they require detailed and well-thought-out answers. Become a listener and let the applicant do the talking.

The Follow-up Interview

It's best to conduct at least a two and sometimes three interview process. Use the first interview to qualify the best out of up to five candidates, and then use the second interview to further evaluate the best two or three from the initial pool. This will give you a better chance of getting to know a candidate, and give both parties a chance to weigh all of the alternatives before making a commitment. Also, be sure to do your due diligence between interviews. Contacting past employers and references can provide valuable insight about the applicant. In most cases, this investigation should stop short of contacting the current employer, for obvious reasons.

Involve the Supervisor

When the candidate is to be under someone else's supervision, include that person in the interviewing process. It may be best to let the supervisor conduct the initial screening and interviewing, and then become involved in the follow-up interview. In

Application for Employment

EMPLOYMENT APPLICATION
(Sample)

Date _____

Name (Last Name First) _____ Soc. Sec. No. _____

Address _____ Telephone _____

What kind of work are you applying for? _____

What special qualifications do you have? _____

What office machines can you operate? _____

Are you 18 years or older? Yes _____ No _____

PERSONAL SPECIFICATIONS

☐ HEIGHT____FEET____INCHES____ ☐ WEIGHT_____LBS. ☐ CITIZEN OF U.S. YES___ NO___

☐ _____

MILITARY RECORD SERVICE

Armed Forces Service _____ Yes _____ No _____ From _____ To _____

Branch of Service _____ Duties _____

Rank or rating at time of enlistment _____ Rating at time of discharge _____

Do you have any physical limitations that prohibit you from performing any work for which you are being considered? Yes ____No ____ Please describe _____

EDUCATION

SCHOOL	NO. OF YEARS ATTENDED	NAME OF SCHOOL	CITY	COURSE	DID YOU GRADUATE?
GRAMMAR					
HIGH					
COLLEGE					
OTHER					

EXPERIENCE

NAME AND ADDRESS OF COMPANY	DATE FROM	DATE TO	LIST YOUR DUTIES	STARTING SALARY	FINAL SALARY	REASON FOR LEAVING

BUSINESS REFERENCES

NAME	ADDRESS	OCCUPATION

addition to freeing up your time, that supervisor will be directly responsible for the hire's performance anyway. It's only logical to involve the supervisor to ensure compatibility. This can also help to build the supervisor's confidence both in him or herself, and in you.

C. Employee Policy Formation
C.1 Employee Orientation and Training

The success of your firm may hinge as much upon your employees' performance as your own. Employee development is as much a dynamic in increasing and sustaining high performance level as your ability to hire the best possible candidate. Employee development should begin on the first day on the job. Don't just deposit the new employee at his or her office or workstation. Start that first day by completing any necessary human resources paperwork, and by taking the time to answer any final questions. Be sure to tour the facility and introduce the new employee to the other employees or those who will have direct involvement, depending upon the size of your organization. Then institute a training program supervised by you, the supervisor, or another employee, to help acclimate the new hire to the position and the new work environment.

The training period should coincide with a probationary employment period of at least ninety days to evaluate the new hires performance. Many firms are now instituting temporary to permanent hire situations in place of probationary programs to make it easier to comply with termination regulations in the event the new hire does not work out. The probationary or temporary period should be concluded with a review or appraisal to evaluate the new hire's performance. This can include a written evaluation as well as a combination of praise and constructive criticism, if need be. Oftentimes, exemplary performance during this period should be rewarded with a pay increase.

Performance Appraisals

Performance appraisals should be conducted at least annually for all employees. This will necessitate developing a uniform means of measuring each employee's performance and developing a standardized review form. Consideration should be given to job proficiency, the ability to work with others, attendance, initiative, and dependability. If a pay raise is in order and affordable, this is the time to initiate it. If not, explain why, and if deficiencies exist, explain why constructively and offer suggestions on how to improve performance-related issues. Remember, employees are looking for guidance and respect constructive criticism almost as much as praise.

A copy of the appraisal should be made available for the employee, and a copy should be made a part of the employee's file. It's always helpful to review an employee's past appraisals too, at the beginning of any current appraisal process.

Retraining Procedures

In today's rapidly changing business environment, initial training must often be supplemented with periodic retraining. There are many reasons to initiate retraining programs including technological advancements, more efficient operating procedures, changes in regulations, requirements to maintain certain licenses, and an increase in responsibilities. Retraining procedures can include apprentice programs, outside seminars, and continuing education classes. When such training programs are utilized, also incorporate some type of proficiency and performance evaluation. Once those have been satisfied, reward the employee with increased responsibility and pay.

C.2 Determining Wages and Other Incentives
Hourly vs. Salary

The initial wage determination will be whether to pay on an hourly or a salary basis. This decision will be influenced in part by the industry and local competition, as well as the level of the position. Those hiring for retail or for general warehouse, factory, or laborer positions will most likely pay on an hourly basis. Management positions will tend to be on a salary basis, and either pay form is acceptable for clerical positions. Regardless of which scale you use, be sure to comply with local, state, and federal regulations regarding minimum wage and overtime pay.

Determining a Salary Range

When determining the exact salary level for a position, take into consideration industry standards, competitor's salary scales, the applicant's qualifications, experience level and current salary, the local cost of living, and your ability to meet the salary requirement. It would also prove advantageous to develop a salary range for each position with a minimum, midpoint, and maximum. This will allow a lower salary for a less experienced employee working at the same position as someone with more experience. It will also inform the employee of financial rewards obtainable at that position or nearing salary limits that may entice an employee to assess opportunities for advancement from within.

Piecemeal Salary Scales

For those with multiple hiring needs that can't quite afford the level of employee you desire, consider a sliding pay scale. This works best in the manufacturing industry, particularly in the assembly-line process. Piecemeal is a form of bonus paid over and above the hourly rate as an incentive and a reward for more productive employees. The scale is set by first determining the average daily output for each worker by units produced. Then simply tack on a pay incentive for each unit produced above that number. The break-even formula can be utilized to determine the level of incentive affordable.

Those considering the form of incentive should implement safeguards to ensure workers don't hurry output to the point of lowering quality or safety standards. Also, be sure there is amiable market for those extra units being produced. You can imagine the operating hardships that you could encounter if those extra units were piling up uncontrollably in the warehouse or if an accident resulted from abating safety standards.

Sales Commissions

For those of you with sales personnel, salaries can be a supplement or made up entirely of commissions. To determine what level of commissions you can afford, again play "what if" with the break-even formula. First, calculate commissions as a percent of the cost of goods sold, and then determine the effects on overall profitability.

An alternative to the straight commission format is a draw against commission arrangement. In this instance, the salesperson is paid only commissions, but is able to draw a percentage of future commissions in advance. This can make the commission arrangement more palatable for the salesperson as they can schedule the pay more systematically to help cover monthly obligations. The drawback to the employer, however, is that the salesperson could quit before those draws have been paid back through earned commissions.

Employee Bonuses

One final incentive is a bonus program. This alternative could be particularly useful for those of you with capital restraints. We've already projected profit levels for the first year. A bonus program could be instituted by simply determining a percentage of any profits exceeding that level to be paid out in the form of bonuses. Then set up a bonus scale for key employees or your entire staff based upon individual performance and salary levels. Normally, bonuses are paid out once a year, but a few companies pay them quarterly.

When determining bonus percentages, be sure to determine the costs of increasing profits so as not to give the entire profit increase, or more, away in bonuses. It would also be advisable to establish an accrual account and set aside bonus contributions on a monthly basis, so you are not caught by surprise by the inability to pay bonuses during the distribution time. Posting accrued contributions for employee review can also serve to improve morale and work performance.

Tax Incentives

One area often overlooked when establishing salaries and pay incentives is tax benefits. For instance, a company car in lieu of a salary increase can offer the added rewards of an investment tax credit and depreciation expense for the employer, while raising the employee's standard of living without increasing his or her tax liability. For now we will assume most of you are starting with a minimum of salary incentives, insurance plans, and no pension or profit-sharing programs. These subjects are, however, covered extensively in chapter 17, and they will certainly become a factor once you've established a profitable operation.

Vacation, Absenteeism, and Dismissal Policies

Company policies should also be established for vacations, absenteeism, disciplinary measures, and dismissal. Among the considerations will be whether vacation and sick days are paid and, if so, whether they can be accumulated to use later or even cashed out. Disciplinary actions are another policy concern. Will you establish a warning policy, such as two or three warning result in automatic dismissal? Will some violations like theft result in immediate dismissal? Will any severance pay be allotted?

Possibly more important than the policies themselves will be the ability to document that the policies exist, that that were discussed in advance with all the employees and that they are being enforced unilaterally. This information is imperative in wrongful dismissal suits or arbitrations. Any reports of disciplinary violations as well as employer actions should be well documented and become a part of the employees' personnel file.

C.3 Employee Productivity

Statistics indicate that in general there has been a decline in the productivity of the American worker. Studies have shown that in a typical eight-hour day, an employer is lucky to get four productive hours from the average employee. I believe this trend is due, in part, to a loss of incentives and, in industries such as fast foods, to a total disregard for the livelihoods of the workforce altogether.

Workers today feel as though their contributions go unnoticed and unrewarded. This is complicated by employer in many industries failing to provide wages that meet minimal living requirements. Many of those employers then subvert governmental regulations by limiting work hours to categorize an employee as temporary or part-time employee. Sadly, the worst offenders are also garnishing millions in tax incentives by claiming to employ the underemployed in federal subsidies.

A Tip from the Japanese

What can be done to correct this imbalance? Japanese companies are managed for the long term rather than to optimize the current quarter's operations. Japanese companies treat their employees as family, and that family obligation continues throughout the workers' entire lives. Give workers a voice as Chrysler did when they gave workers a seat on the board of directors. If you establish bonus and incentive programs, distribute them throughout your workforce, not just senior management, like General Motors and so many others. Look upon your organization as your second family, and treat every member as an integral part of that family.

D. Chapter Summary

Remember, as projections guide your operating performance, organizational policies guide your staff toward their fulfillment. Employees want to take pride in their work, and the need to be recognized and rewarded for their contributions. Remember too that gratification does not always have to be in the form of money. Peer recognition often is as important, and such things as title incentives, extra vacation days, and even an occasional pat on the back, can go a long way in showing your appreciation.

CHAPTER 14

Building an Effective Marketing Strategy

Many small business owners tend to overlook the importance of marketing, often because they feel the least qualified in this area. Yet without an effective marketing strategy, one can never improve upon an existing business or get a new business off the ground. To put it more succinctly, marketing is the key ingredient for meeting and maintaining sales forecasts.

To plan an effective marketing strategy, we must first further segment our targeted market, determine how to make the product or service known to that market, develop a need, set an optimal pricing structure, and determine the most cost-effective distribution method. Once these procedures have been completed, they must then be coordinated into one standardized marketing policy.

Some of you will also have to take into consideration the source of your product or raw materials, as well as the costs and the time restraints involved in meeting delivery schedules. Selling terms and credit procedures may also have to be taken into consideration. These variables will be discussed in greater detail in chapter 16, which covers credit and inventory policies. The remainder of this chapter will be devoted exclusively to those areas directly involved with marketing policy.

A. Defining Your Company's Image
A.1 What's in a Name

Where better to begin our marketing discussion than with choosing a name for the business? There are no simple steps or formulas for doing this, but the best approach involves some degree of common sense. For those purchasing an existing business, it is usually best to continue trading under the same name. This will prove less disturbing to the existing customer base, and help to provide for a smoother ownership transition. Of course, this will require the consent of the previous owner, and this condition should be spelled out clearly in the buy/sell agreement.

There will be times when it will prove more advantageous to change the name. If you are considering changing the scope or nature of the business, for example, a name change would help to accentuate a new image. A name change would also prove beneficial to those purchasing a declining business to help serve notice or advertise that a change of ownership has occurred. Most existing and potential customers, and those that might have been previously driven away, will be anxious to see the changes.

When choosing a name for a new, keep it short and simple so that it's easy to remember. Try to make the name unique so that it will prove memorable as well as easily identifiable with your business. If possible, identify your product or service within the context of the name. This will serve as a helpful advertisement for those who may be unfamiliar with you or your business. Finally, be sure to register the name with the appropriate county clerk to ensure you are not infringing upon someone else's trade name, and that you are adequately protecting your own name against future infringement.

A.2 Market Positioning

The name you choose will have a profound effect on how your company is perceived within the marketplace. Certainly you have an idea of how you would like your company to be perceived, but we have yet to define it. We did identify a customer base during our initial research, and now let's establish a posture toward that market. Though the decision will have far-reaching implications, the strategy itself is quite simple. Do you intend to become a large-volume low-markup operation, a lower volume high-markup operation, or do you plan on taking a middle of the road approach? How your company is perceived will be influenced by many operational areas, but none will affect it more than your positioning within the market.

Industry Mandates

Obviously, this discussion will be influenced by the industry itself. Wholesaling, for example, is generally considered a high-volume low-markup industry, while a retail jeweler might be considered just the opposite. There are, however, varying degrees within each industry. A Kay's Jewelry outlet, for example, operates within a completely different segment of the market than say a Tiffany & Company outlet. Market segmentation is affected by such variables as location, competition, product line, and by any personal traits that might be personified in your business.

Market Segmentation

Like our jewelry store example, there are legal firms that charge $100 an hour and those that charge $700 or more, and many in both categories are successful. Both operate within the same marketplace, yet each has geared its operation to a different segment of that market. It will be up to each of you to survey your targeted market in terms of your location, competition, product quality, and personal preferences, and to position yourselves accordingly.

Once you have decided upon a positioning, incorporate that decision into an overall company image. Don't be afraid to write it down and display it. Make it part of your mission statement. This will help to remind your employees and yourself of the purpose or principles upon which the business was founded. To be most effective, these ideals should be carried over into every operational area.

For once, those in the start-up phase will be at an advantage. Those purchasing an existing business will inherit a preconceived image that may or may not be to your liking. It's certainly easier to create an image than to change what has already been etched into a customer's mind.

B. Developing a Pricing Policy

Market positioning will be the major determinant to pricing limits or ranges, but each of you will have a degree of pricing freedom within that range. The price you finally do choose will directly affect the unit sales volume for that product or service. To determine optimal pricing levels, you must decide which price and volume combination will net the highest gross profit margin. Though this is most indicative of a retail or wholesale establishment, it will also hold true for manufacturers and servicers.

B.1 Price/Volume Volatility

Let's suppose you manufacture baseball bats, and during your first month in business you sold ten thousand bats at $120 a bat. The next month you decided to raise the price to $150, and unit sales dropped to eight thousand bats. Which of these sales figures would provide the larger net profit? The answer, of course, depends upon the correlation between unit sales and variable expenses, since a fluctuation in unit sales volume will have a direct effect on variable costs. This in turn will affect the gross profit margin.

In the preceding example, sales by dollar volume would be $1.2 million for both months. If we assume variable costs, or the cost of goods sold, were $50 per bat, your cost to manufacture and sell ten thousand bats would be $500,000, but only $400,000 to manufacture and sell eight thousand bats. Assuming fixed costs weren't impacted at either sales level, your gross profit as well as your net profit before taxes would be $100,000 higher at the lower unit sales level, even though you sold two thousand fewer bats.

Less Price-Sensitive Products

While all products are price sensitive, there are those that are less sensitive than others. Reasonable price fluctuations for these products or services will have little or no effect on sales volume. This is most true in the service industry. A lawyer who currently charges $100 an hour would probably experience little or no customer attrition if he or she raised that hourly rate to $125. There is, of course, a point of diminishing returns at which even less sensitive products or services become price sensitive. If this same attorney were to raise the hourly fee to $250, he or she would probably experience a noticeable loss in clientele.

Reverse Price Sensitivity

There are times when raising the price may actually increase in sales volume. This would be true if your product or service is one that is considered prestigious or one in which a certain price level is associated with quality. Again, using our legal example, there are those who might feel quality legal service requires paying a fee of at least $250 an hour. If that same attorney dropped the hourly fee to $150 in hopes of attracting more business, there's a strong possibility some of the existing customers would feel an erosion of services and they might seek representation elsewhere.

B.2 An Optimal Pricing Formula

For products and services that are subject to a reasonable amount of price sensitivity, we can adapt the logic used in the baseball bat analogy to construct an optimal pricing formula. The mathematical formula is: 100 − (Units Sold × Cost Per Unit × 100/$ Sales) = Gross Profit Margin. The formula isn't as difficult to complete as you might first think. First perform the calculations within the parentheses. That answer will be the cost of goods sold or variable expense to sale quotient, which when multiplied by 100 will be converted into a percent of sales equivalent. This figure is then subtracted by 100, which represents 100% sales figure, to arrive at the adjusted gross profit margin. The higher the gross profit margin, the better the unit sales figure from a profit standpoint.

If we work the formula through for the baseball bat analogy, the 10,000 bat sales level would calculate as follows: 100 − (10,000 × 50 × 100 / $1,200,000) = 100 − (50,000,000 / 1,200,000) = 100 − 41.67 = 58.33%. By comparison, the 8,000 bat sales level would calculate as 100 − (8,000 × 50 × 100 / 1,200,000) = 100 − (40,000,000 / 1,200,000) = 100 − 33.33 = 66.67%. To prove the answer, multiply each quotient by the dollar sales volume to convert them back to gross profit by dollars: $1,200,000 × 0.5833 = $699,960, while $1,200,000 × 0.6667 = $800,040. The difference of $100,080 represents the initial gross profit differential, plus an extra $80 we lost originally by rounding.

Accounting for Market Pressures

Eventually a point will be reached where any increase in unit sales volume will result in an increase in either fixed expenses or in the variable expenses to sales percentage.

Theoretically that point would represent your optimal price point and unit sales volume level at your present operating capacity. Any increase in unit sales beyond this point would require an additional capital outlay or an increase in fixed costs. The optimal sales level is of course a textbook application, and does not take into consideration other variables that would have an impact on sales. These include the quality of your product, its availability and seasonality, the maximum amount your customers are willing to pay for that product, and the underlying economic conditions.

Adapting the Pricing Formula

During the projections' modeling phase, we determined the cost of goods sold and gross profit as a percent of sales. From this we established a projected sales volume in dollars. We can now establish the optimal price and unit sales volume for each product or service by incorporating those figures into our pricing formula. Again, once optimal prices are determined, they may need to be adjusted to be compatible with your competition and with what the market itself will bear.

Those purchasing existing businesses will have a much easier time determining obtainable unit sales volume, since you will have past performance records to help guide you. Those in the start-up phase can do little more than establish a well-educated guess at this point. All of you should keep accurate sales records on a daily, weekly, and monthly basis to appropriately measure how price changes affect your unit sales volume, and then adjust prices accordingly.

C. Advertising

Undoubtedly, advertising will be one of the most essential elements of your marketing strategy. While marketing is the overall procedure for meeting and maintaining sales forecasts, advertising is the vehicle for generating those sales. It will be particularly important to the start-up concern that will have to allocate a larger initial advertising budget to develop its customer base.

Those purchasing an established business will already have an existing customer base. Don't fall into the trap of thinking you can really depend exclusively on existing customers, however. There is a certain amount of customer attrition associated with any business, and a change in ownership might impact that attrition rate further. New customers will have to be generated to replace those lost, and there is no better way to spearhead this than by advertising.

C.1 Establishing Market Boundaries

We identified our target market during the initial research phase, and we have since further defined that market in compliance with pricing strategies. Now let's identify the boundaries of that market. Do you intend to establish a local, state, regional, national, or international customer base? The larger the geographic area, the better the chances you will have to generalize your advertising. Though perhaps long forgotten, Wendy's "Where's the beef?" is a perfect example. It's a message that applies to consumers of all ages and walks of life.

For some of you, a better alternative will be to segment your market, and gear dissimilar or multidimensional advertising campaigns to reach specific segments or geographic regions of your market. General Motors is a perfect example of multidimensional advertising. They place general ads to promote their brands nationally, and more specific ads to promote better-selling products per region. They know pickup trucks sell better in the Midwest and Deep South, while luxury sedans are more popular on the East and West Coasts. They supplement their general national ads with regional ads geared to the most popular products in each of those areas. While I doubt there will be many of you with the market share or advertising budget of a General Motors, there is certainly a lesson to be learned from this example.

Defining Communications Preferences

Once you have identified the geographies of your market, you will have to determine how best to reach that market. Does your audience listen to FM radio or do they stream music and news? What type of music do they listen to? Which newspapers or magazines do they read, and by online editions or print? What effect would billboards or cable TV ads have? What about mass mailings or catalogs, e-mail blasts and social media?

In most cases, a combination of these alternatives will work best based on the personal preferences of your customer base, the standards for your particular industry, the geographic boundaries of your market, and your capital limitations. A retail store with a localized customer base might use local publications and radio stations, possibly localized postcards with a discount coupon, a company website, and social media outlets such as Facebook. A regional wholesaler might utilize regional or trade publications and regional television ads to reach a larger geographic area in conjunction with Internet presence and a social-media campaign.

C.2 Establishing an Advertising Budget

Many of you may have included advertising in your original projections or grouped it with other operating expenses. Let's now determine a more definitive advertising outlay. The best approach to establishing an advertising budget is to set an annual figure based on a percentage of your cost of goods sold or services. This annual budget should be either affordable in terms of maintaining projected profits, or easily passed on to the customer by means of a slight price increase.

For some of you this may be as little as 1%, but for others up to 8%, and for still others—cosmetic distributors for example—upwards of 50%. Again, consult your research materials for industry averages as a starting point. Those purchasing an existing business can check past financial statements as well as review past advertising methods for guidance. Observing your competitor's advertising methods can also provide keen insight.

Once you have established an annual advertising budget, it is best to redefine that budget into a monthly advertising plan as part of your short-term operating projections. If your business is subject to seasonality, you'll want to target larger portions of that budget toward peak selling periods. Subdividing your annual budget into monthly allotments will also help you to enact better spending controls, lest you wake up on April 1 and realize you've already spent the year's advertising allotment.

Advertising Assistance

Some of you will have the need and the budget to hire an outside advertising agency or an in-house advertising or marketing director or specialist. Many of you, however, will have to rely upon your own skills to design and place ads, at least at the outset. Again, study your competition, but don't just mimic what they do; analyze and improve upon their methods. Most advertising salespeople can also be helpful in layout, design, and placement assistance.

Additionally, advertising salespeople should provide a media guide that will have statistical data to support the number of homes their station, publication, or website reaches, as well as a profile of their average reader, listener, or viewer. This information can be helpful in determining the effectiveness placing an ad with that supplier as well as a reference to see if those they reach are a good fit for your targeted customer base. Keep in mind these salespeople are being paid by commission, and though they can be extremely helpful, they may also have a tendency to upsell.

C.3 Designing Ads

Regardless of the media or your budget, there are certain general considerations to keep in mind when designing ads and writing advertising copy. First, your ad should tell a story that can be conveyed through words—a picture, visual format, or both. Second, that story should be educational so that the reader learns about your product or service, and why he or she should use it. Let the audience know what sets your product or company above the rest. Finally, that story should be geared to your targeted market. If you are distributing cosmetics for teens, you're not going to want to use thirty-year-old models or terminology associated with parental markets.

If at all possible, create a catchphrase or jingle. Ads are easily forgotten, but a short catchphrase or jingle used repeatedly in all of your ads will instill a permanent impression. It's also important to identify both your company and your product in that catchphrase. We can test the importance of this by means of example. We can all identify the company and product behind the "Pepsi Generation," but do you remember who popularized "Try it, you'll like it?"

Utilize Your Creativity

Though many of you will be on limited budgets, don't make the mistake of restricting or neglecting advertising. At the risk of being repetitive, advertising will create sales, and there are inexpensive yet effective ways to go about it even on a limited budget. Personally distributing ads or pamphlets, community bulletin boards, e-mail blasts, referral discounts for existing customers are just a few examples. You must be creative when designing effective ads. If the situation warrants, use that creative spark to create a cost-effective advertising campaign.

Public Relations

There is another channel that should be incorporated within your marketing and advertising campaign. This is public relations. Certainly, larger firms realize the importance of this segment. Many employ a separate public-relations person or staff. Every company, regardless of size, should take full advantage of public relations and community service activities. While it's primary emphasis is, of course, community service, free or inexpensive exposure is certainly an important side benefit.

When something newsworthy or of importance happens to your company or a key employee, issue a short press release and distribute it to local news sources. Do this on a regular basis. Additionally, your company's name on the front of a youth sports uniform or on the inside of a school gymnasium can often provide more business than a series of paid advertisements. Make public relations a vital part of your advertising.

Websites and Social Media

Most of you will establish and maintain a company website. It is important to update and add new information on a regular basis to give viewers a reason to keep coming back. If you can sell your products or related merchandise through your website, you can develop another distribution channel that can significantly increase your reach and your customer base. You can also use your website to educate and institute changes, provide discount coupons, and create links to related organizations. Oftentimes you can even establish advertising arrangements ancillary servicers' that can provide yet another source of income and help introduce your company to new customers.

Social media should be viewed as another public-relations platform. Facebook, Twitter, Instagram, and so on, all offer opportunities to expand and advertise your business at a low cost or even for free. Facebook can also provide data to help research and define your market. Google too, can be extremely helpful in this area. It is also important to update and add new information to social media accounts on a regular basis to give viewers a reason to keep coming back.

D. Sales Distribution

The final area of our marketing strategy discussion is sales distribution. This could encompass retail counter sales, telephone and mail solicitation, Internet sales, salespeople covering specific clients or territories, or an independent distribution network. This discussion will prove beneficial even to those of you who do not have designated salespeople, since every business involves some degree of selling. A professional such as a lawyer, doctor, or hairstylist must sell themselves and their skills if they wish to be successful, and those skills must deemed price and quality effective.

Educating Employees

Though sales distribution methods will differ for each of you, this function must be proceduralized and coordinated with your overall marketing policy and remaining operational policies if it is to be effective. This will necessitate providing those employees with direct and indirect customer contact, a thorough knowledge of your pricing methods, advertising strategy, and your preconceived company image. They should also be made knowledgeable about the products or services rendered so that they can talk intelligently to your customers, and accurately answer any questions that might be asked. Also, once credit and inventory controls have been established, these same employees must be versed on any time restraints involved in fulfilling orders as well as the proper credit standards that might be required.

Open Communications

In short, your business will run most effectively when open channels of communication are maintained, and when employees have a working knowledge of all operating functions in which they are directly or indirectly involved. This principle is particularly important with salespeople and employees who have direct customer contact, since they are the ones conveying your company's policies and attitudes to the general public. This is equally important whether you are a retailer, wholesaler, manufacturer, servicer, or franchisee.

Sales Territories

Those of you with true sales networks will have to set up territorial routes and delivery schedules, the optimal number of customer accounts to be handled by each salesperson.

You could evenly distribute your best accounts, or assign them all to the salesperson you most trust. You could also consider territories along with account assignments, and then divide up customers by geographies. Though the solutions to these types of procedural questions will vary by situation, the best course of action will always be one that is most harmonious to the customers, employees, and your operating procedures.

E. Management Reporting

The availability of data for reporting purposes will depend upon the complexity of your accounting function. Those with a product or measurable service to sell will want to compile some sort of gross sales report on a daily, weekly, and monthly basis. This will enable you to see which products or services are being most readily accepted, and allow you to fine-tune or restructure marketing approaches accordingly if need be.

Those of you with a sales force may want to subdivide sales results by salesperson to help assess individual performance. Sales results should also be compared against sales projections on a regular basis to help determine any operating changes that might be necessitated by lagging or excessive growth. Sales statistics can also be used in conjunction with inventory and cost information to help determine inventory requirements and optimal product mix.

F. Chapter Summary

Certainly the aim in marketing is to generate sales, the master link in the chain to building a successful business. But, as we've shown in this and preceding chapters, sales for sales sake can sometimes prove detrimental to the health of the business. As in our projection model, measuring the cost of sales, setting effective pricing, and measuring the performance of key products and sales personnel, are all as important to an effective marketing strategy as advertising policy itself.

CHAPTER 15

Accounting and Professional Matters

I n this chapter we will continue our discussion of operating procedures. We will begin with a general discussion on accounting geared to those who intend to keep their own books. Then we will assist in helping you to define your own accounting needs, both internal and external. From there we will turn our attention to insurance. We will discuss the various types of coverages available and, again, define your individual insurance needs. We will conclude this chapter with a discussion on ancillary banking services and the legal profession.

A. A Word about Single- and Double-Entry Accounting

Before we delve into defining bookkeeping and accounting requirements, let's further our discussion on accounting principles. This will serve a two-fold purpose. One, it will help outline basic bookkeeping functions for those who intend to keep their own records. Two, it will help improve the basic understanding of accounting for those who intend to hire a bookkeeper, accountant, or an independent accounting firm. This basic discussion should help all of you improve your ability to evaluate cash budgets, projections, financial statements, and other types of management reports.

Anyone who has to keep track of expense records for an expense report, or completed an income tax return, has utilized the single-entry accounting system. It is a simple compilation of revenues received and expenses incurred. For those of you owning sole proprietorships with the simplest of accounting needs, this system will work fine. An example might be a realtor or a beautician working out of his or her home.

The vast majority of you, however, will require much more control and assurance than can be provided through single-entry accounting. You will need to institute a double entry accounting system. Simply stated, double-entry accounting is a system that requires two entries for each accounting transaction as a means of insuring accurate reporting.

Let's refer back to our discussion on accrual accounting to help explain the concept of a double-entry system. If you recall the correlation between sales, accounts receivable, and cash during our cash-budgeting exercise, you'll remember that when a sale was made on credit, an account receivable was generated. The two accounting entries for this transaction would be an increase in sales revenue, and a corresponding increase in accounts receivable. When the receivable is collected, another double entry will transpire. There will be an increase (debit) to cash, and a corresponding decrease (credit) to accounts receivable.

Our financial statement discussions involved analyzing and understanding the finished products, but understanding double-entry accounting will provide us with the knowledge to comprehend the processes used to compile those financial statements. Simply stated, these double entries represent the nuts-and-bolts-type procedures, which effect changes to all assets, liability, equity, sales, and expense accounts, from one accounting period to another. To prepare the actual balance sheet for the year ending 7/31/X2, for our example Superior Jewelry, we would add or subtract from the 7/31/X1 balances all the entries that took place to each account during the subsequent twelve-month period. The ending balance for each would then be the figure reported on the 7/31/X2 balance sheet.

B. A Basic Double-Entry Accounting System
B.1 The Chart of Accounts
The first step in preparing a double-entry system is to compile a chart of accounts, a sample of which is provided on the following page.

As you can see the chart is nothing more than a listing of possible assets, liability, equity, sales, and expense accounts. This is by no means a complete list, and many companies will have additional account headings. There is also a corresponding numerical title for each account with assets typically starting at 100, liabilities at 200, and so on. This is done for convenience since there is less time involved in copying or inputting a number than the account title itself.

B.2 The Cash Disbursement's Journal
The double-entry system requires a series of journals to enter or post each transaction. These will be templates in canned programs like Peachtree or Quicken. They can also be constructed in Excel, or even purchased to handwrite entries at most business supply stores. The first journal we will discuss is the Cash Disbursements Journal, which is merely a form of a checking account register. Consider cash disbursements in the same vein as paying your monthly bills. When a bill is paid, the entries are posted to the appropriate account or account from your chart of accounts. The amount paid will be added (debited) to the appropriate expense account, and subtracted (credited) from the cash account.

A debit is an accounting term signifying an increase to an asset, equity, or expense account, while a credit is an increase to any liability or sales account. Subsequently a decrease to an asset, equity, or expense account would be a credit, while a decrease to a liability or sales account would be a debit.

CHART OF ACCOUNTS

ASSETS
100 Cash in Bank
110 Cash on Hand
120 Accounts Receivable
125 Allowance for Doubtful Accounts
130 Employee Advances
140 Inventory
150 Prepaid Expenses
160 Equipment
165 Accumulated Depreciation
170 Furniture & Fixtures
175 Accumulated Depreciation

LIABILITIES
200 Accounts Payable
210 Notes Payable
220 Accrued. Payroll Taxes Payable
230 Accrued Income Tax Payable
240 Other Accrued Expenses Payable
250 Long Term Notes Payable

CAPITAL
290 Capital Stock
295 Retained Earnings

INCOME
300 Gross Sales

DIRECT OPERATING EXPENSES
400 Cost of Goods Sold
402 Materials
405 Direct Labor

GENERAL & ADMINISTRATIVE EXPENSES

410 Salaries	465 Repairs & Maintenance
415 Payroll Taxes	470 Advertising
420 Employee Benefits	475 Supplies-General
425 Rent	480 Taxes & Licenses
430 Utilities	485 Telephone
435 Insurance	490 Travel
440 Interest	495 Dues and Subscriptions
445 Legal & Accounting	
450 Office & Postage	
455 Depreciation	
460 Donations	

B.3 The Accounts Receivable and Payable Journals

Let's add another element to the conversation. Most of you will have slightly more complex accounting needs and will prefer to utilize an accrual accounting system that will enable you to recognize a sale when it's transacted rather than when the cash changes hands. This necessitates setting up two additional accounts and journals—Accounts Receivable and Accounts Payable. In accrual accounting, again, when a credit sale transpires, sales would be credited by that amount and the offset would be accounts receivable (debited) rather than cash. Then when the cash is collected, accounts receivable would be credited and cash would be debited.

Accounts payable transactions are similar. Say you receive a bill that you do not intend to pay for forty-five days. You would still add or debit that bill to the proper expense account, but rather than credit cash you would credit (or add it) to accounts payable. Then forty-five days later when you pay it, you would write a check that would reduce or credit your cash account. You would also debit or reduce accounts payable by the same amount. Again, remember the correlation between debits and credits. A credit increases liabilities but decreases assets. Subsequently, a debit increases assets but decreases liabilities.

B.4 The Payroll System

Many of you will want to separate the payroll function, and utilize a separate payroll checking account. The Payroll Journal is a bit more complex than those previously discussed. While there is only one gross pay amount, there are at least four accounts affected. The gross amount of the check would be your debit to the Salaries expense account, but the credit to the cash or payroll checking account would only be for the net pay amount. The remainder will have to be divided between the FICA. Withholding account for social security payments, the Federal Income Tax Withholding account and, in most cases, the State Income Tax Withholding account. Some of you will also have to withhold for local or city tax accounts and for retirement contributions.

Accruing Payroll Taxes

It will be up to you as an employer to accrue payroll taxes and file quarterly reports with the state and federal governments. There are also state and federal unemployment taxes that you as the employer must pay directly. You will also be required to complete W-2 forms for all employees, or 1099 Miscellaneous Income forms for subcontracted workers. Once you have been through this a few times, you will realize it isn't as complicated as it seems. If you do need assistance, ask your accountant.

Automated Payrolls

Most small and midsized businesses today utilize automated payroll services. This service can be established through many of the larger banks as well as separate payroll service providers like ADP or Paychex. You simply give the servicer the payroll information for salaried employees, or prior to each pay period for hourly employees. The servicer then issues the corresponding paychecks or direct deposits, and takes care of all of the entries and reporting requirements, provided of course, that you make the necessary deposits. The payroll servicer will also provide you with an accurate accounting of all transactions on a per-pay-period basis, monthly, quarterly, and annually. Again, they will also complete all government reporting requirements including W-2s and 1099s. Payroll servicers relieve you off all of the payroll accounting and reporting burdens, and usually at far less than the cost of administering your own payroll program.

The Fixed Asset Ledger

If you have heavy investments in fixed assets, you will want to maintain a Fixed Asset Ledger. This ledger is similar in detail to the fixed-asset depreciation schedule utilized for income-tax reporting. It contains a description of the asset, the date of purchase, the purchase price, the estimated useful life, the salvage value, the method of depreciation and the amount of periodic and accumulated depreciation. This ledger can be extremely helpful in scheduling fixed-asset maintenance and purchases, and in keeping informed on the remaining value and useful life for each particular item detailed.

B.5 The Inventory Log

The next area of our accounting discussion is inventory. The primary tool for maintaining inventory records will be the Inventory Log. Two samples are provided—one for a retailer or wholesaler, the other for a manufacturer. Again, those of you with canned accounting software will have templates for these functions provided, or you can build your own using Microsoft Excel.

As indicated, the log lists the date an item is ordered, received, and sold by cost and selling price. Each time additional items are ordered and received, they will have to be entered into the log, and each time items are sold, they will have to be deleted from the log. The Manufacture's Log is a bit more complicated since it requires the distinction between raw materials, work in progress, and finished goods. A physical inventory count should be taken at least once a year for all companies with inventory accounts to verify the accuracy of the log.

The Inventory Log can tell you what items were on hand at any given time, and what has been sold during any given period. From this you can gleam information like, which products are selling best, which products are laggards and may require sales incentives, and which products need to be reordered and in what quantity. The log is also helpful in managing the time requirements needed for ordering, receiving, manufacturing, and selling a product. This information is vital in maintaining inventory controls, a subject that will be discussed at great length in chapter 16.

INVENTORY LOG
(Wholesalers and Retailers)

| Location: | Unit Value: | | Time required to obtain: | | | | |

| Maximum Stock: | | Minimum Stock: | | Reorder Point: | | Ordering Quantity: | |

Date	Description	Quantities in terms of units of issue:					Remarks
		On Order	Rec'd	Cost	Date Sold	Price	

INVENTORY LOG
(Manufacturers)

Description _____   Min. Quantity _____   Ordering Point _____

Code _____   Max. Quantity _____   Amount to Order _____

Unit of Issue _____

RAW MATERIALS					WORK IN PROGRESS			FINISHED GOODS			
Date	Cost	Rec'd	Reserved	Balance	Date	Reserved	Balance	Date Complete	Date Sold	Price	Balance

B.6 The General Ledger

All of you will want to compile financial statements on a regular basis that necessitates the use of a General Ledger. The General Ledger ties together all of the aforementioned systems. If you think back to our discussion earlier in this section regarding compiling a financial statement, you'll get a better understanding of the correlation with the General Ledger. It's basically a booklet that includes a page for each account in your chart of accounts along with their opening balances. Each of the logs and ledgers we have already discussed are typically totaled once a month and those totals are also posted to the appropriate account in the General Ledger. In this manner, year-to-date balances are maintained, and if so desired, financial statements can be prepared from the closing balances as often as monthly.

C. Determining Internal Accounting Requirements

Those of you purchasing an existing business will be at an advantage when evaluating your initial accounting needs because, hopefully, the accounting function will already be in place. You merely need to evaluate and, if need be, improve upon the existing system. Those in the start-up phase will have to determine the complexity of your internal accounting needs on your own.

Under either circumstance, start the process by evaluating how much of the work you plan to do yourself. Consider both your accounting abilities as well as the time restraints involved in this determination. Though accurate accounting is undoubtedly one of the most important management functions, it is after all still one of many important functions. You as the owner will have to oversee the entire operation. This can best be accomplished by disassociating yourself with all of the day-to-day labor involved in any of the management reporting functions, including accounting.

If you do have to complete any of bookkeeping and accounting functions yourself, do them in the evening or when they will not affect your other duties. If the situation warrants and you can afford it, hire a bookkeeper. If it is not a full-time function, make it a part-time position or utilize other employees' time for other duties.

For those who need additional assistance in making this determination, seek it from the most logical source, a local bookkeeping, accounting or, preferably, a certified public accounting firm. Any of these sources can be used on a part-time basis to establish accounting systems and procedures and to help with management reporting, compiling financial statements, and completing local, state and federal tax returns.

C.1 Accounting Personnel
The Bookkeeper

For many smaller businesses seeking accounting personnel, the best bargain may be an experienced full charge bookkeeper. A bookkeeper with five to ten years of experience can often prove more knowledgeable than a recently graduated accountant or CPA, at about one-third the cost. The reason is very simple. Though accounting principles can be taught, like many professions, becoming a good accountant requires years of practical experience. An experienced bookkeeper usually has learned those principles on the job while also acquiring that edge of practical knowledge. The drawback is that without credentials, it will be up to you to authenticate if the bookkeeper does in fact possess the knowledge that is required.

The Public Accountant

Those who will require the aid of more than one bookkeeper, say a payroll clerk, an accounts receivable clerk, and an accounts payable clerk, will probably also require the aid of an in-house accountant to supervise the accounting function. Though a few of you may find a bookkeeper who can fill this role, most of you will require a degreed accountant knowledgeable in management reporting and financial statement preparation. A public accountant is someone with an accounting degree who has not yet fulfilled the requirements to be certified as a CPA. Again, the costs will be less than if you hired a CPA, but authenticating the knowledge base will be more subjective.

The Certified Public Accountant (CPA)

To earn a CPA distinction, an accounting graduate must complete thirty credit hours over and above the undergraduate degree requirements, gain at least two years of practical experience at a CPA firm, and pass an extensive written examination conducted by the American Institute of Certified Public Accountants. The CPA distinction should help to alleviate any uncertainty as to an accountant's level of practical accounting knowledge.

Those who will need a CPA are those whose business is either large enough or complex enough to require qualified or audited financial statements. In most cases, you will not have to make this determination alone. It will often be a requirement of a lender, a customer contract, a government licensing requirement, or possibly the requirement of an investor or stockholders.

Again, this does not mean you have to have a CPA on staff. In fact, qualified and audited statements require an independent CPA's opinion letter. It only means you must retain an independent CPA firm to oversee financial statement preparation. Your internal accounting function can be supervised by a bookkeeper, public accountant, CPA or even you, provided the contracted CPA firm oversees financial statement preparation and verifies proper accounting procedures are being followed.

C.2 PC's Level the Playing Field

You can imagine the amount of time and manpower required to compile all of the accounting functions for a large corporation using a manual system. It wasn't that long ago, in fact, my career began during this Dark Age. The computer has enabled the automation of all operational and accounting functions. This has greatly enhanced the ease, speed and accuracy of management reporting and has enabled the compilation of data in almost any configuration you desire. The result has been the catapulting of accounting to the forefront of management planning.

Not long ago, accountants were locked away in a backroom to crunch numbers that were typically three months in the rears. These numbers were used to compile financial statements for periods long since closed, and they had little intrinsic value with regards to management reporting. Today accounting functions are often completed in real time, and the data can be extrapolated and turned into projections and meaningful reports instantaneously. Moreover, the advent of low-cost PCs and accounting software has enabled any size business to maintain a computerized accounting and management reporting function that is as sophisticated as those used by the largest corporations.

D. Determining External Accounting Requirements

The need for an outside accounting firm and the level of services required will vary for each of you. Some small retailers, for example, may be able to do their own bookkeeping, but utilize an outside firm to complete their tax returns. Many in this category may even get by with using a bookkeeping service or an H&R Block to provide this function. Why pay more for what you don't need?

Most of you, however, will be large enough to require at least an annual financial statement. Many of you will require semiannual or quarterly statements. My advice to you would be to hire a CPA firm but, unless you are conducting business at more than one location nationally or internationally, a smaller local firm will generally be more cost effective than one of the "Big 4" firms.

Ancillary Accounting Services

As with those utilizing banks and lending institutions, those who use a CPA firm should take full advantage of their services. Use their insight into your own operations by having them review your accounting and reporting methodology periodically. CPAs can also prove invaluable in tax planning and investment strategies, but be sure to weigh that advice with that from other professional advisors such as your lawyer, broker, financial planner, or banker.

Locating an Outside Accounting Firm

How do you find a qualified CPA or accounting firm? Once again, by asking for referrals from business associates like your banker or your lawyer. Bankers can be extremely helpful in choosing an accounting firm. Most experienced commercial lenders have reviewed financial statements, and have had personal contact with a vast majority of the CPA firms in their area. They learn the good from the bad very quickly. Surprisingly, the level of service can vary dramatically among CPA firms, and usually with no decrease in the cost. Take the time to interview more than one referral, and hire a firm that has come both highly recommended and one that provides a high degree of comfort. Remember, poor accounting advice can oftentimes be more detrimental than no advice at all.

E. Evaluating Insurance Needs

The scope of your insurance needs will also be determined by the size and complexity of your business. Insurance needs can be broken into four major categories: life and hospitalization, property damage, personal injury, and business interruption. Let's discuss each of these areas on an individual basis to determine the types of coverages available, distinguish which might be applicable for your particular situation, and determine liability limit requirements.

E.1 Property Damage Coverage

Property damage could include protection for the business premises and its contents including inventory, equipment, and fixtures. Property insurance can be purchased to protect against fire loss, vandalism, theft, wind and rain damage, flood damage, and other natural disasters ranging from hurricanes to earthquakes. Certainly you will need most of these coverages, although natural disasters will be dependent upon geographic area and location, and can be extremely expensive or excluded in some instances. If you are renting or leasing, insurance requirements will normally be built into the terms of the lease. Those on a triple-net lease will have to shoulder the insurance requirements of the property owner.

Theft and Fraud Coverages

A word of caution: vandalism, burglary and theft may all be defined as separate coverages. Be sure any policy you bind includes coverages for all three definable areas. In some cases, these coverages will also exclude thefts by employees. This could necessitate additional coverage needs supplemented by a fidelity bond if employees will be handling large amounts of cash or expensive inventory. Those in this category may also wish to purchase fraud insurance to guard against customers or employees who may try to pass items like bad checks or credit cards.

Liability Limits for Property Coverages

To determine the liability limits required, simply estimate the replacement value of the assets to be covered. Coverages should carry liability limits at least equal to the replacement value of the insured assets. Also be sure to take seasonal requirements into consideration. For example, if your inventory fluctuates by season, make arrangements to carry a minimum liability equal to your highest inventory levels of the year. If possible, slide the limit to fit the season. Also, be sure the coverage applies to all locations, and to items in transit.

E.2 Personal Injury Coverages
Worker's Compensation
All employers are required by law to provide a safe working environment, hire and properly train competent employees, and install proper safety measures. Worker's Compensation coverage is also a governmental requirement to protect employees in the event of an injury on the job. Though the coverage is mandatory for all employers, you will have a choice as to whether to purchase the coverage from a private insurer or directly from the state government in which you do business.

For those of you purchasing Worker's Compensation from a private company, make sure the liability limits coincide with the state's minimum requirements. Additionally, make sure the limits are sufficient to cover the costs of law suits or catastrophic injuries that might arise as a direct result of an employee injury. Be sure also that the coverage extends beyond the boundaries of your physical location, if necessary, to cover employees during deliveries or during travel for business.

Business Interruption Coverage
Property insurance coverage will replace inventory or equipment in the event of, say, a fire, but what effect would a temporary closure resulting from that fire have on your operations? How would fixed expenses be paid, payroll requirements met, or loan payments maintained. Ongoing expenses and any anticipated profits can be insured and replaced through business interruption insurance. Determining liability limits for business interruption insurance should be as easy as reviewing your projection model. In the event of a catastrophe, business interruption insurance could be as important to your business's survival as property damage coverage. I would advise all of you to purchase and maintain both types of coverage.

Personal Injury Coverage
Personal injury coverage will be necessary for those who must insure against injury to customers or pedestrians. In some cases, product liability coverage may also be necessary to insure against injuries that might arise out of the use of your product. The limits of liability on these coverages must also allow for the possibility of catastrophic circumstances, be they medical injury bills or law suits demanding punitive damages.

E.3 Life and Hospitalization Coverage
Additional Employee Coverages

Life insurance coverage is a nice side benefit that usually adds little cost to the overall insurance bill unless, of course, the employee is in a high-risk situation. This isn't the case with medical coverages, however. Hospitalization, major medical, eye, and dental care are increasingly expensive coverages. Until recently, many larger employers historically provided these or a portion of these coverages as an employee benefit. The skyrocketing costs of medical coverages has made this practice all but obsolete.

Employers with fifty or more full-time employees are now required to provide affordable health coverage. Today, most employers only share in the cost, however, and employees are required to pay a portion of their premium through payroll deductions. Some employers are also manipulating the definition of a full-time employee, which is categorized by a thirty-hour or more work week, by limiting employees to twenty-nine or fewer hours a week. The fast-food industry is notorious for this practice.

To determine the extent of employee coverages needed, talk to your competitors, and study trade journals and research information. Attracting and keeping good employees necessitates benefits packages that match or exceed those offered by the competition. There could also be tax advantages for those of you who are incorporated. These will be discussed in chapter 17.

Malpractice Insurance

Those of you engaged in various professional endeavors will also require some type of malpractice coverage. This coverage is no longer the exclusive property of the medical profession, but also spills over to law and accounting. Again, liability limits for malpractice coverage need to be sufficient to cover lawsuits and punitive damage claims.

Those who must purchase malpractice insurance should discuss the need with other members of their profession, or places of contractual employment. Since malpractice insurance is possibly the most expensive coverage available, many professions are seeking less expensive alternatives. These include bonded programs and self-insurance plans. Be sure to weigh all of your alternatives before purchasing standard malpractice coverage.

Key Man Life Insurance

The death or disability of one or a few key persons, particularly in a small business, can severely impact the continued success of that business. As discussed earlier, this risk can be minimized by purchasing term life and possibly disability insurance for owners and key personnel. Dependent on the situation, coverage limits should be in amounts adequate to permit a smooth management transition or provide income to family members in the event the business must be closed or sold.

E.4 Choosing an Insurance Company

How do you choose an insurance company? Not always by the cheapest quote. After all, what good is coverage if the company isn't around when it comes time to pay on a claim. You will be safe with coverage from any of the major companies, but if an agent offers coverage from an unknown company, ask for ratings verification on that company.

There are several publications that rate insurance companies. The most popular is *Best's Insurance Guide*, which is used both by consumers and by investors. Your agent should be able to provide a one-page summary for any companies he or she recommends. I'd be suspicious if they can't provide one.

Best rates companies on a scale of A++ to F based on the financial strength and integrity of the insurance company. The scale includes six secure ratings:

- A++, A+ (Superior)
- A, A− (Excellent)
- B++, B+ (Good)

The scale also includes ten ratings for companies deemed "Vulnerable":

- B, B− (Fair)
- C++, C+ (Marginal)
- C, C− (Weak)
- D (Poor)
- E (Under Regulatory Supervision)
- F (In Liquidation)
- S (Rating Suspended)

Most commercial lenders will also have access to *Best's Guide,* and can share information too. They are also a good reference source for finding a reputable insurance broker.

I would strongly recommend obtaining two or three insurance quotes for your initial coverage. Prices can vary dramatically, and while I certainly don't prescribe to always taking the lowest quote, if that quote also included companies with A++ and A+ ratings, then yes, thank you very much. I would also advise each of you to purchase coverage in those areas that are directly applicable to your business. The extent and limits of those coverages will again differ under each circumstance. Use common sense when choosing areas of coverage. Though you don't want to be underinsured, excessive coverage will result in an unnecessary operating expense.

In addition to ensuring fair pricing, three quotes will provide you with three different perspectives on your insurance needs by three different insurance professionals. Utilize those perspectives to make a more educated final decision when deciding the limits and types of insurance bind.

F. Legal Assistance

Most of you will only need legal assistance on a limited basis. For most that will be at the initial purchase or start-up phase. Many of you will require an attorney to draft a partnership agreement, LLC, or articles of incorporation. Many will need assistance reviewing and drafting the conditions of a buy/sell agreement. For those in this category, it would not be cost effective to keep a legal firm on permanent retainer. I would, however, advise you to remain in contact with your attorney and, for those who incorporate to possible, appoint him or her to your board of directors.

Only those with larger and more complex businesses will need to place a legal firm on permanent retainer. These would include those who have numerous contractual agreements, be they with suppliers, customers, or employees. It will also include those of you engaged in endeavors with significant governmental or environmental impact, as well as those whose operation, product, or service could be subject to far-reaching legal liability.

Choosing an Attorney

Choosing an attorney is best done by referral. Most of you should have a friend or relative who's an attorney. If not, talk to your banker or accountant. Most lawyers and law firms tend to specialize in one or a few legal areas. If a legal acquaintance practices primarily in another area, he or she will still usually know lawyers to refer you to who are better suited to your needs. Make sure you chose an attorney who specializes in business law and, more specifically, in business formation and continuation.

G. Furthering Banking Relations

Larger commercial banks provide a host of services in addition to standard deposit and lending functions. These ancillary services can include issuing debit and credit cards, credit card merchant status, money management, and trust services including pension, profit sharing, and retirement planning. All of you will need at least one bank account initially, and as your business grows, so will your need for additional services. The sooner you develop a strong banking relationship, the better.

This is true even if those have been turned down for bank financing. A turndown shouldn't be viewed as a personal affront, but rather as the bank deeming your proposal too risky of an investment. There's good reason banks maintain high credit standards. Most of you will start off with a debt to worth ratio of four to one or less. A bank is leveraged to three times that extent. This leaves little margin for error when choosing investments, most of which are loans. And if you have been turned down, you can gain a certain level of satisfaction from proving their initial decision wrong, all the while using their other services to improve your own operating performance. Then, as your business grows in stature, so too will the number of services the bank will be amenable to place at your disposal.

Choosing a Banker

Choosing a bank or banker is like choosing any other professional. You want someone who is trustworthy, who you feel comfortable working with, and someone who will go to bat for you. Like all professional areas, referrals are the best source for finding the right banker or bank. A good banker's reputation will precede him or her. So too will a bank's areas of expertise. Most banks are proficient in only a few areas, so be sure to choose a bank whose strengths are suited to your needs.

You may also have to choose between an international bank, a national bank, a regional bank, and a local bank. In general, the services available rarely vary despite the size of the bank. There will be trade-offs, though. Relations are likely to be more personal at a smaller bank, and fee structures will be simpler to understand. Larger banks will tend to apply more analytical methodology to their approval processes. Smaller banks are likely to give a higher regard to a lender's gut instincts and the personality strengths of the customer.

Banks are also limited by their size as to how much they can lend to any one borrower, both in terms of a maximum and aggregate loan amounts. This could restrict with borrowing needs in the millions from utilizing a smaller bank. Larger banks would also be best for those with regional, national, and international business affairs. The size and scope of your business could be the best barometer for the size of the optimal bank.

H. Brokerage Firms

Banks have been traditionally conservative in the investment and trust areas, which often translates into lower than market investment returns. Those of you with larger investment portfolios or more discretionary income, if you haven't already, establish a brokerage account and perhaps a relationship with a financial planner. Take the time to investigate all of the investment alternatives at your disposal, and take an active part in managing your investments. Get to know the underlying securities, insurance coverages, and any guarantees for any investment or deposit account. Map out short and long-term investment strategies that are consistent with your situation and stage in life. Diversify your investments to limit risk. Coordinate your business goals to coincide with your current needs and your retirement goals.

I. Chapter Summary

Regardless of whether the accounting function falls upon your shoulders, your spouse's, an employee, an independent accounting firm, or a combination thereof, no business today can run effectively without proper accounting controls. There is accounting help available in every price range. Don't skimp on services because of budget limitations. Design the system that best optimizes your operations, and if need be, find creative solutions to institute it. The same holds true for insurance coverage. Don't let a minute pass without proper business and personal coverages. By the same token, purchase insurance based on an objective assessment of your needs. Professional associates are there to assist you. Learn to utilize them, as well as all of the resources at your disposal.

CHAPTER 16

Creating Credit and Inventory Policies

T his chapter will be devoted to forming credit and inventory policies. These policies will be your staff's guidelines for maintaining optimum levels of receivables and inventory, as established during our projection modeling process. Maintaining these projected operating levels will be essential in reaching your projections and optimizing cash flow.

A. Establishing a Credit Policy

Each of you will generate sales or revenues, but have you determined if you will extend credit and, if so, the terms of those credit sales? Have you determined the credit criteria by which a customer will be approved for credit or for establishing individual credit limits? Have you zeroed in on a system for recording payments, or collecting past due accounts? Establishing a uniform credit policy will require proceduralizing all of these areas and formulating them into one functional credit policy.

A.1 A Check Cashing Policy

Those of you who will accept checks in addition to cash will have to establish a check-approval process. You may want to establish a dual identification system requiring a driver's license and major credit card. You may want to add an additional step to include management approval. You may want to stipulate the customer's name, address, and phone number appear on the check, and that any missing information be copied onto the back of the check. You'll most likely want to establish a charge for returned checks. You may even have a register system that records and verifies checks automatically similar to those used in a grocery store. The system you choose is less important than having one, and making sure that your employees follow it systematically.

A.2 A Credit Card Policy

What about debit and credit cards? Which, if any, will you accept? Did you know that the bank or servicing company charges a fee for credit card transactions, anywhere from

0.25% to 6% of the transaction amount? Those of you who plan to accept credit cards should shop servicers' rates to obtain the lowest transaction rate possible. Be sure to factor in the cost, if any, for the processing equipment and any necessary supplies when comparing servicers' rates. You may also wish to stipulate a credit card approval process. You may want to stipulate a minimum sales amount for using credit cards, or possibly utilize the same identification process as in your check cashing policy. Again, having and following a uniform policy is your goal.

A.3 Establishing Credit Standards

Check cashing and credit card procedures are primarily systems for identifying the customer. In both instances, the customer's credit worthiness and repayment abilities will have been, for the most part, predetermined by the institution extending the service. Those of you who extend your own credit terms will not be afforded this underlying assurance. You can, however, develop a system for providing that assurance by modeling your credit standards after those utilized by financial institutions. The key to setting credit standards is to know your customer's repayment abilities and repayment habits prior to extending credit. For those of you dealing with large-ticket sales items, initial and periodic submission of financial statements should be part of the credit approval process.

The Credit Application

The credit approval process should begin with the completion of a credit application. Depending on the complexity and the cost of the transaction, your application could be as detailed as a bank loan application, or as limited as a grocery store checking cashing application. It should at least contain the desired credit limit, the applicant's name and address, social security or tax identification number, deposit accounts, major bank and credit-account information, and, if a corporation, a corporate authorization to borrow. Most importantly, the application must give authorization by the customer agreeing to the credit verification process. Standard credit applications can be purchased at most office supply stores, or downloaded from templates from programs such as Microsoft Office.

The Credit Investigation

The credit application will serve as the basis for your credit investigation.

The investigation should begin by obtaining an employer reference to help substantiate job stability and salary levels. The customer's bank and major creditors should also be contacted to verify deposit and credit accounts, and to establish a repayment history. A mortgage holder or landlord inquiry should also be an integral part of your investigation. All of this information will prove vital in establishing realistic credit limits and terms.

Credit Reporting Services

There are many formalized investigative reporting services that will appeal to some of you. Those of you whose customer base consists primarily of other companies can obtain formalized credit reports by subscribing to companies like Dun & Bradstreet or Equifax. Those whose customers are mostly individuals can subscribe to TransUnion, Experian, or Equifax directly, or utilize a third-party servicer. All of these companies will provide a credit history by account as well as a credit score based on an overall ratings scale. While credit reports can be crucial for the approval process, 75% of them contain some inaccuracies, so follow-up on any concerns with the customer directly. Any customer who is turned down because of information contained in a credit report must be notified to give them an opportunity to refute and correct any misinformation. It is also common practice to charge an application fee to cover the costs involved in the credit reporting process.

Requiring Financial Reports

Those of you whose customer base is primarily other companies may wish to require annual financial statements from customers to directly evaluate their financial position as part of the credit approval process. Those in this category can utilize the financial statements to provide a limited working-capital analysis, debt to worth determination and conduct a brief liquidity test. Statements should be submitted at least annually and, if possible, supplemented with the latest interim financial statement.

Establishing Customer Credit Limits

Once you have compiled all of the information for the credit investigation, you will need to assess it to make a determination on whether credit should be extended and, if so, to what extent. You will want to establish credit approval standards normally grounded in good payment histories, and a minimum overall credit score. You may also want to establish a maximum debt to income ratio to qualify repayment ability, or a minimum length of employment history. If sales or accounting personnel have input or a history with the customer, you will want to include them in the credit process as both will be directly affected by your determination.

For those customers deemed unworthy of credit, there are alternative measures you can use to try to keep them as customers. These include requiring personal guaranties, bank-issued letters of credit to guarantee payments, or even COD terms. Finally, when establishing credit terms, they will have to be compatible with those of the industry, those of your competition, and with your overall company policies.

Maintaining Customer Files

Those of you establishing credit standards should also maintain customer credit files as means for storing and documenting past and present credit decisions. You may wish to review and possibly revise credit terms for each customer on at least an annual basis. This review should be supplemented with a credit investigation update and, if required, the latest year end and interim financial statements.

A.4 Payment Terms for Credit Customers

If you offer credit sales, you will have to decide on the terms of those sales. This could be net thirty days, or possibly a 1% or 2% discount if paid within ten days. Those of you selling large ticket items may wish to extend terms of ninety days or longer. Most of you will also want to impose a 1% to 5% monthly penalty for late payments, or impose an interest charge for those on extended payment terms of six months or more. The longer the term, the more significant the negative impact on your cash flow and profitability. It's only fair that the customer share in that added expense. Let's take a moment to examine the impact of a customer paying late.

Say, for example, a past due or extended receivable of $50,000 necessitated your borrowing an equivalent amount on a thirty-day basis from your line of credit. The cost of you borrowing that money for thirty days at say 10% would be $416.67 ($50,000 × 0.10/ 12 months = $416.67). It's only fair that the customer responsible for you having to borrow should have to pay a penalty or an interest charge at least equal to your additional costs. By comparison, a 1% monthly late fee on $50,000 would net you a return of $500, and a 2% late fee a return of $1,000.

A Cost of Doing Business

Before you begin counting the money you might net from interest charges and penalties, I must warn you, they are extremely difficult to collect, even from otherwise well-intentioned customers. Additionally, if your credit terms are more restrictive than your competitors, those terms and their enforcement could result in lost sales. There are situations when you will be forced to absorb the increased costs of a late-paying customer or risk losing that customer altogether. This is commonly referred to as a cost of doing business.

If you find yourself in this situation, define those costs and include them in your projection scenario. In this way the effects will be known and can be budgeted into your operating plan. If you find a customer squeezing your profitability too significantly, I would suggest raising the price for that customer even at the risk of losing them.

Some of you may also find yourself at the mercy of much larger companies as customers. Companies like US Steel, for example, have a history of purposely extending their creditors payment terms to improve their own cash-flow positions. The burden of borrowing to supplement cash flow is then shifted to you, the smaller company who can usually less afford to pay the interest costs, but can ill-afford to do without the customer's business. In this situation too, it's best to predefine your costs rather than fly blindly into the night.

Customer Communications

This situation doesn't have to be the norm when dealing with slow-paying customers or larger clients. If that customer has a need for your product or service and respects your abilities to produce it, they may be willing to pay more promptly if confronted in a sensible manner. As with employees, communication is the key to happy customer relations. If you have a need for prompter payments, discuss it and try to arrive at an amenable solution. Don't expect your customers to anticipate your needs. They have enough concerns of their own.

Selling Customer Contracts

Those of you selling large ticket items like electronics, appliances, jewelry, motorized vehicles, or industrial equipment have another possible credit solution, selling the contract to a third party. Many manufactures maintain subsidiaries to purchase and finance installment sales contracts from their distributors. Many banks and finance companies such as GMAC or General Electric Credit Corporation also private this service to unrelated third parties. In most cases, there will be little or no cost to you, as the underlying customer will pay interest on the installment sale directly to the lender. Third-party contracts are a great way to free up your cash flow and increase your sales volume, while offering yet another sales alternative to your customer base.

A.5 Recording Credit Accounts
The Customer List

We have discussed the terms of payment and the conditions for extending credit; now let's establish a system for sending out bills and recording payments. The first order of business will be to complete a customer list. This is simply an alphabetical listing of your customers by name, address, and phone number, as well as the contact information for the owners or key contacts. You may also find it beneficial to compile a potential customer list for those you would like to add to your customer base. Customer lists will prove invaluable not only for billing purposes, but for collection activity and sales promotions.

The Invoice

Recording sales presents another problem. Are your sales transacted over the counter; by a sales or distribution network; by telephone, mail, or Internet; or a combination thereof? Will you also have to coordinate product shipment with billing? In most cases, sales will be registered on an invoice or sales receipt. In the event that other operating functions must be coordinated with the credit function, the invoice should be made out in duplicate or multiplies.

The invoice should provide a detailing of the purchase. It should list the date of purchase, the items purchased or services rendered the price per item or service, a subtotal, any tax charge, and finally a total sales amount. You may also wish to include columns for previous balances and past due amounts. In addition to the customer information, you will also want to include your company's name, address, phone number, and website address prominently at the top, as well as include any payment terms and remittance instructions. Sample invoices can be purchased at any office supply store. They can also be designed from templates in Microsoft Office or accounting programs like Peachtree and Quicken.

The Billing Function

It will be up to each of you to determine a central gathering place for completed invoices, both those used for cash and credit sales. Again, depending upon the size of your organization, this could be with your bookkeeper, accounts receivable clerk, or on your desk. This person in turn will be responsible for bookkeeping entries, mailing or e-mailing invoices, and possibly recording payments. You must also determine the frequency for mailing invoices, most often monthly. Remember that the quicker you bill, the soon you will receive payments, although competitor practices and industry standards play a factor.

Ledger Cards

For those of you whose accounting system isn't fully computerized, you may want to keep a ledger card for each active client. This is simply a listing of each transaction, both purchases and payments to an individual customer's account. Ledger card transactions are listed by date and amount, possibly including the payment method, and include a running outstanding balance. If any of you are utilizing a pegboard or one-write manual accounts receivable system, the ledger card can be included as one of the carbons. The ledge card can also be helpful in compiling invoices and scheduling collection efforts.

A.6 Collection Procedures

Usually collection activities should begin by the thirty-day past due stage. For businesses like property management, collection procedures often begin as quickly as ten days past due. You'll want to start the process with a polite reminder notice or e-mail, graduated to a more formal letter or series of letters, supplemented with telephone inquiries. For the chronic delinquent, legal threats and eventual legal action might be necessary. A collection agency may also prove a necessary alternative for the most chronic delinquents.

If and when collection procedures are mandated, there will be the added question of when to discontinue or restrict further sales to that customer, possibly place them on COD terms. As discussed earlier, communications are essential. Try and determine reasons for the customer getting behind and try to work out amenable solutions. Try to exact a payment plan or promise from the customer, and follow up if they don't adhere to that plan. Again, while credit and collection policies will be different for each of you, it is essential to establish them, train your employees to understand and follow them and to take appropriate action when they breakdown.

A.7 Management Credit Reports
The Monthly Accounts Receivables Listing
The final area of credit policy will be management reporting. I would recommend a minimum of two reports to be compiled on a monthly basis. The first is a month-end accounts-receivable listing, detailed by the customer, contact information, and out-standing balance. This will be helpful in reviewing overall receivables and in calculating the receivables turnover rate and the number of days receivable on hand. These results can then be compared to past statements, your projections, or the RMA statement studies to provide an accurate measurement of the success of these operational areas. It can also alert you to policy changes that might be required.

The Accounts Receivable Aging
The second report I would strongly recommend is a monthly accounts receivable aging. I'm sure you will recall, this too is a listing of outstanding receivables by customer, but for-matted by those who are current, thirty, sixty, ninety days, and over past due. This report will apprise you of what amounts and percentages of your company's receivables are past due, and by whom. This report will prove instrumental to your collection efforts. It can also be helpful in your working-capital planning, evaluating customer credit standings, and determining which receivables should be deemed uncollectible for accounting purposes.

Additional Sales and Credit Reports
Those of you with more complex needs can devise a multitude of reports from credit and sales data. Some of you may wish a listing of past-due accounts by a salesperson, for example, to determine if that employee is too lackadaisical in adhering to credit policy. Or you may want a listing of sales by product or service to help identify and track your best-selling items or help project gross profit margins. There are as many ways to compile data as there are identifiable needs. Each of you will have to evaluate your own requirements, and then design reports that compile quantifiable data into the most use-ful informational formats to assist with you operational planning.

A Final Credit Policy Reminder

Credit policy can sometimes result in internal strife. A sales force will often seek less restrictive credit controls than an accounting department. Under such circumstances, it will be up to you to affect an amicable solution, and to ensure that all parties abide by that solution. When formulating any area of credit policy, keep in mind, though the happiness of your employees is certainly a priority, your primary concern will be the profitable and orderly continuation of your business.

B. Inventory Controls

We have partially discussed inventory on several occasions. It's time now to tie those discussions together, and formulate them into a standardized inventory policy that includes supplier relations, determining optimal inventory levels, and establishing inventory controls. Those who are manufacturers will also want to establish quality control methods to ensure a standardized and reliable finished product. Controls should also be instituted to discourage theft or waste.

At the cost of sounding repetitious, we cannot overemphasize the importance of inventory controls and their relationship to profitability. This presupposes you have inventory, but even those who don't will have many of the same procedural requirements. Motel owners for example will in effect have an inventory of rooms. These will require a scheduling procedure to optimize the total number of rooms occupied at any one time, particularly during peak seasonal periods. Those of you who are professionals will have to determine work flows and the time restraints involved in completing your particular service, like a manufacturer, if you wish to effectively manage time and costs.

B.1 Establishing Supplier Relations

Naturally before you can sell a product, you must first stock or manufacture it. This requires establishing relations with suppliers to purchase raw materials or finished goods. The professional and servicer will also have to establish supplier relations. The motel operator will need furnishings, linens, and possibly food purveyors. The professional will need office supplies and furnishing and possibly specialized equipment. Regardless of the industry, every business will have to establish and maintain buying standards.

Direct and Indirect Supply Sources

There are two general types of suppliers: direct and indirect. As the name implies, direct sources are those producing and selling a product such as manufacturers, mines, and farmers. Indirect sources are those who act as a middle person like wholesalers, jobbers, and brokers. Neither type should be considered preferential. Rather, explore all sources to determine which can provide the best assortment and highest quality of products or raw materials at the fairest price. Consideration should be given to variables like transportation methods and costs, delivery schedules, and support services, in addition to pricing.

Terms of Sale

Terms of purchase will be another important consideration when choosing suppliers, particularly to those working on limited budgets. Most suppliers will offer discounts often from 1% to 5%, for paying within a reasonable term, usually from net ten days to net thirty days, depending upon the industry. Some suppliers will even offer dating terms ranging from ninety days to six months as an added incentive for purchasing their products. This occurs frequently for seasonal type products such as those sold at Christmas or perhaps in the spring or fall. The savings or hidden costs of any such programs will be discussed during our quantity discount discussion later in this section.

Locating and Developing Suppliers

Though suppliers or their salespeople will eventually call on you, it will be up to you to make the initial contact. This will be most important to those starting their own business, since a network of suppliers will not as yet have been established. Initial relationships can be cultivated at trade shows and conventions, through trade publications, and in discussions with out-of-area competitors. As with other professional services, recommendations are advisable whenever possible.

As you develop relationships with suppliers remember the "golden rule," "treat your suppliers as you would expect your customers to treat you." Always deal with them in a friendly and honest manner, and pay your bills on time. Viable supplier relationships will be extremely important to the success of your business, and at times when special considerations might be required such as having to return defective merchandise or if a specialty order is needed.

Suppliers as Informational Sources

It's also important to remember that suppliers are often better informed about product developments, changes in customer buying trends, and other economic factors that might affect your business. The better your relations with suppliers, the more likely they are to keep you abreast of trends affecting the industry. Also, try to establish relations with a number of suppliers. This will enable you to stay abreast of optimal pricing opportunities, and keep you from being dependent on one or a few select suppliers.

C. Establishing Inventory Procedures

Inventory controls should begin when an order is placed. Many of you may wish to incorporate the ordering function with the inventory logging procedures. Others may wish to utilize a separate order form to list the date, items, and quantity of merchandise purchased, as well as from whom it was ordered and the expected delivery date. Procedural steps should also include steps on who can place orders, from whom, in what quantity and at what price. Again, the size and complexity of your business and the abilities of your staff will be key factors in determining your policy requirements.

Supplemental Logging Procedures

When an existing business is being purchased, a physical inventory count should be conducted on the date of transfer as a condition of the buy/sell agreement. All of you, both in the purchase and start-up phase, should update the inventory log with a physical inventory count at least on an annual basis. The physical inventory count can be a slow and tedious process, but it is a necessary step to ensure the continued accuracy of the inventory log, and to help appraise the need to write down or delete lost, stolen, misplaced, or obsolete items.

Those with separate logging functions will also find it helpful to list reorder points directly on the log to help keep abreast of reordering requirements. The manufacturer's inventory log should also list quantities reserved, and should be supplemented with a subtotaling of raw materials, work in process, and finished goods. Though the logging process is a fairly simple procedure, don't regard it too lightly. An accurate and current inventory log is the key to maintaining proper inventory controls.

The Professional's Time Log

A professional's or servicer's time log is a lot like a manufacturer's inventory log. Your knowledge represents the raw materials, and the time needed to complete a project represents the time it takes to manufacture a finished good. Accurately forecasting time requirements and measuring time utilization will be vital to controlling your costs and effectively pricing your services rendered.

Inventory Storage and Verification

Many of you will require inventory storage procedures to assure optimal inventory life and turnover ratios. Those in the shoe business, for example, will have to be concerned with storage by gender, style, color, as well as by size. A grocer will be more concerned with the date the merchandise arrives and possibly expires when proceduralizing inventory controls. Those of you with raw materials or products that require special handling will have additional considerations. While these areas were discussed during location requirements, special logging and accounting procedures may also be needed to help ensure effective inventory turnover and controls.

Many of you will also have to coordinate shipping, receiving, and payments to suppliers. In all cases, this can be accomplished by giving a copy of the invoice to the appropriate accounting person, and by verifying the quantity and price of the items received match the initial order. The items should also be inspected for defects and any possible damage that may have occurred during shipping.

Account Payable Payment Procedures

As with accounts receivable, procedures will have to be instituted for paying accounts payable. The system design will be very similar to a receivables system. Bills will have to be logged by the appropriate person, bookkeeping entries performed, and payments made. Ledger cards could be beneficial here too for those few without a computerized accounting system. Procedures will have to be established on who can pay the bills, the timing for those payments, whether or not to take advantage of discounts and whether or not to withhold payments if a bill is in dispute. Again, the level of proceduralization will depend on the size and complexity of the business.

C.1 Determining Inventory Requirements

There is a fine line between too much and too little inventory on hand. You could carry a large enough inventory so as never to run short, but this would dramatically add to the costs of carrying your inventory. These costs could easily reach 30% of your initial inventory costs when taking into consideration obsolescence, insurance, storage, and possibly interest costs. You could minimize these hidden costs by carrying fewer inventories, but that creates the added concern of not having enough inventories on hand to fulfill orders promptly. This could lead to lower sales volumes and even the loss of customers.

The Optimal Inventory Level

The optimal inventory level is one that turns over often enough to minimize carrying costs, while providing enough of a cushion to cover seasonal needs and specialty orders. How is this optimal level determined? Believe it or not, optimal inventory levels have already been defined within the context of the cash budget in your short-term projections. For our sample, Superior Jewelry, we decided upon a 194-day supply. Those with more than one product will also have to define the optimal inventory mix by determining the optimal inventory level for product or category.

Ordering Intervals

Determining when to order is also a simple procedure. Begin by determining the quantity of each product used and the time it takes to place and receive an order for that product. Next, choose the amount of each product you would like to maintain on hand. Combining these two figures will give you your reordering point. Remember to include seasonal considerations too. For some of you this might necessitate establishing seasonal and off-season reordering points.

Quantity Discounts

There may be cost advantages to purchasing in quantity, which should also be taken into consideration when determining ordering procedures. The effectiveness of quantity discounts can be measured by comparing the savings they generate against the cost of utilization. If, for example, the money used to purchase inventory would be earning interest in a money market account, compare the amount of interest income lost, plus any hidden costs, against the offsetting discount.

Conversely, cost savings through volume purchasing could also make it advantageous to borrow, at times, to purchase inventory. Again, measure the discounted saving against the interest and carrying costs to make this determination. Keep in mind though, the risk of inventory obsolescence will be greater when purchasing in volume.

C.2 Management Reporting

The Inventory List

An inventory assessment on at least a monthly basis is essential for effective inventory management. Those in retailing and wholesaling may even wish to complete an accounting on a weekly or daily basis, or as a part of the ordering process. This is best accomplished by means of an inventory listing, which simply tabulates the date an item is received, its cost, the number on hand, the number of each item sold during the period, and the optimal number to be stocked.

The inventory listing can help appraise the accuracy of your inventory procedures. It can also help to determine when write-downs, mark-downs, and sales promotions are needed. This information can be combined with operational data from other areas as well to measure the efficiency of key departments or personnel in the production, purchasing, and sales areas. Again, operational data can be compiled in any number of ways to best suit your requirements.

D. Chapter Summary

Building and reducing inventory levels in accordance with seasonality will require purchasing and selling decisions be made far in advance of those seasonal periods. Again, effective planning is the key. Though distinctively different in nature, credit and inventory controls should be considered as interdependent functions. All the sales in the world won't make a company profitable unless they are optimally priced, collected in a timely manner, and accomplished under a controlled expense environment. Costs of goods sold, by their variable nature, are those costs that have the greatest impact on profitability, often to as great an extent as increasing sales volume itself. Don't examine one without considering the other.

PART VI
MONEY, PLANNED EXPANSION, AND BEYOND

CHAPTER 17

Conserving the Wealth

I've always been dismayed when movies span time with subtitles. Every time I see "six months" or "three years later" flash across the screen, I can't help but think of subtler ways to get the point across. I now find myself in a similar position, and for lack of a cleverer approach, let's just say it's "eight months later." We will further assume your first eight months of business proved modestly successful, and that you are still trending upward.

Everything seems to be rolling along smoothly. For the first time since you began this quest, you can actually sit back and catch your breath. Though you're not yet rolling in dough, you are showing a profit. You've even accumulated some excess profits, which your banker, broker, accountant, and insurance agent would all like to invest. The sudden attention is kind of flattering, but also a bit confusing. This chapter will be devoted to minimizing that confusion through discussions on money management, tax planning, pension, and profit-sharing programs and estate planning.

A. Effective Money Management

Just as too much inventory can slow the working-capital cycle, too much cash in non-interest bearing accounts can result in money mismanagement and unrealized profits. Though large corporations have been investing excess cash for decades, money management is a fairly recent discovery for the small and midsized business. The reason is twofold. Competitive pressures have forced banks and brokerage firms to lower minimum deposit requirements for certain interest-bearing accounts, and the computation of the accounting function has enabled smaller firms to utilize the same sophisticated cash-management tools previously only available to much larger firms.

Let's examine how larger corporations invest their excess cash to see if we can employ similar strategies. Microsoft, for example, is currently sitting on about $100 million in excess cash. Only a little over $2 million of that cash, or 2%, is sitting in general operating accounts. Over half, roughly $51.7 million is invested in cash equivalents and short-term investments. A third, roughly $31.7 million is invested in US government and agency securities. Another $12 million is invested in corporate notes and bonds, and the remaining $2 million is invested in mortgage-backed securities. Most large firms employ similar cash-management strategies. You should too.

A.1 General Operating Funds
Minimum Operating Cash Requirements

To determine how much you can invest, you must first determine how much cash we be needed to comfortably maintain operations. To do this, you must determine how much working capital is necessary to meet your company's ongoing operating expenses, taking into account any seasonal requirements. This calculation has already been completed in our short-term projection model. Another easy method is to divide the past year's total operating expenses by twelve to give you a monthly average. In either case, a minimum of two months' worth of operating expenses should be devoted to your general operating accounts. Any, balances above those minimums can be considered excess cash.

A.2 Excess Cash Accumulations

Keep in mind, you can increase the amount of interest income earned by maximizing the amount of time monies are held in an interest-bearing account. For example, when you mail a check to a supplier or creditor, there will be a few days before that check is actually drawn against your account. Utilize that float time to your advantage by holding those monies in investment accounts for two or three extra days to help maximize investment returns. Additionally, if you are saving money for a specific purpose like to pay off a note to a previous owner or for a down payment to purchase additional equipment, match the timing of those needs to investment maturity dates to help maximize investment returns.

Maximizing Cash Investment Returns

There are two main strategies you need to uphold when it comes to investing excess business cash. First, you need to invest the money in relatively safe investments. Your objective is to increase profits through interest and investment income. Losing money on more speculative investments will have a negative impact that few of you can absorb. Second, you'll need to keep the funds as liquid as possible so they can be accessed to meet operating expenses, if necessary. The last thing you'll want at this stage is to have cash available that you can't utilize because of mismatched maturity dates or other illiquidity factors. Your goal will be to generate the highest possible return on the excess funds within these two aforementioned parameters.

Business Money Market Accounts and Mutual Funds

Every business will require at least one general checking account. Sole proprietorships will have an advantage in this area because they are treated like individual consumers in this regard, and are able to open money-market checking accounts with unlimited check writing ability. Those in this category that can afford the minimum deposit requirement, typically $1,500, may want to utilize this type of account as your general checking account.

Partnerships and corporations are also eligible for money-market accounts, but these carry limitations. They typically allow only three withdrawals by check a month. You can, however, make deposits as often as you wish. Some of you may find this type of account useful by depositing all of your funds into it, and then by formulating a withdrawal strategy to transfer funds to your general operating account at three key times each month.

The money-market accounts and business mutual funds offered by most banks are typically insured up to $250,000 per depositor by the Federal Deposit Insurance Corporation (FDIC). While interest rates are admittedly, at historic lows, more importantly, the accounts offer maximum liquidity.

Time Certificates

You can greatly increase interest income by choosing investment vehicles with longer maturity dates when possible. The most popular of these is the certificates of deposit (CDs). These are a good option for relatively large sum of excess cash that you know you won't need for at least three to six months. CDs generally pay a higher rate of interest than a business mutual fund or money-market account, but you'll also sacrifice some liquidity, so again make sure you won't need the money before the CD matures. Though the rates paid on CDs usually increase as the maturity rate lengthens, occasionally market conditions can force shorter term rates higher. Be sure to compare rates throughout the maturity spectrum to capitalize on the highest rate obtainable before making your investment decision.

Business Sweep Accounts

As the name implies, these are bank accounts that automatically "sweep" excess funds above a target minimum balance into short-term or overnight investment vehicles. Funds are then swept back into your checking account as needed to cover operating expenses. The beauty of a sweep account is that all of this is done automatically, enabling you to easily maximize your return on excess funds. Many smaller banks don't have the sophistication to offer sweep accounts. Those who would like to utilize this service will likely be forced to deposit with a regional, national, or international bank.

Federal Issues

The federal government has its own series of accounts that can be purchased on denominations ranging from $1,000 up to a limit of $5 million. The most popular of these is the Treasury Bills, which offers maturity dates of up to one year. The second option is Treasury Notes, which are similar, but are issued with maturity dates of two, three, five, or ten years. For long-term investors, the federal government offers Treasury Bonds with maturities of thirty years.

All of these issues can be purchased online from the government at TreasuryDirect. Most corporate purchases, however, purchase them on the secondary market through their bank or broker. Most fixed-income mutual funds own Treasuries, some own Treasuries exclusively. There are also exchange-traded funds (ETFs) that track Treasuries without owning them.

Treasuries may offer a higher yield than business CDs due to the longer timeframe, but again, you have to consider your company's potential liquidity needs. Also, if interest rates rise in the future as many are predicting, the value of your bond may fall. Interest rate sensitivity is a consideration that must be factored into the decision process for any mid and longer term investments.

Another popular federal issue is a series of instruments administered by the Farmers Home Administration. They offer both variable and fixed rate instruments with a minimum investment of $1,000 and maturity dates ranging from overnight to ten years. Often these pay a little more interest than Treasury instruments. They too can be purchased through most regional, national, and international banks.

Repurchase Agreements

The money market accounts and CDs offered by most banks are generally insured by the FDIC up to a maximum of $250,000. Larger banks also offer alternatives to time deposits known as Repurchase Agreements. These are not federally insured, but they usually pay a higher interest rate than CDs. These are accounts in which the bank will buy long-term certificates issued by another institution, usually the federal government, and then resell shorter term participations in those same certificates. What makes "Repos" so attractive is they can be purchased with maturity dates as short as overnight. Minimum deposit amounts are usually $1,000.

Bankers' Acceptance and Commercial Paper

Two similar accounts are bankers' acceptance and commercial paper. These too are longer term certificates that are purchased by the bank, who in turn resells shorter term participations. The difference is the issuer—bankers' acceptances are issued by larger banks and commercial papers, or certificates are issued by larger corporations. These generally carry maturity dates ranging from a minimum of 14 days to a maximum of 270 days. Minimum deposit requirements are typically much higher than with other investment alternatives, and because they are not federally insured, their degree of safety would parallel the investor's faith in the issuer.

A.3 Additional Cash Considerations

Though I would urge all of you to maximize your interest and investment income, there will be times when there will be better uses for your money. Cash utilization should be planned with an eye toward maximizing operational benefits and minimizing the overall income tax burden. Operational considerations such as purchasing new equipment, deferred maintenance requirements, and planned expansion, which will be discussed in the next chapter, must all be factored into your cash investment scenario. The remainder of this chapter will be focused on reducing your income liability, and planning for your personal financial security.

B. Tax Planning

Visions of your first year's income-tax liability should come into play at about the tenth month of operation or your first relaxing moment, whichever comes first. This will also be the time to institute a tax planning or reduction program. The lower your profits, the lower your tax liability, and of course, profits can be lowered by increasing expenses or by reducing revenues. I apologize if this seems too simplistic, but that in a nutshell is the basic premise behind effective tax planning.

Those of you utilizing outside accountants should get a call ninety days before your year end to discuss tax planning. If you don't, I would strongly suggest you initiate that call, and perhaps review the competency level of your accounting firm.

B.1 Fiscal Year-End Adjustments
Forestalling the Recognition of Income

All of you will have sales occurring near the end of each taxable year, which could be legally deferred until the next taxable year, provided you are on an accrual tax reporting system. A simple example would be a retailer who forestalls the billing and delivery of orders placed during the last week of the taxable year until the following week. Lowering revenues in this manner will directly lower pretax profit and the subsequent income-tax liability. True, the revenue deferred will have to be declared the next taxable year, but at least that gives you time to plan additional tax reduction strategies; and it defers having to pay any corresponding tax liability for up to 12 more months.

Accruing and Prepaying Expenses

You can also increase year end expenses by using similar rationale.

Planning a January inventory purchase? You may wish to consider making that purchase in December instead so that you can expense that purchase during the current fiscal year. The same holds true for any year end operating expenses including bonuses or pension contributions. Expense whatever you can during the last month of the taxable year, even if you have to accrue the payment of that expense. Depending upon the expense, you will have from 30 to 90 days after the year end to pay it for tax reporting purposes. If you have excess cash, you may even want to consider prepaying expenses like insurance premiums or interest expense again to lower profitability and the corresponding income tax liability.

While accruing and prepaying expenses will lower overall profitability and the resulting tax liability, these are more crash than planned tax savings strategies. Their benefits are short-lived because they are merely deferring income or accelerating deductions until the following year. Now let's look at programs which can provide long range tax benefits, both for the company and its owners.

B.2 Indirect Compensation

The term indirect compensation refers to tax deductible business expenses which provide increased personal benefit to the owners and/or employees of a company without increasing their personal tax liabilities. These deductions are available to proprietorships, partnerships and corporations alike; however, the benefits are intended for employees. There are restrictions for owner participation for those of you operating as a proprietorships or partnerships. For those of you considering indirect compensation programs, it would be highly advantageous to incorporate as these restrictions are lifted for owners of corporations who draw salaries.

Indirect compensation can include non-cash benefits such as contributions for medical insurance, life insurance, retirement accounts and other employee services. They can also include country club and business organizations memberships and dues, business-related travel expenses, business-related meals, tuition reimbursement and entertainment, and the cost of trade shows and seminars.

Company Cars

Company cars or a car allowance is another important indirect compensation category for many of you to consider. Company can provide a host of ancillary tax expense benefits like the cost of gas, oil, repairs and maintenance, and insurance. Lease payments or interest on any loans to purchase company vehicles are also tax deductible, and the company can take full advantage of any investment tax credits available as well as allowable depreciation.

Deferred Compensation

Deferred compensation refers to a contractual arrangement between an employer and an employee, which stipulates a predetermined portion of that employee's salary be withheld until a later date, quite often retirement. Under a deferred compensation program, the employer receives the full advantage of expensing the salary, but the employee doesn't have to pay taxes on the deferred portion until it is received. This can provide a tangible tax savings to employees nearing retirement age, and to owners who may not need the benefit of their entire salary, but would like to utilize the business deduction. This program is only available to corporations.

B.3 Real Property Purchases

Most of the benefits associated with company cars apply to the purchase of any fixed asset. These include possible investment tax credits, depreciation, loan interest or lease expenses, insurance costs, and the costs of repairs and maintenance. Imagine the tax savings you can generate from the business owning its own operating premises just in mortgage interest and depreciation alone. There is even a way to double your pleasure, and that is to buy the fixed asset personally, then lease or rent it back to the company. This of course will require the company to be a separate entity, preferably a corporation.

The Purchase/Lease Back Arrangement

The purchase and leaseback will allow you to deduct the normal operating expenses of maintaining that fixed asset from your personal income taxes. You will also be able to deduct depreciation, interest costs, and take advantage of any investment tax credits offered. Likewise, the business can deduct any amounts paid to you in rent or lease payments as well as the cost of any leasehold improvements.

True, you will have to report the rental payments as income, but in most cases that will not exceed the mortgage interest and depreciation expense, at least for the first few years. There should be more than enough discretionary tax savings between these and other building expense deductions to shelter at least a part of your salary. Additionally, rent payments and other expenditures can be adjusted upward or downward through changes in the lease agreement depending upon who needs the benefit of the added expense.

There is another consideration here as well. The owner of a fixed asset will derive the most tax benefits during the first few years of ownership since this is when interest and depreciation will be at their highest. You can capitalize on this benefit twice by selling the asset to the company once you have derived those initial benefits personally. In this way you can start the depreciation process over again and, depending upon the financing arrangements, possibly the interest expense as well.

C. Pension and Profit-Sharing Programs

There are no laws requiring an employer to establish or maintain a pension or profit-sharing program, and most recently formed companies will not be able to afford one. However, once you reach the stage where profits exceed operating needs, a pension and profit-sharing program will become a viable alternative for a portion of your excess profits. Normally this stage will occur at the three to five-year juncture.

Pension and profit-sharing programs can prove a major benefit to both owners and employees. They can serve to improve employee performance and morale by providing the added security of accumulated retirement benefits. If structured properly, they can be funded primarily from income-tax dollars and in this way provide a major tax shelter as well. There are a number of programs available that can be tailored to fit almost any circumstance. Let's discuss each type individually to better determine which, if any, suit your needs.

C.1 Proprietorships and Partnerships
IRAs, Roth IRAs, and SEPs

The most elementary form of retirement account is the Individual Retirement Account (IRA). IRAs are available to all who work, including those who are self-employed, and they can be established and funded by either the employee or the employer. There are two types of IRAs available to individuals: Traditional and Roth.

Traditional IRAs are a good choice for those who are seeking a tax deduction now, whose income is too high to be eligible for a Roth IRA, or who expects to be in a lower tax bracket at retirement. Roth IRAs are a good choice if you are seeking tax-free withdrawals in retirement, if you want to avoid required minimum distributions beginning at age seventy and a half, or you feel you will be in the same or a higher tax bracket at retirement. With either type, contributions can be made up to $5,500 a year if you are less than fifty years old, and up to $6,500 a year if you are fifty and over. In either case, the funds in the IRA can be invested in many types of investments including stocks, bonds, and mutual funds.

IRAs established by an employer are known as Simplified Employee Pension Individual Retirement Arrangement (SEP), and they can be used to fund retirement accounts for owners and employees. Employers can contribution up to 25% of an employee's salary into an SEP account up to an annual limit of $53,000.

Keogh Accounts

A Keogh plan is another popular tax-deferred retirement account for the self-employed and unincorporated businesses. There are two types of Keogh plan: a defined-benefit plan, and a defined-contribution plan. In a defined-contribution plan, a fixed contribution is made each pay period. The defined-benefits plan is more complex. It relies on an IRS formula to calculate the rate of contributions. As in other types of retirement plans, the funds in the plan can be invested in many types of investments. Like the SEP plan, contribution levels can be much higher for a Keogh than an IRA. Employer contributions can be up to 25% of an employee's salary up to $53,000 annually.

Keogh plans are best for individuals with a high level of income. They do require much more administrative paperwork than IRAs and SEPs, though. While most small business owners can set up and manage IRAs and SEPs themselves, Keogh plans require professional help to establish. In recent years, they've been largely replaced by SEPs, which have the same contribution limits but much less paperwork.

C.2 Corporate Preferred Plans

Retirement plans available to corporations come in three general categories: pension plans, profit-sharing plans, and employee ownership or trust plans. Each of these plans must cover a general cross-section of employees, and any employee age twenty-five or older with a minimum of three years of service must be included. Salaried owners are of course eligible.

These plans can be wholly funded by the employer but more frequently provide an opportunity for an employer to match the contributions of the employee up to a fixed limit. The concept of matching affords the employer another advantage, a vesting period. This creates a lock-in time frame, whereby an employee isn't entitled to all the contributions until he or she satisfies a preestablished waiting period. This is often regarded as a "golden handcuff" as employees are penalized if they do not stay with the employer until the vesting period has expired, usually three to five years.

Common Tax Advantages

Although each of the three plan types has limitations on the maximum allowable annual contribution, all of them are considered "qualified" by the IRS, meaning the contributions are tax deductible. For all, contributions are formulated on a pre-tax basis, and the earnings within the plan grow tax deferred. Likewise, employees pay no tax liability on their contributions until they are withdrawn. In the event of an employee's death, distributions are excluded from estate taxes, provided beneficiaries do not receive the proceeds in one lump sum. The similarities between these three types of plans end there, however, making it necessary to discuss each individually.

C.3 Pension Plans

Pension plans come in two broad categories: Defined Contribution Plans and Defined Benefits Plans. Under both types, contributions are fixed and based upon a predetermined formula. The formula is based upon the amount of contribution necessary to accumulate the predetermined retirement benefit. Contributions must be made annually, but they can be accrued and funded the following year if necessary. Additionally, excess contributions can be paid during periods of higher profitability and deducted in later years.

Defined Benefit Plans

A Defined Benefit Pension Plan is exactly what the name implies. The employer makes all of the contributions, and the employee receives a fixed monthly benefit at retirement. The amount of the monthly benefit is based on the employees' salary level and years of service. All investment decisions are made by the employer, and the employee has no control over the funds until reaching retirement age.

Defined benefit pension plans used to be the most common type of employer-sponsored retirement plan, at least until the 1970s. Today they are fairly rare, and most have been replaced by defined contribution plans.

Defined Contribution Plans

Defined Contribution Plans are the most popular corporate plans today, and the 401(k) plan is by far the most popular type. With Defined Contribution Plans, the contribution is the predetermined factor in the calculation formula, and not the benefit amount. Contributions are funded primarily by the employee, but often employers participate with at least a partial matching contribution. The employee also chooses which of the investments offered by the 401(k) plan in which he or she can invest his or her contributions. The employee also has complete control over the proceeds upon reaching retirement.

Should an employee withdraw the funds prior to retirement, those funds can be rolled over either into a traditional IRA or into the 401(k) plan of another employer, without incurring taxes or early withdrawal penalties.

Any funds withdrawn, but not rolled over into another qualified plan, will be subject to ordinary income taxes as well as a 10% early withdrawal penalty. Annual contributions are limited to $18,000 if the employee is under age fifty. There is a catch-up provision allowing additional contributions of $6,000 for those fifty year and older.

Another alternative is the Roth 401(k) plan. These provide the benefits of a regular Roth IRA, but the employee contributions are the same as those for a regular 401(k) plan. The main advantage to this plan is that distributions are tax-free, at fifty-nine and half years of age, as long as the employee has been in the plan for at least five years. Employers can offer a partial match on a Roth 401(k) too, but the employer's contribution must be placed into a regular 401(k).

C.4 Profit-Sharing Plans

A Deferred Profit-Sharing Plan (DPSP) is a plan that gives employees a participation in the profits of a company. This is a great way to reward employees while instilling a sense of pride and ownership. Another advantage is, there is no predetermined contribution requirement. Instead, the employer determines when and how contributions will be formulated. Annual contributions are not mandatory during periods of low or no profitability if so elected. Contribution amounts are usually determined quarterly or annually, and are based both on an employee's salary level and the firm's profitability. Annual contribution limits are up to 25% of an employee's salary not to exceed $53,000 annually.

C.5 Employee Stock Ownership Plans

Employee Stock Ownership Plans or Trusts (ESOPs) are similar in nature to profit-sharing programs. Annual contribution limits are, in fact, the same, but are paid out in the form of company stock rather than cash. This can prove a great advantage to cash flow as well as for reducing tax liabilities, since contributions are tax deductible, just as if they were made in cash.

ESOPs can also be used as a means of raising capital because the plan is allowed to borrow money to purchase stock options. The loans are then paid back through deductions of cash contributions. This can effectively help to lower loan costs as well, since the deductions are made with pretax dollars. ESOPs can also provide an excellent means for transferring the ownership of a closely held corporation upon the death or retirement of a major stockholder.

The one major drawback to an ESOP program is the dissolution of ownership interests since the program does increase the number of stockholders. Many owners of smaller businesses find this dissolution unacceptable for fear of losing overall management control. If structured properly, however, this situation is easily avoidable and is most often an unfounded fear.

Professional Assistance

I would strongly recommend that each of you seek the counsel of a tax lawyer and your accountant before implementing any type of pension or profit-sharing program. When that time comes, you would be well served to also have these experts evaluate your estate planning needs. Though this may not be of immediate concern to the new business owner, there will come a time when a succession plan will have to be developed for your business. When you've reached the stage of implementing pension or profit-sharing programs, that time has most likely arrived. For your family's sake, the sooner that planning occurs, the better.

D. Estate Planning

We have alluded to estate planning several times: during our discussion of partnerships and buy/sell agreements, in our discussion of insurance coverages, and in our discussion of pension and profit-sharing programs. Effective estate planning will, after all, utilize a combination of all these areas along with a will and possibly living trust accounts. In terms of the business within your estate plan, you'll only have three options: continue, sell, or liquidate.

Those who wish to sell or liquidate should prearrange the terms and conditions of that sale within your estate plan. Those who wish the business to continue should consciously plan effective management succession in conjunction with planned ownership succession. This will mean training your successors to the best of your abilities, be they family members or unrelated parties. It will also mean making arrangements for the distribution of profits. If more than one successor is involved, procedures should be instituted to effect smooth interrelations between those successors.

Accumulated Appreciation

For most of you, the primary concern of estate planning will be for the care of your surviving family members. You will want them to have a financially secure life, regardless of your decision of how best to dispose of the business. In most cases, a business that has been in existence for a number of years will also have appreciated substantially in value. This will necessitate your making arrangements to cover the added tax burdens from that appreciation within your estate plan.

Professional Assistance

Estate planning can be effected in many combinations including pre-death gifts, living and private trusts, business liquidation agreements, buy/sell agreement, ESOP plans, insurance or annuity payments, stock redemption plans, or a combination thereof. Since regulations change frequently in this area, this brief discussion is meant only as a reminder. I repeat, for those in need of estate planning assistance, seek professional guidance, and above all, exercise caution! Anyone can call themselves an estate planner. A tax or estate lawyer working in conjunction with your accountant and bank trust officer or financial planner will prove your best option.

E. Chapter Summary

I seem to be harping on a familiar theme, effective planning. As in all operational areas, planning is the key to successful cash management, tax preparation, pension and profit-sharing programs and estate planning. While pension and profit-sharing programs and estate planning may be less immediate needs, they will require your attention sooner than you might think. To quote an all-too-familiar truism: "Don't lock the barn door after the horse is already out."

CHAPTER 18

Planned Expansion

The business stage we are about to discuss will come at different intervals for each of you. It will come at a time when you've finally gained control of your operations and business environment. This could be in one year, but most likely three to five years, depending upon the amount of time it takes for your business to begin to mature.

There will be two exceptions to this natural course of development—those plagued or blessed, depending upon your adaptability, with uncontrollable growth, and those experiencing insufficient sales volume. Since there will most certainly be some overlap of the first two business stages, those in either exception category will also find comfort in the discussion pertaining to planned growth. Conversely, for those who have no desire to expand, complacency can spell disaster. Grow or die applies to business just as to biology.

Stage One Development

The average life span for a successful business is twenty-nine years. The first three to five years are the most volatile and, consequently, are those to which we have dedicated the majority of this text. As discussed previously, these first few years are a learning stage and management errors are not uncommon. This stage is usually further complicated by fluctuating sales volume, which, in turn, can cause difficulty in controlling expenses and financial stability. We need not dwell on this stage, since each of you now possess the necessary skills to excel during this most difficult period. Rather, we will further our discussion to the second stage of a business's life cycle.

A. The Second Business Phase

We will define the second stage of a business's life cycle as a period of controlled and sustained growth. It will be characterized by a knowledgeable, yet still energetic ownership or management. Sales will still be growing, but at a more controlled or predictable level. Expenses too will be more predictable, and profit trends will have been established. Organizationally, your staff will be well experienced and functioning as a team. Any operational bugs will be well behind you. In short, your business will be running like a finely tuned engine.

A.1 The Tune Up

Even though your business should now be well meshed, let's begin the second stage as we did the first, with a little preventive maintenance. Compare this maintenance phase to the ten thousand mile service for your automobile. The "break in" period is now complete, and after an oil change and a few minor adjustments, your car is now ready to achieve and maintain optimal and peak levels of performance.

Our scheduled maintenance will consist of an operational reevaluation. Its intent will be to maximize profits at current sales levels. The main objective will be to reduce unnecessary expenditures. This will include optimizing balance-sheet performance vis-à-vis improving inventory and receivables turns, reducing payables and notes, and possibly updating equipment.

By now, all of you should know how to perform this evaluation. You need to merely ask yourself, "How can my business run more efficiently?" The answer or answers will of course require the same procedures we conducted during our initial evaluation. The only difference will be the financial statements used in this evaluation will be, at least in part, your own. Likewise, the analysis will be that of your own operating performance. For those of you who have continued to make and update projection models, in effect, you've been conducting an ongoing business reevaluation. This next phase will prove a simple task.

The Organizational Reevaluation

It's quite possible your reevaluation will result in the ability to reduce your staff. Under most circumstances, the ability to improve operations through staff reductions would of course be advisable, but not at this juncture. At this stage, let's keep one eye on the future, since the expansion stage could quite possibly necessitate having to add employees. What better place to find these employees than within your own organization? For one, they will already be at least partially trained. Two, this will provide upward mobility opportunities for your entire staff, which will improve both morale and job performance. And three, a layoff followed by a rehiring would only serve to frustrate and confuse your remaining staff.

Not only will expansion necessitate adding to your staff, in all likelihood, it will necessitate upgrading your present staff's responsibilities. If as yet you haven't done so, now is the time to shed your entrepreneurial cocoon. During the first business phase, you were probably fearful or couldn't afford to delegate many managerial duties. Now, you can ill-afford not to. This is the time to promote, delegate, and retrain in anticipation of the expansion phase. During this phase, your goal will be to build an effective organization that can literally run the business by itself.

The Operational Reevaluation

The reevaluation stage could take up to a year to institute and implement. Look upon it as a gearing-up stage, and use the time to evaluate your expansion alternatives. More than likely this will involve two paths: expanding your current market, either in terms of customer base or geographies, or taking on additional products or service lines. For some of you, this expansion might necessitate adding additional locations.

There are of course other alternatives available. You could purchase or start a second business or division. Some of you may even decide this is the right time to sell out to raise capital for retirement, or to purchase or start an even larger business. These choices will be discussed in the next chapter. For now, we will limit our discussion to expanding our markets or product lines.

B. Expand Products or Markets?

The choice of whether to expand your market or product line may be somewhat predetermined by your particular industry. Those of you in retailing, for example, might be hard pressed to expand your market base without adding an additional location, unless of course you expand that base through Internet sales. For you a less expensive way to expand might be to increase your product lines, provided of course you have the existing floor space or capacity to easily accomplish this.

B.1 Expanding Product Lines

When expanding product lines, your first consideration should be to expand in related areas. For most of you the majority of your sales will be generated by just a few of your products or services. Examine those key products and services, and utilize that information to help develop products for expansion that will be attractive to this preferred customer base. If you own a women's apparel shop, for example, that sells primarily to women professionals, look to products that would appeal to them, possibly make up or shoes.

These changes would be far less costly than to expand into unrelated areas that might require much larger capital outlays for items such as leasehold improvements or the costs associated with attracting a new and unfamiliar customer base. Also, since related products can be sold as a crossover or with less disruption to your existing customer base, this will limit the risk of upsetting or losing that original base during the transition period. Related products will also fall within your area of expertise, thereby further improving the chances for a successful transition.

For those who have yet to reach your original projections, you may find it necessary to make a more drastic change in the emphasis of the business. Even for you, related product areas will prove the best alternative for all of the same reasons. Be sure, however, to analyze the shortcomings of your original plan before proceeding to this next phase.

B.2 Expanding Markets

By comparison, those who are light manufacturers will find that adding product lines could require additional manufacturing capabilities. In most cases this will prove the more expensive of the two alternatives. In all likelihood, your initial expansion would be best accomplished by increasing your market share or size. This too would result in additional expenditures, possibly more advertising, selling expenditures, inventory costs, and so on, but these expenditures would still be far less costly than adding additional manufacturing capacity for new products.

There are a number of ways to expand your geographic market or market share. These include increasing your sales force or marketing efforts, adding retail or wholesaling components, providing a delivery service and increasing Internet sales. Each of you will have to determine the most cost-effective means for expansion based upon the industry and your individual situation. As in many prior examples, it will help to list your alternatives and the advantages and disadvantages associated with each. Again, much of this information will be readily available from your initial research, and your operating results to date.

C. Expansion Requirements

Projecting Expansion Costs

Determining the optimum expansion alternative will require a cost-benefit analysis. If the costs of your expansion plan are solely expense items, you can utilize the break-even formula discussed earlier to determine the impact on your operations (Total Fixed Costs / Gross Profit Margin = Break-Even Sales). Understandably, this will require identification as to whether those costs are fixed or variable.

The break-even point can be determined for the expansion requirements alone by isolating the fixed and variable costs associated with the expansion to the projected revenue increase. The formula can also be utilized to determine the effects on the entire operation by combining the expansion projections with your actual revenue and expense figures.

Fixed Asset Requirements

Some of you will have expansion requirements that will necessitate additional fixed asset purchases. Again, the same formula can be utilized to project profitability at various sales levels, or to determine the increase in sales volume required to cover the cost of the new equipment. For those who intend to finance the equipment purchase, the costs will have to be annualized to determine the annual payback, if the analysis is to be truly effective.

The Hidden Costs of Expansion

In most cases there will be hidden expansion costs over and above any projected expenditures or capital outlays. Consider for a moment any other balance-sheet changes that might be necessitated by your expansion plans. How will expanding sales impact your accounts receivable and inventory requirements? How will equipment purchases impact fixed assets and consequently cash or notes payable? As with our original projections, determining the true cost of expansion will require measuring the effect of income statement changes on the balance sheet.

Measuring Balance-Sheet Changes

You can, of course, forecast the balance-sheet changes by utilizing the same techniques developed during our projection modeling phase. First, utilizing your last fiscal year-end balance sheet, determine each accounts correlation (percent) to total sales found on the corresponding income statement. Total sales again represent 100%. Next, multiply each of your account percentages by the projected sales level. This will provide you with a balance-sheet projection based upon your expansion requirements.

The projected balance sheet is of course estimation, and nowhere is that more apparent than in the fixed asset section. For our projection, any level of sales increase will result in increases to fixed assets. In reality, a certain level of sales increase can be accomplished without having to add to fixed assets. Once that level is exceeded, then additional equipment would be required, but at its actual cost, and not its projected percentage increase. For those anticipating equipment purchases, use actual cost information to project any changes to the fixed asset section.

Updating Your Projections

As you can see, business cycles really do run in circles, and the expansion planning phase is conducted in much the same manner as our original projection modeling. In fact, once an expansion plan has reached the implementation stage, your short and long-term projection work sheets are for the most part updated. I would suggest finalizing any portions that haven't, so that you are in a position to utilize them to chart your new course.

D. Funding Expansion

Once you've decided upon your expansion plan and determined the costs of implementation, you will have to determine the best means for funding that expansion. Some growth can be funded entirely through operations, while others will require increased borrowings or capital injections. Before discussing alternative capital sources, let's quickly review debt structuring for those who intend to borrow.

Structuring Expansion Borrowing

The balance-sheet projection will be helpful in identifying whether borrowing needs are of a short or long-term nature. Again, a certain level of increase in receivables and inventory will have to be expected given those increases an air of permanency. The amount of borrowing needed to increase these and any other current assets to higher base levels should be considered as permanent working capital, or a long-term borrowing need. As such, borrowings for this purpose should be structured as a term loan and paid back on a scheduled basis.

D.1 Uncontrollable Sales Growth

A few of you will experience such uncontrollable growth that management by conventional means will be next to impossible. This will happen well before the typical expansion stage, but will require the same expansion processes. The reason should be fairly obvious provided of course you've had time to run projection calculations. For those in this category, sales will expand so rapidly, growth will exceed your operating capabilities and your borrowing capacity. You will have three options: temper growth, raise additional capital by going public, or soliciting additional investors or franchise.

Tempering Sales Growth

Trying to keep pace with uncontrollable sales growth will most often result in declining profit margins, and eventually financial instability. Tempering sales growth is often the most palatable solution. For those in this category, begin by reevaluating your capabilities. First, determine an obtainable and realistic level of sales volume that would be optimal from an operational standpoint. Next, choose the most effective means for terminating the sales above that point. In most cases, this will necessitate identifying and eliminating your least profitable customers.

Keep the channels of communication open during the purging process. Tell the customer it is purely a business decision necessitated by an unprofitable or low profit relationship. This will enable you to part ways on friendly terms, leaving the door open for future relations. In some instance, you may even find clients are willing to pay more to preserve the relationship.

Franchising

Franchising may be an option for a select few. To be viable for franchising, your business will have to have a unique product or service or have a revolutionary marketing or operating concept. Additionally, this concept will have to be standardized and proceduralized into an easily patternable operation. For those few in this category, first consult with your attorney and accountant. Upon their approval and only with their continued guidance, seek out an investment banking firm, which specializes in franchising, to help guide the development and roll out.

Investor Solicitation

Those of you seeking sources for investor alternatives need merely to review our previous discussions, as well as the advantages and disadvantages associated with each. Again, seek the investment type that best suits your specific needs. If your needs are limited, seek a limited partner or individual investor, possibly a family member. If your needs are larger, find a specialized investment banker or venture capital firm. Some in this category may find it's time to take your company public, which is the focal point for our next chapter.

E. Chapter Summary

Again, the second or expansion stage is in many ways a repeat of the initial business stage. It is, or will be, your chance to atone for all those errors you made the first time around. Utilize your experience and knowledge wisely, as well as that of those around you. Keep in mind, a business must grow to stay healthy, but that growth should be planned, funded, and managed in a manner that best suits you and your organization. Remember too, a business's growth and continued development can be more enjoyable the second time around.

CHAPTER 19

Public Offerings, Mergers, and Acquisitions

Many of you who find growth exceeding borrowing capacities will find going public an optimal solution. Though there could be several reasons for going public, our discussion will center on raising expansion capital. Additionally, while there are several capital vehicles that could be used to fund this expansion such as the sale of preferred stock, debentures or bonds, our discussion will be limited to the most common initial method, common stock offerings. We will also discuss two possible outgrowths of public offerings: mergers and acquisitions.

A. The Advantages of a Public Offering
Funding Without Payments
Despite many commonly held fears, when structured properly, the benefits of a public offering are many and any disadvantages can be all but eliminated. Obviously, the major advantage is that expansion capital can be raised as equity rather than as increased borrowings. Simply stated, this means the funds don't have to be paid back as loan funds would. Although it could be necessary to declare dividends sometime in the future, most knowledgeable investors purchase first issues under the assumption their investment return will be in the form of stock appreciation, and not dividend income. As such, there will be little pressure to declare dividends, at least in the foreseeable future.

Improving the Financial Position
Since the proceeds of a stock offering are injected as capital, this serves to strengthen the company's financial position rather than weaken it, as is often the case with increased borrowings. Often a public offering will improve the financial position enough that increased borrowings are again possible. There are times when additional borrowings can be obtained in conjunction with capital injections. In a dual arrangement such as this, much more cash can be generated than would ever be possible by conventional means.

Minimizing the Risks of a Public Offering

As with an ESOP plan, the major concern with going public is loss of management or ownership control. This will not be a factor, however, if the offering is structured properly. Most first offerings don't involve more than 30% of a company's common stock. Though we would advise retaining at least a two-thirds majority, operating controls can be maintained with as little as 51% of the voting shares for a closely held company. Additionally, good underwriters purposely discourage large block purchases that might further dilute others' ownership interests by enabling a pooling of interests by a few large block owners in an attempt to exercise management control.

The Costs of Going Public

Why then doesn't everyone go public? Very simply, a company must first prove itself or its product or service before enough interest can be generated to ensure the stock will sell. Public offerings can also be very expensive, usually approaching from 15% to 25% of the gross capitalization amount, when including accounting and legal fees. Unless the underwriter is willing to guarantee the offering, you will be required to pay the expenses as they occur and absorb them directly if the offer doesn't sell.

Who Best Qualifies

Those who will benefit most from a public offering will not need a list of guidelines for assurance. Most of you will already be incorporated. Most will have been recently turned down for a loan, or have expansion or development plans, which are too expensive for conventional borrowing alternatives. Some of you will also have legal and accounting counsels pointing you in this direction. Let me reemphasize, the decision to go public should only be made with the complete agreement and cooperation of your accountant and lawyer.

B. Types of Public Offerings

There are three major types of public offerings: intrastate registrations, Regulation A issues, and S-1 filings. A full public registration, or S-1 filing, is the most popular format. However, the intrastate and Regulation A methods are both less expensive and less time-consuming. Either of these methods could be better suited to those of you with smaller capitalization requirements. Before conducting our discussion of the three types of public offerings, let's discuss one other alternative means of raising capital known as a private placement.

Private Placements

Some broker-dealers specialize in private placements that comprise the sale of stock or securities to wealthy and sophisticated (accredited) investors instead of to the general public. Private placements do not need to be registered with the SEC; however, the private placement agent is required to be registered.

Accredited investors are basically individuals or institutions that have the resources and the knowledge to invest in risker, unregistered securities. To be deemed as accredited, an individual must have at least $1 million in assets and must have earned in excess of $200,000 during the two years, $300,000 if married. He or she must also expect to make at least that much in the current year.

Although the SEC does not require that a disclosure statement be offered to accredited investors, most issuers do provide a Private Placement Offering Memorandum, which is very similar to a prospectus. After all, sophisticated investors too, like to know about their investments.

B.1 Intrastate Registrations
The Requirements and Advantages
The intrastate registration is by far the easiest and least expensive format. To qualify, the stock subscription must be sold to residents of just one state, which must also be the state in which you are incorporated and in which you conduct a most of your business—a minimum of 80%. This is the only public offering format that does not require a Security and Exchange Commission (SEC) registration, nor does it require a formal prospectus or specific financial statement requirements. As such, the intrastate offering can usually be accomplished with the company acting as the underwriter, rather than having to employ an outside firm. Legal and accounting assistance will be required though, under all circumstances.

An advertising or marketing strategy will also be necessary to stimulate interest in the stock issue. Consider marketing stock subscription's as you would any product or service. Target your market, determine which media are best suited to reach your market and gear your advertising accordingly. Capital requirements and budget restrictions will help determine whether this marketing effort is on a local, selected area, or statewide basis.

Limiting the Risk Exposure
As mentioned previously, those who utilize this format will have to absorb the costs until the offering sells, and permanently if it doesn't. The proceeds from an intrastate filing must be impounded until the offering sells out. The costs associated with this type of filing can be minimized by offering those providing professional assistance stock certificates as a portion, or in lieu of, their fees. True this will further dilute your ownership interests, but structured correctly, it will have a limited effect and help spread the risks more evenly.

B.2 Regulation A Stock Issues
The Requirements
For those with needs of less than $5 million, but requiring interstate or national exposure, a short form registration or Regulation A, will prove the best and least expensive alternative. Since the short form is an interstate registration, filing with the SEC is required at least ten days in advance of the sale. An offering sheet or prospectus is also required, which in most cases will necessitate the hiring of an independent underwriter to coordinate the registration efforts. Again, even when hiring an independent underwriter, your accountant and lawyer will play important roles in the registration process, and in helping to oversee your continued ownership and management control.

The Prospectus
For those unfamiliar with a prospectus, it is simply a booklet or pamphlet published by the company to inform the general public of the stock offering. The prospectus is formatted in much the same fashion as our loan package, and is intended for much the same purpose. It will usually begin with a summary, and then discuss the proposed capitalization structure and the uses for the proceeds. This will be followed by financial statement summaries, which must be audited in the case of a full S-1 filing, and a corresponding narrative. If an outside underwriter is utilized, the final section of the prospectus will summarize the underwriting agreement.

Advantages of the Regulation A Registration Format
Prospectus requirements are not as stringent for the short form filing, nor are audited financial statement a requirement for the filing. Therefore, the costs and the time element involved in completing the registration process are much less restrictive than with a full S-1 filing. In most cases, the costs will be no greater than with a venture capital firm providing your capital requirements, and you will lose far less management control.

Minimizing the Risks
As with the intrastate filing, the major drawback to this format is you will have to absorb the initial costs. Again, the proceeds of the sale will be impounded until the issue has been sold out. The risks associated with this format can also be minimized by offering compensation in the form of stock certificates to both professional associates and the underwriter. Many underwriters will even agree to defer their fees by means of a consulting contract. We've now mentioned underwriters several times. Let's digress for a moment and define just who they are.

B.3 The Underwriter

According to Webster, an underwriter is one who agrees or signs his or her name to a subscription, thereby lending to its authenticity, and who often assumes any loss or risk exposure. A subscription can take the form of an insurance policy, in which case the issuing insurance company would be the underwriter, or a bond issue, in which case a bank, public company, or a government entity might be the underwriter. For the remainder of this discussion, we will assume a subscription represents a common stock offering and an underwriter, a brokerage or investment banking firm. There must be an underwriter for any public-stock offering; however, in the case of an intrastate registration, the company will often act as its own underwriter.

Choosing an Underwriter

Those of you requiring an underwriter's assistance would be best advised to choose a firm that is a member of the Financial Industry Regulatory Authority, Inc. (FINRA), which is a private self-regulatory organization that succeeded the National Association of Securities Dealers, Inc. (NASD). FINRA is a nongovernmental organization under the jurisdiction of the SEC that oversees member brokerage firms and exchange markets including the New York Stock Exchange.

This is the largest and most respected association of brokerage firms. Additionally, though you will be dealing with only one underwriter, selling a stock offering usually involves the participation of many brokers. Choosing a FINRA member will help to ensure a network of willing participants exists to help sell your stock offering. Again, the best sources for locating underwriting prospects will be your lawyer, banker, or accountant.

B.4 S-1 Registrations

By far the most popular form of stock offerings is the S-1, or complete SEC Registration. Of the three major types, it's also the most expensive and the most time-consuming. An S-1 filing requires a more extensive prospectus than the short form filing, and it requires fully audited financial statements. It will also necessitate you to hire an outside underwriter to work in conjunction with your attorney and accountant.

There are three main underwriting categories associated with an S-1 filing: the best effort commitment, the all or nothing commitment, and the firm commitment. Most firm commitment underwritings will also contain a market-out clause, which allows the underwriter to be released from liability, if events occur, making the sale of stock difficult or impossible. Conversely, some commitments may contain a standby clause in which the underwriter agrees to purchase any part of an issue that has not been purchased by current stockholders through a rights offering. The underwriter then exercises and maintains a trading market in those rights, and then offers the stock acquired to the public.

The Best Effort Commitment

The best effort commitment establishes a time period during which the stock will be offered and sold to the general public. The monies collected during that period will again be impounded. The underwriter makes no guarantee as to the salability of the stock, and only commits to assuring its best effort in selling the offering. Again, if the offering should have to be withdrawn, the company presenting the offer would be responsible to absorb the costs incurred.

Under the best effort agreement, if an offering isn't sold out during the allotted time period, alternative arrangements can be made. If enough of the stock has been sold to meet the company's immediate needs, for example, the owners can withdraw the remaining shares for sale. The owner or underwriter could also decide to purchase the remaining themselves, or file an extension to allow additional time to sell the remaining shares. The situation will dictate the appropriate alternative, but it's important to note that there are other options available, if needed, with the best effort commitment.

The All or Nothing Commitment

The next category of underwriting assurance is the all or nothing commitment. Under this arrangement none of the options available under the best effort format exist. The funds are again impounded during the sales period. However, if all of the shares are not sold in the allotted amount of time, the offering must be withdrawn and the proceeds collected to date must be returned to the purchasers. Again, there are no other options or alternative available under the all or nothing commitment, and the company would be responsible for any expenses incurred.

The Firm Commitment

The safest and most desirable form of assurance is the firm commitment. Under this arrangement the underwriter agrees to purchase all of the shares in advance for resale to the general public. The underwriter rather than the company assumes the risk in the event the offering does not sell out, or sells below the predetermined price. The underwriter also receives the benefit of any appreciation in the market value if shares begin trading above the predetermined price. Most of you will find the costs and risks associated with an S-1 filing necessitate the need to attempt it only on a firm or best effort arrangement.

C. Determining the Size and Price of an Offering

Those of you employing an underwriter will have much, if not all, of the concern involving pricing and the number of shares issued assumed by the underwriter. For those underwriting your own programs, your lawyer and accountant will be able to assist in these areas. Regardless, each of you should develop at least a basic understanding of the concepts involved in these determinations.

C.1 Meeting Capital Requirements

The primary consideration for a public offering will be the company's immediate capital requirements, whether they are to purchase equipment, fund additional locations, increase manufacturing capabilities, fund research, provide working capital, or a combination thereof. The initial offering will have to provide enough capital to meet these requirements plus the expenses incurred from the offering itself.

Par Value

Before a price per share can be determined, an arbitrary selling price will have to be established for your company. In this situation, an earnings multiplier is the pricing method used most often, and the corresponding value will closely parallel the company's book value. Then, once the total number of shares has been agreed upon, the price per share or par value, can be determined by dividing the total number of shares issued and outstanding by the gross selling price or book value. Any paid-in capital or retained earnings will need to be deducted from this calculation.

Market Value

Keep in mind, the par value is merely your determination, with the aid of your accountant or underwriter, as to the stocks true value. Once the stock goes on sale, the market will establish its own value or price. This could be higher or lower than the one you've determined, depending upon the market's perception of your company's financial strength and future potential. Generally, the market value of a major stock runs from six to twelve times its earnings per share. Growth stocks can easily reach a price per earnings ratio of 30:1. First issues are often nearly immeasurable. Again, the investor will be gauging potential as well as past performance. It will be up to you and your advisors to attempt to accurately predict investor response.

C.2 Determining the Number of Shares Required

Since the price per share will be somewhat restricted, the total capitalization derived from an initial stock offering will be determined more by the number of shares issued for sale, than by the price established for each individual share. Those contemplating a public offering should also take into consideration the possibility of any future offerings at this juncture. These shares can be issued or authorized now without having to be sold during the initial offering. By issuing these shares concurrently, you can save the time and the expense of having to reapply to the secretary of state for permission to issue additional shares or affect a stock split at a later date.

An Analogy

Assume your capital requirements, including the cost of underwriting, are $1 million, and you've established a price per share of $12, which arbitrarily represents a ten-to-one earnings multiplier. Let's further assume that you want to retain two-thirds of the stock issue for your personal holdings. Under this scenario, you would have to sell 83,334 shares at $12 per share to reach the $1 million request.

In all likelihood, you would want to offer 100,000 shares for public sale in the event a slight drop in the market value occurs once shares begin to trade. This would require a stock issue of at least 300,000 shares in order to retain a two-thirds majority. It would also necessitate an earning level of $360,000 per year for the ten-to-one multiplier to remain constant ($360,000 × 10 / 300,000 = $12).

Stock Dissolution

There is one final disparity that must be discussed when determining the number of shares involved in an offering. The earnings multiplier and market value per share will always change in correlation to the number of shares outstanding. Though we assumed a ten-to-one multiplier for the preceding example, $360,000, this assumption was based on the total number of shares issued and outstanding of 300,000.

Now let's assume you are already incorporated with the same earnings level as in our prior example, $360,000, with the same ten-to-one earnings multiplier. Let's further assume that originally only 50,000 shares were issued, but again your present needs call for a total of 300,000 shares. Under these assumptions, the price per share at the 50,000 shares level would be $72 ($360,000 × 10 / 50,000 = $72). This value would decrease to $12, however, once the remaining 250,000 shares were issued. This difference is known as the "dilution" value. Be sure the earnings multiplier and price per share you establish are after dilution, or you could find yourself with less of a capital injection than you intended.

Recapitalization

Most of you who are already incorporated will find yourselves in this situation and will have to issue additional shares of stock to meet your capitalization requirements. Again, let's assume that your initial stock issue was fifty thousand shares, and that the preceding example matched your needs and performance level. You could effect the necessary recapitalization in one of two ways. One, you could apply to the secretary of state for approval to issue 250,000 additional shares, or two, for approval to effect a stock split—in this case six to one. Under this second scenario, the original shares would have to be turned in, or retired, and replaced with six new shares.

The Decision to Go Public

The commitment to enter into a public offering should not be regarded lightly. Regardless of which format you choose, the three general steps: planning, meeting the requirements, and selling the stock issue can easily take a year to complete. In many cases, financial statement reporting methods will have to be upgraded, and in some cases, a major accounting firm might be required to add reliability to the prospectus. Additionally, your company will have to display a sufficient net worth or enough growth and earnings potential to attract potential investors. Again, seek advice from your professional advisors or a reputable underwriter before making the final decision to go public.

C.3 Life in the Aftermarket

Let's take a moment to discuss the effects or ramifications of going public on future operations. Those of you who were not already incorporated will be required to appoint a board of directors, which, in most cases, will include you as its chairman. Use this body to its full potential. Appoint those who can give a blend of management assistance or lend prestige to your firm's identity. In most cases, this should include your lawyer, accountant, and banker.

Retaining Control

Just as you must ensure the retention of ownership interests by retaining a majority of shares issued, you must also structure the corporate bylaws to retain management control. These controls should be set in place during the initial planning stages. Though common stockholders have voting rights, as the majority stockholder, you will want to control the voting actions of the group. Provided the bylaws are structured properly, life in the aftermarket should go on much as it had previously.

Added Benefits

There can be additional benefits to a public offering. Since open market trading will establish future values, you will no longer have to concern yourself with the company's true value. This may or may not be a blessing, but it will take much of the guesswork out of your estate planning. Additionally, the predetermined market valuation can aid in taking the proper steps in passing on the business to your heirs or successors. It will also make it easier to establish a price for buying out another's interests or in selling your own. Finally, since there will be a marketable value placed upon the stock, a portion of your personal holdings could be utilized to collateralize personal borrowings, or a portion could be sold to raise cash.

D. Selling Out

As remote as this may seem now, some of you will want to sell your company sometime in the future. As with the initial purchase, the conditions or circumstances for that sale will help to determine the optimal terms of sale. There are, however, selling alternative available only to corporations that could prove advantageous for many of you.

Trading Corporate Securities

As in the earlier example of the carry-back note, capital gains can be deferred by taking payment in the form of corporate securities rather than in cash. If at least 90% of the sales price is received in the form of corporate securities, the portion not taken in cash qualifies as a tax-free exchange. These securities could be in the form of common or preferred stock, debentures, bonds, or notes. However, if the purchaser is another corporation and the securities received by the seller are those of the purchasing corporation, then the securities received must be in the form of common stock if the sale is to qualify as a tax-free exchange.

The securities exchange method can prove extremely advantageous to those who take back common stock in a growing corporation. As that company prospers, the value of your holdings will appreciate, enhancing the original selling price. When cash is needed, you can simply sell enough of your shares to fulfil that need. You will only be taxed on the amount sold, and only on the amount of appreciation over and above its original value. One obvious rule of thumb when considering a securities exchange is to never trade for stock you wouldn't be willing to purchase outright as an investor.

E. Mergers and Acquisitions

Sellers wishing to start or purchase another business may also want to weigh the advantages of a tax-free exchange. For example, you could arrange to exchange the stock you receive from the purchaser of your business for the stock of the business you wish to purchase. You could even arrange for the purchaser of your present company to first acquire the business you wish to buy, and then orchestrate a tax-free exchange by transferring stock between the two companies. The first example is a crude form of acquisition, and the second, a merger with a spin-off sale. Acquisitions and mergers are, after all, forms of buying and selling businesses, but ones with considerable tax advantages.

Asset Redistribution

There could be assets or even a whole division of the business you wish to acquire that have no interest to you, but that could be of interest to the purchaser of your original company or to an independent third party. The distribution of any such assets could be negotiated within the terms of the sale to either lower the selling price or to raise additional cash. Other benefits could be derived from any unused investment tax credits or past losses that can be carried forward. Again, if you're not in a position to utilize any of these benefits directly, the sale can be structured in such a way as to pass these benefits on to another party to lower your overall purchase price or raise additional cash.

Using Past Tax Credits

Those of you acquiring a business with unused investment tax credits or past losses, should structure the acquisition as a division of your original company or of the company you are forming to enable you to utilize these benefits. This would allow the recipient to file a consolidated tax return and to utilize the benefits going forward. If the company you are purchasing displays potential, this type of acquisition can prove a bona fide bonanza, since the acquisition can provide an excellent tax shelter while helping to strengthen your original organization.

E.1 Measuring the Operational Effects

As is true with adding product lines, acquisitions often involve related products or stages of product development. For instance, a manufacturer of computers could decide to purchase the retail outlets that distribute those products. The processes involved in analysing the acquisition will be identical to those discussed in chapters 5, 6, and 7. What will change is the organizational structure of your original business. Company acquisitions, like product additions, will have a severe impact on your overall operation. This impact should be one of the major considerations in your decision. Unlike product additions, in the acquisition stage, opposite organizational or operational structures do attract.

The Benefits of Dissimilar Operations

Those of you with rapidly growing sales, an unquenchable appetite for working capital and with few fixed assets or a less than favourable net worth, could strengthen your company by acquiring or merging with a company that demonstrates the opposite operational characteristics. Likewise, those whose companies might be reaching the maturation stage characterized by a levelling of sales combined with a heavy investment in fixed assets and years of underutilized retained earnings growth might find purchasing a young, high-flying sales organization a much-needed shot in the arm. Always look for these types of enhancements when considering possible actuations.

F. Chapter Summary

The more successful you become, the more often offerings, mergers, and acquisitions will loom. Financing and credit arrangements will also be much easier to arrange. The differences between this stage and your original start-up or purchase stage will be more than just operational and financial stability. Your management abilities will likewise be honed and proven, resulting in your ability to negotiate from a position of increased strength, wisdom, power, and respect. All of which you will have earned!

EPILOGUE

During the course of this text, I have tried to cover the natural course of a business's progression from the owner's personal requirements, to planning, start-up or purchase, operating, expanding, acquisitions, and selling out. I have also tried to cover as many potential problem areas as possible within each of these operational stages. I know you will find the management techniques shared within this text beneficial. I trust they will help you to better anticipate and thereby better plan to overcome or avoid any operational pitfalls. Certainly, situations will arise that aren't covered in this text. Again, I trust you will have gained the ability to solve these problems as well—either on your own or with the aid of a professional associate.

I hope our association will continue into the future and that you will find this text helpful as a reference tool. I would be pleased if it's of benefit in solving any forthcoming problems, as an aid in future operational planning, or simply as a means to recall management techniques. The challenge you are about to undertake can, and will, be the most rewarding career experience of your life. Enjoy it as you do all other areas, and may God bless you all with success!

ABOUT THE AUTHOR

David D. Hasley has owned and operated two successful businesses over the course of his career, which together span twenty-five years of continuous operation.

Hasley's more than forty years of business experience also include contributions as a lead commercial lender and administrator for a regional bank in California and as a principal and vice president for a national investment management firm.

GLOSSARY

ACCOUNTING—a system of principles that permits the recording, classifying, and accumulation of sales, purchases, and other transactions of a business or individual

ACCOUNTS PAYABLE—a current liability representing the amount owed by a business or individual to a creditor for the merchandise or services purchased on open account

ACCOUNTS RECEIVABLE—money owed by a business or individual for merchandise bought or services rendered on open account

ACCRUAL BASIS—an accounting system by which income is recorded when earned and expenses are recorded when incurred, even though the cash may not have been received or paid out

ACCRUED EXPENSES—expenses incurred during one fiscal period but not paid out (deducted from cash) until the next fiscal period

ACCRUED INCOME—income earned during one fiscal period but not actually received during that period

ACCUMULATED AMORTIZATION—an accumulation on the balance sheet of amounts expensed to write off the cost or value of an intangible asset over its estimated valued life

ACCUMULATED DEPLETION—an accumulation on the balance sheet of amounts expensed to write off the value or cost of non-replaceable assets such as mineral reserves, oil, or gas reserves

ACCUMULATED DEPRECIATION—an accumulation on the balance sheet of amounts expensed to write off the cost of a fixed asset over its estimated useful life

AGING ACCOUNTS RECEIVABLE—grouping customer accounts according to due dates, usually by current, thirty days, sixty days, and ninety days past due

AMORTIZATION—the gradual reduction of a debt by means of periodic payments sufficient to meet current interest and liquidate the debt at the maturity of the obligation

APPRECIATION—the increase in the value of an asset in excess of its depreciable cost due to economic and other conditions

ASSET—anything owned by an individual or business having commercial or exchange value

BALANCE SHEET—an itemized statement that lists the total assets and the total liabilities of a given business or individual to portray its net worth

BALLOON PAYMENT—the balance due at the maturity of an obligation that has not been fully amortized

BOND—a certificate indicating that its issuer has borrowed a set sum of money from the bondholder, usually with an identifiable maturity date at a specified rate of interest

BOOK VALUE—the tangible net worth of a company as reported on its balance sheet, often stated in terms of the value of a share of common stock for a corporation; also applies to the balance-sheet valuations of inventory or fixed assets

BOOKKEEPING—systematic practice of recording the transactions affecting a business

BREAK-EVEN POINT—the volume point at which revenues and costs are equal

BUSINESS—the enterprise of providing people with goods and services for an intended profit

BUSINESS INTERRUPTION INSURANCE—insurance that provides for the uninterrupted flow of income when a fire or other disaster causes a company to temporarily shut down

CALENDAR YEAR—January 1 to December 31

CAPITAL—the amount subscribed and paid by stockholders; the net worth of an individual or business; the monies used to fund a business

CAPITAL STOCK—the ownership shares of a corporation as authorized by its articles of incorporation, including both common and preferred stock

CAPITALIZATION—the monies used to fund a business

CARRY BACK NOTE—refers to any amount of the purchase price of a business or asset carried by the seller in the form of a note

CASH BASIS—the accounting method of recording income and expenses only when cash is actually received or paid out

CASH FLOW—a concept used in analyzing financial statements to determine cash earnings from operations, taking into consideration all noncash expenditures and the effects of changes to the balance sheet

CERTIFIED PUBLIC ACCOUNTANT (CPA)—accountants who meet a state's requirements for education and experience, including passing an examination prepared by the American Institute of Public Accountants

COLLATERAL—some specific valuable item or items pledged to secure a loan in which the lender can seize ownership in the event the borrower fails to repay

COMMON STOCK—stock that has last claim on distributed profits, but receives voting rights on a pro-rata basis in the management of a company

COMPENSATION—the payment of employees for their work

CONVERTIBLE BONDS—bonds that may be paid off by a conversion to stock

CORPORATION—a type of business organization chartered by a state and given many of the legal rights as a separate entity

COST OF GOODS SOLD—the amount determined by adding the beginning inventory for a period to the net purchases for that period and subtracting the ending inventory for that period

COVENANT NOT TO COMPETE—a formal and binding agreement covering a specific time frame and geographic territory by the seller of a business with the purchaser of that business not to compete in any form or fashion

CURRENT ASSETS—the assets of a company that are expected to be converted to cash during the next twelve-month period

CURRENT LIABILITIES—liabilities to be paid within one year

CURRENT RATIO—current assets divided by current liabilities

DEBENTURES—unsecured bonds issued by a corporation that are often convertible to stock

DEBT TO WORTH RATIO—a relationship determined by dividing a company's net worth into its total liabilities to establish how many dollars of debt are outstanding for each dollar of net worth

DEPRECIATION—the amount of expense charged against earnings by a company in writing off the cost of a depreciable asset over its useful life

DIVIDEND—that portion of a corporation's earnings that are paid out to the stockholders

DOUBLE ENTRY BOOKKEEPING—a system by which two entries are recorded for every accounting transaction

ENTREPRENEUR—one who assumes the financial risk of the initiation, operation, and management of a business

ESTATE—the entire group of assets owned by an individual

ESTATE TAXES—the federal and state taxes levied on the right of transfer of property from the deceased to his or her heirs

EXPENSES—the costs that arise in generating revenues for a business

FACTORING ACCOUNTS RECEIVABLE—the actual selling of accounts receivable to a financial institution or the assignment of collection for a fee

FIFO (First In First Out)—a method of inventory valuation by which the cost shown for the first shipment of the respective item is used for valuations for subsequent purchases

FINANCE—the management function of effectively obtaining and using money

FISCAL YEAR—any twelve consecutive months, usually indicative of an accounting or tax year

FIXED ASSETS—permanent investments in buildings, equipment, land, and other tangible property

FRANCHISE—the agreement between a franchiser and an individual business to market the franchiser's products

FRANCHISER—a corporation that grants an individual or group the exclusive right to use the franchiser's name in a certain territory

FRANCHISING—a form of retailing that offers local business people the opportunity to buy and operate their own businesses under the emblem of a larger company

GENERAL ADMINISTRATIVE EXPENSES—the expenses that arise out of the overall administration of a business

GOODWILL—that intangible possession determined at the time of sale of a business, which enables a business to continue to earn a profit in excess of the normal or basic rate of profit earned by other businesses of similar type

GROSS PROFIT—the amount by which a business's net sales exceed the cost of goods sold

GROSS SALES—the total dollar amount of goods sold by a business

IMPROVED PROPERTY—real property improvements such as a building placed on vacant land

INCOME STATEMENT—a statement that details a business's revenues and expenses over a given period of time

INFLATION—a general rising in the level of prices

INTANGIBLE ASSETS—items of nonphysical nature such as goodwill, patents, and trademarks that are of value to a company

INVENTORY—raw materials, work in progress, and finished products on hand for a business

INVENTORY CONTROL—determining the best quantity of various items to have on hand and keeping track of their movement and use

INVENTORY TURNOVER—the number of times a business turns over its inventory during a period, which is determined by dividing the ending inventory for the period by the cost of goods sold

JOB DESCRIPTION—a specific statement of the tasks involved in the job and the conditions under which the holder of the job will work

LIABILITIES—the debts of an individual or business

LIMITED LIABILITY—the legal responsibility of shareholders of a corporation, or limited partners of a partnership, which is restricted to the extent of their investments

LIFO (Last In, First Out)—an inventory valuation method by which the price shown on the last shipment of the particular item is the one that will be used for current valuations

LINE OF CREDIT—the maximum amount of money a lender is willing to lend a business during a specific period of time

LIQUID ASSETS—those assets deemed readily convertible to cash

LIQUIDATING VALUE—the anticipated value of a particular asset that would be realized upon a distress sale

LIQUIDITY—a term used to describe the solvency of a business referring to the degree of readiness in which assets can be converted into cash

LONG-TERM DEBTS—obligations that will not be due for at least one year

MARKET RESEARCH—a study to determine consumer product or service needs as well as the marketing and selling practices most likely to appeal to those needs

MONEY MARKET FUNDS—a pooling of investor funds to purchase securities

MUNICIPAL BOND—a bond that is issued by a town, city, state, port authority, or the like and used to finance new public services such as housing, schools, or roads

NET INCOME—the amount by which total income exceeds total expenses for a fiscal period

NET SALES—the final sales amount for a period determined by subtracting the amount of sales returns, allowances, and sales discounts from the total amount of sales

NET WORTH—the equity or ownership interest of the owners of a business

NOTES PAYABLE—written promises to individuals or businesses to pay stated amounts at specific intervals

NOTES RECEIVABLE—written promises from individuals or businesses agreeing to pay stated amounts at specific times

OPERATING EXPENSES—the costs of operating a business that aren't directly associated with the costs of manufacturing or selling a product or service such as general and administrative expenses

OWNER'S EQUITY—an owner's net worth in a business

PARTNERSHIP—a legal association of two or more persons in the co-ownership of a business

POINTS—a term used for loan fees (one point is equivalent to 1% of the loan amount)

PREFERRED STOCK—corporation stock that grants its owners certain preference rights on payments of dividends and the distribution of assets but does not provide for voting rights

PREPAID EXPENSES—supplies on hand and services paid for but not yet used

PRIME INTEREST RATE—the interest rate set by individual banks for their largest and most credit-worthy business customers

PROFIT—the money remaining after expenses have been deducted from all sums received for sales

PROFIT SHARING—a program whereby employees receive a portion of the company's profits

PROPERTY INSURANCE—insurance that covers the insured company or individual for physical damage to, or destruction of, property in the event of unavoidable peril

PUBLIC ACCOUNTANTS—accountants who operate in a service capacity, and who are independent of the businesses and other organizations they serve

RATIOS—arithmetical relationships between two amounts

RETAINED EARNINGS—total profits of all previous periods, including the current period, which have not been paid out to stockholders

REVENUE—money a company makes through sales, rents, and services

SALARIES—the compensation of an employee based on a week, month, or year

BONDS—issues that offer bondholders specific collateral backing for their bonds

SECURED LOAN—a loan backed by a pledge of a specific item or items in the form of collateral

SOLE PROPRIETORSHIP—a business owned by just one person

STOCK—shares of ownership in a company

STOCKHOLDER—a person who owns shares of the capital stock of a corporation

TANGIBLE NET WORTH—the net worth or equity of a business, excluding the valuation of any intangible assets

TARGET MARKET—a particular market to which a firm attempts to sell its products or services

TAX-FREE BONDS—bonds that enable the investor to earn an income that is legally exempt from federal income taxes

TREASURY STOCK—stock certificates that have been repurchased from shareholders by the corporation

UNIMPROVED PROPERTY—real property such as vacant land to which no improvements have been made

UNLIMITED LIABILITY—the condition that any damages or debt that can be attributed to the business can also be attached to the owner

UNSECURED BONDS—issues that are not backed by any specific collateral

UNSECURED LOAN—a loan that requires no collateral

VARIABLE COST—an operating expense that varies directly with sales or production

WORKING CAPITAL—the pool of resources readily available for a business's operating needs and defined by the excess of current assets over current liabilities

WORKER'S COMPENSATION INSURANCE—insurance covering claims by employees against employers if they are injured on the job selling its products or services

www.ingramcontent.com/pod-product-compliance
Lightning Source LLC
Chambersburg PA
CBHW080906170526
45158CB00008B/2013